12TH STREET RITA

BY

SHIRLEY SANDY

Copyright © 1997 by Shirley Sandy

All rights reserved. No part of this book may be reproduced, stored in a retrieval system, or transmitted by any means, electronic, mechanical, photocopying, recording, or otherwise, without written permission from the author.

ISBN 1-58500-109-0

In the late 60's and early 70's I was a well-known prostitute in Kansas City, but this isn't the *Mayflower Madam* or *Hollywood's Heidi Fleiss*. This is not about the rich and powerful. It is a true story about your everyday prostitute.

I've titled the story *12th Street Rita* because Rita was my "street name" and 12th Street was where I worked. I have written the story in three parts. Part I, "Journey to 12th Street" begins at age 11 when both my parents die and my brother, sister and I are sent to live with abusive relatives. Part II, "The Life" is about prostitution in Kansas City in the 60's and 70's. Part III, "The Awakening" is just that, coming out of a dream world and facing reality. The story ends at age 26.

Over the years I'd thought about writing this story, but I didn't have time. I was a single mother trying to make ends meet after my prostitution career ended. As the years went by, I married and acquired in-laws I worried about. I didn't want them to know about my past. Then the grandchildren came and I said I'd never write the story.

Almost three years ago I had open-heart surgery. I almost died several times, but I didn't. I survived when everyone had given up hope. At that time, I realized I wanted to tell my story, because it too is a story of survival.

The book contains profanity, but I couldn't be true to the story without it. This is a fast-paced, hard-hitting story, not for children, and not for those offended by adult language or sex.

Wilma Wilcox
December 2000

PART I   Journey to 12th Street   1

PART II   The Life   86

PART III   The Awakening   211

PART I

JOURNEY TO 12TH STREET

My dad sat on the side of my bed, "Wake up, Shirley. Get dressed and come out to the living room. I want to talk to you kids."

It was December 31, 1959. My birthday was in 5 days. I'd be 11 years old. I knew my dad wanted to say something about mama. As long as I can remember, my mama had always been sick. It had something to do with her kidneys, but I wasn't sure exactly what it was.

I knew my mother was in the hospital, and in the night I heard my great-aunt Jean say to someone on the telephone, "Virginia passed." I wasn't sure what that meant, but I felt I would soon find out.

I got out of bed and dressed quickly. We had been staying at my great-aunt's house since Christmas, because dad spent all of his time at the hospital.

When I got to the living room, everyone was there. My dad, my great-aunt Jean, Jean's husband, Buck, my sisters Sandra, Barbara and, my brother Jim. Daddy and my brother were crying. Why were they crying? Didn't Jean say mama had passed? Didn't that mean everything was okay?

Daddy spoke first, "Shirley, your mother passed last night." I just sat there, I didn't understand. Death had never touched my life before. We had a couple of dogs and a billy goat that died, but never someone close to me.

Daddy had started a mournful sobbing that seemed to last forever in the silence. I wanted to comfort him but I was rooted to my seat. I felt very confused. What's going on?

The morning sun slipped in through the Venetian blinds and landed in bright stripes on the carpet. I looked at the strips of Sun, afraid to raise my head and look at anyone.

Suddenly, daddy sobbed, "You're never going to see your mother again!" It took him a long time to say each word, he was sobbing, and his chest was heaving in and out. He was gasping for every breath Tears were streaming down his face.

"A-A-A-H-H-H-H Virginia" he began to moan like a chant.

Daddy's aunt Jean spoke next, "Gordon, you're going to have to pull yourself together. There's nothing you can do, you must go on with your life." She spoke with authority in her voice, like the priest at Church.

He stopped his sobbing long enough to say matter-of-factly, "I can't live without her." Aunt Jean took over then, "We've all got to get cleaned up and straighten the house, people will be coming over. Gordon, you'll have to go home and get clean clothes for the kids."

*****

Gordon and Virginia's home was 20 miles outside of Kansas City. Gordon was a carpenter, and he had built a small cracker box house for his family. He had worked at the government ammunition plant in Sunflower, KS. during World War II. He and another guy at the plant, Bill Dolan, bought some farmland together and built their houses.

Over the years, Gordon added to his home; first a two-car garage, and later a huge living room and another bedroom. Dolan's house never changed from the original cracker box.

The house was in the country, there were lots of woods, and cow ponds, and creeks, and pastures to explore. In the summer we hauled the mattresses outside, and watched the stars in the black, country night. In winter, we rode sleds down the slopes of the hills, on the fresh fallen snow.

I took my life for granted. Everything had always been the same. I didn't know what change was, I'd never experienced it.

I didn't do well in school. When I started kindergarten, I would pee my bed during the night. My mother would throw a dirty, wrinkled uniform on me, without cleaning me up or combing my hair. My mother was too sick, or maybe she was too lazy, but I started school, smelling like an outhouse. One day the teacher sent a note home to my parents saying I had a "pungent odor". Daddy got mad at Mama and she started to clean me up before school. But it was too late. For the rest of my years at that school, the kids always held their noses when I approached and called me "stinky".

The only thing I liked about that school was my uniform blouse. On the collar was embroidered the initials of the school, which were also my initials; SJS- - Saint Joseph School - - Shirley Jean Sandy - - I liked that.

When I was at home in the country, I was happy. Ol' Man Dolan had many children, and together these children had many adventures in the country. We were always getting in trouble and got spankings all the time. We usually deserved the lickings we got - - we ran that country like dirty, wild animals, always into mischief.

On the last day of 1959, I did not realize that the death of my mother would change the course of my life forever. Not only did I not realize the importance of this event. I refused to accept it.

While everyone around me cried, I handled it calmly. I knew it wasn't true, but I didn't tell anyone, I kept it to myself. I thought my mother wanted to get away for a while, take a vacation, and she didn't want to take anyone with her, she wanted to go alone. So, she pretended to die, but I knew she was coming back.

*****

"All kinds of people started coming to Aunt Jeans' house, bringing different dishes of food, neighbors, people from daddy's work, church members and relatives from down South. These relatives cried and hugged me, calling me poor, motherless child. I didn't really know these relatives, they were just names I'd heard my parents mention, they didn't really have anything to do with me.

Gordon sat in the living room, smoking a cigarette, acknowledging no one, and eating none of the food. He was totally wrapped up in his black mood. Everyone, except Aunt Jean, was afraid to approach him. He was famous for his bad temper.

Everyone was either in the kitchen, fixing food, or in the dining room eating it, when a voice from the living room yelled, "Somebody better get in here, the carpets on fire and Gordon has passed out!"

Poor Daddy, I thought, I wanted to tell him it would be all right. Mama was coming back, but I was afraid of the black mood that surrounded my father.

When Gordon woke up, he started to talk of death and what it was. "There is no heaven or hell," he said, "There's no afterlife. When you're dead, you're dead and that's it."

"Now, Gordon," Aunt Jean spoke up, "That's blasphemy, you can go to hell saying such things. You were raised in the Catholic Church and you know what the Bible teaches. You're just upset right now. You don't know what you're saying."

"Yes, I'm upset" he replied, "but I know what I'm saying, the only part of the Bible I believe is ashes to ashes, dust to dust, and that's where it ends, there's nothing after that. When you die it's over, and I can't wait!"

"Gordon! Don't ever talk that way in front of the children!" Aunt Jean said. Jean was the only one brave enough to enter into the swirling black mood. Jean and Gordon were very close, always had been, she was the sister of his dead mother, who died giving birth to him. She had always looked out for her nephew. Childless herself, she treated him as the son she never had.

Virginia's wake was held at the funeral home. When Virginia's father, who had a bad heart, went in to view the body, he had to be helped from the room. Gordon went in and looked down on the face of his dead wife, the woman he'd been married to for 17 years. A woman who, at the age of 34, died after a long illness.

Gordon grasped the sides of the coffin and began to rock it back and forth, he started to yell, "Get up, Virginia! Get out of there right now and let's go home." The rocking and yelling became more violent, people ran to grab Gordon and stop him before he dumped the body on the floor.

When I went in to view my mother's body, I looked down and saw a doll. This isn't my Mama, I thought, Mama didn't wear her hair curled like this, and she never wore pink lipstick, only red. And what are those pink blotches on her cheeks? No, this isn't Mama, why can't everyone else see that? I looked down again, the smell of carnations was overpowering in the room. This isn't Mama.

The next day was the funeral. It was a perfect day to bury someone. It was raining, the sky was dark and threatening-it was a sad setting for a sad event. As they started to lower the coffin into the ground, the sky opened up and the rain fell in sheets. Mourners began to run for cover, except one, Gordon stood there over the coffin of his dead wife and cried in the rainstorm. All that rain couldn't disguise his teardrops. He stood there and watched as they lowered the coffin, he stood there drenched with rain, or was it his tears, until someone led him away.

After the funeral, they returned to Aunt Jean's house. Jean was from the South, Memphis to be exact, with all the mannerisms and attitudes of a Southern Belle. She wasn't the helpless type of Southern Belle, but rather the kind that would take over the plantation and run things if she had to. She was a strong woman. She spoke to Gordon firmly, "I know you're upset, but you have to go on for the sake of your children. You need to take your children and go home. Get on with your life. Virginia's gone and she's not coming back.

Gordon packed up his kids and went back to his house in the country, the house he'd built for his wife. Jean hired a housekeeper to come in and watch the kids, but mostly to clean up and cook meals.

Two days after we returned home was my 11th birthday. The housekeeper baked a cake, something my mother had never done, probably because she'd been too sick. Everyone bought me presents, which was also unusual, since I usually received a Christmas/Birthday gift, because Christmas was 10 days before my Birthday. This Birthday was different, there was cake, ice cream, and lots of presents. Everyone felt sorry for me now, or maybe they needed to celebrate something after all the sorrow that had just passed. Everyone, that is, except Gordon, my dad.

Gordon returned to work, his children returned to school, the housekeeper was running the house. On the surface, it appeared that everyone was healing.

*****

My birthday was on a Tuesday. By Friday, the end of the workweek, my dad wanted to return to his aunt's house. He couldn't bear the thought of spending the weekend in his house - - he was depressed, he didn't want to be alone with his memories.

"No," Jean told him. Being childless, she really didn't want a bunch of kids in her house. Although she had raised my sister, Sandra, who was now 16, the rest of us were raised in the country. Jean's house wasn't decorated for children.

She had lots of knick-knacks and breakable things, fine upholstery on her furniture that she didn't want spots on and white carpeting she didn't want dirty little feet walking on. She was still upset that my dad had passed out and burned a hole in her carpet. The week we'd stayed at Jean's house, we kept her kitchen dirty and the kids pissed in her beds, she complained. Sandra had grown up in Jean's environment and had adapted to it, but the other children, except for the week of our mother's funeral, had been there only a few times.

Jean didn't want to be bothered with my Dad or his kids. "You need to stay home and get on with your life - - you have to get over this, Gordon. I know it's hard, but in time everything will be better." She replied to his plea for comfort.

My Dad stayed home that weekend. He acted strange, but he'd always been a little unstable emotionally, even before my mother had died. No one took notice of his behavior.

In fact, everyone tried to stay out of his way. No one was there with him but his 3 children for the housekeeper didn't come on the weekend.

*****

My Dad was 36 years old at the time of my mother's death. He was a small man, only 5'8", but his body was strong and muscular. His hair, what was left of it, was golden blonde. Although he was becoming prematurely bald, it only added to his brooding good looks. My Mother, Virginia, was part American Indian, and equally good-looking. She was a tiny woman, only 5-foot tall. They were a striking pair - - him very blonde, and her very brunette.

When they married he was 19 years old and she was 17, it was 1942 and most couples didn't wait to get married during WWII. They didn't know what tomorrow might bring, better do it today, while you still can, was the way people felt.

Gordon didn't know how he would ever get over his grief. The welfare of his children never entered his mind. He was our father, he took care of us, but we weren't really people to him, only the by-product of his and mama's sex life. He didn't feel emotionally bound to his children, he only cared about his own feelings. He was a spoiled, selfish man who always got his way. Now his wife was dead, and no amount of tantrums, black moods or angry fits was going to bring her back.

*****

I was glad to be back home. My great-aunt always thought I was dirty, or my hair needed to be combed. She never told me I was pretty, or smart, but criticized me, making me feel ashamed. I was glad to go home. Sandra and Jim had inherited our dad's blonde looks, while

Barbara and I took after our mother with dark hair. Aunt Jean never liked Virginia and only felt close to the children that looked like Gordon, rejecting the other two as plain.

I really didn't care about Aunt Jean's feelings. I didn't want to live in a house where you had to tiptoe around and not touch anything. I was perfectly happy running around in the country like a wild animal. I had my father, whom I adored, and my mother would be back, as soon as she got tired of traveling.

I woke up on the Sunday after my birthday. I shared a double bed with my sister, Barbara, who was still asleep. It was cold, too cold to get out of bed, but I heard the car running. I got up and looked out the window. The window on the north side of the room gave me a perfect view into the garage. Daddy had built his two-car garage on the north side of the house, next to our bedroom, and he had left the window there.

My dad was sitting in the car, reading the Sunday paper, smoking a cigarette. It was nothing unusual, he was probably warming up the car and going to work. I got back in my warm, comfortable bed and went to sleep.

I woke up again, I don't know how much time had passed, I heard the car motor - - still running. I jumped out of bed and looked out the window, into the garage. My Dad was slumped over in the seat and the garage was full of smoke.

"Barbara! Barbara get up, daddy's sleeping in the car and the garage is full of smoke! What should we do?"

I ran from the room and woke my 13 year-old brother. "Jim, wake up! Daddy's sleeping in the car, and the garage is full of smoke!" Jim leaped from the bed, immediately awake, dashed through the house in his underwear (he was always very modest) went to the garage, pulled the car into the driveway, called the fire department and called "Aunt Jean. He was in complete control and I was very impressed.

It seemed only seconds before the fire department arrived. They pulled my dad out of the car and laid him in the driveway while my siblings and I looked on. They worked over my dad for what seemed a long time. One young fireman looked up at us, "I'm sorry, he was still alive when we got here," the fireman looked away from the children, feeling uncomfortable. "We couldn't save him, we tried but it was too late."

Jim, Barbara and I waited for Aunt Jean and her husband, Buck to arrive. It didn't take them very long, we gathered a few changes of clothes and left with our aunt and uncle. At that moment, I didn't realize sitting in the back of Buck and Jean's car, headed for Kansas City, that my life had just taken a 180 degree turn and would never be the same. My childhood was over, I was on my own. No one told me I was on my own, and I didn't know it yet. I was sitting in the back seat, looking at the interior of that car, (turquoise with little black dots, very popular in the 50's) all I could think was that Daddy's going to take that trip with Mama. I wonder how long they'll be gone.

*****

People were bringing food to Aunt Jean's house, but not as much this time. After all, they'd just done this 10 days before. There was no sobbing, fainting and shaking of caskets this time. Most people didn't feel much sympathy for my Dad. Most people criticized him and were shocked at his actions. Suicide is a sin. How can he be buried next to Virginia in Catholic ground? The funeral was postponed a few days, until they received permission to bury him in the Catholic cemetery, from the Archbishop of the Diocese.

My Dad was declared "temporarily insane" by the Archbishop, insanity caused by his grief, and laid to rest for eternity by his wife, Virginia.

There seemed to be no question that we would live with Buck and Jean. They were the only family we knew, and they had raised Sandra. Everyone agreed it was best to keep the children together.

All our relatives were glad to be relieved of the responsibility of four orphan children they didn't even know very well. Buck and Jean were called saints by neighbors, friends, Priest and nuns. "God will reward you for what you're doing, Mrs. Comte," Monsignor Spurlock whispered to Aunt Jean, while holding her hand and giving her comfort.

Jean enjoyed this adoration from others, and to all outward appearances, played the role of the loving great-aunt who had taken in her poor orphaned nieces and nephew. Inside, Jean was burning with anger. "Damn Gordon to hell, for doing this to me," she whispered to herself before going to sleep.

My Dad left a modest amount of money when he died, but most of that went for my mother's hospital bills. The estate was handled by the Probate Court and Buck and Jean were appointed our legal guardians and executors of our estate. The house in the country was sold. The money was divided among the four children and put into escrow accounts until each turned 21. It wasn't a lot of money, about $2,000 a piece. Buck and Jean received almost $100 a month for each child from Social Security Benefits. An extra $400 a month was a tidy sum in 1960.

Buck was a mechanic at the TWA overhaul base. He made a good living and didn't need the money, but they were glad to have it. Jean liked shopping. She always wanted pretty things. They lived in a little bungalow in Kansas City, KS. It wasn't a fancy neighborhood, but it wasn't the slums either. If only they could get the money without keeping the children.

Buck was a skinny guy. Very short and very skinny, with thick black hair he kept combed straight back. He had a thin cadaverous face. His eyes, light blue, sunk in beneath thick black eyebrows. Often his mouth was curved in a smile, more like a sneer, for there was nothing amusing about his smile. Some say he had Cajun Blood, but his background was rather fuzzy, and people weren't sure where he came from.

Buck was always standing off to the side, a cigarette dangling from his mouth and a smirk on his lips. He let Jean make most of the decisions and that was fine with him. He liked the idea of Jean being a Southern Belle, she had class, she was a lady, and he was proud she was his wife. She knew how to do things properly, where he might make mistakes. He came from a family of dirt-poor sharecroppers. He had never owned a suit or eaten in a nice restaurant until he met Jean. He appeared to be happy in his role, standing back, letting Jean handle everything.

With the arrival of Gordon's children, he found a new role thrust upon him - - disciplinarian. Often you could hear Jean's shrill voice calling, "Buck! Buck you better get in here, these kids are out of control!" In he would come, taking off his belt as he entered the room, swatting the offending party several times, then leave and return to whatever he'd been doing. After he left, Jean would snicker, "I guess that'll teach you to get smart with me." There was no love or affection in that house. Everything was accomplished through fear. Often Jean told us that she never wanted us, and how miserable her life had become since we arrived.

Buck was pretty easy-going, nothing seemed to offend him, but Jean was real picky about everything and all discipline was doled out at her urging. Jean chose the child that Buck would punish and most of the time she chose me.

I tried at first avoid this punishment. They kept telling me I was a bad girl, and I knew this must be true, or why would they keep punishing me? I tried to be good, but I just naturally did bad things. I figured I must have been born bad, because no matter how hard I tried to be good, again and again, Jean would cry, "Buck! Buck get in here, Shirley's getting smart with me." Then she'd turn to me and say, "You little bitch, I'll show you!"

What did I do that was so bad? I sat on the front porch with out permission- - although I'd never been told to ask permission. One time I tried some pink lipstick and was severely punished, even though Jean had said I could try some on. When I was found wearing the lipstick, and said Jean gave me permission to do so, Jean narrowed her eyes, "You little liar, I never said you could put on lipstick, and parade around like a slut." The deeds that I committed weren't bad at all, but I didn't know this, I thought I was bad, and couldn't help it.

After awhile the reasons for the punishment were overshadowed by the punishment itself. No one could remember what I'd done, but they certainly remembered the punishment I received. I was very confused. No matter what I did, I always ended up doing something bad. They don't do this to Sandra, Jim or Barbara, I thought, it must be true, I must be bad, there's something wrong with me. I need to figure out what it is so I can fix it, so people will like me. These thoughts filled my mind as I lay in bed at night. Out of my frustration in trying to understand what was happening, grew a terrible bitter anger.

No longer did Jean have to look for excuses to start yelling, "Buck! Buck get in here, Shirley's sassing me!" When Jean hissed, "Bitch," I hissed it right back at her.

When they threatened to send me to my mother's family in Arkansas, I screamed back, "Buy the ticket, I'm ready to go!" For this remark I received a couple of punches on my head from Buck's fist.

As far as I was concerned, I was going to get those punches whether

I said anything or not. I'd already tried to be good, it didn't work, and my frustration at not being able to avoid this punishment, made me daring in my speech and manner.

I didn't get punished everyday, sometimes weeks went by when nothing happened. But the threat of this punishment was always in the air. I lived and breathed it daily. There was no escaping it, and nowhere I could hide. It was always on my mind, ready to strike at any moment.

My life consisted of dusting the knick-knack shelf three times a week before school, mopping the kitchen floor three times a week after school, and taking turns with my brother doing dishes. On Saturday's, I did everyone's laundry and ironed all the clothes. Plus any other little chores Jean could find for me to do. The rest of the time I spent in my room reading or listening to records. I tried to avoid my aunt as much as possible. No one living outside the home knew what was happening, or would have believed it. But all those who lived there blamed Buck - - all except me, I knew every beating I received was initiated by Jean.

Once Buck began to viciously beat me with his fist, Jean would cry, "Buck, that's enough, now." Acting like she was innocent, and Buck got carried away, and she couldn't control Buck. But I knew who was beating me, although it was Buck's fist doing the punching, he never did anything without Jean's okay, and that included beating me. Not once did I get a beating because Buck had gotten angry, it was always Jean.

I felt trapped, but when I lay in bed at night I thought about my Mom and Dad. If they knew about this, they would come home. Surely they'll be home soon. It's been almost two years now. How long can they keep traveling? I would daydream about their homecoming; they would come and ring Buck and Jean's doorbell, everyone would be so happy they were alive, we'd all leave together, and return to our home in the country. We'd be a happy family again, no more fear and punishment.

Then the thought would creep into my mind "Maybe they left because I'm such a bad girl? Maybe they don't want to come back?"

Confused and unhappy, I had no one I could confide in. There was no adult person in my life that cared about me. The priest at Church and the nuns at school thought my aunt and uncle were "fine God-fearing people, who gave shelter to their orphaned nieces and nephew." If I seemed troubled and withdrawn, well, that was only natural. After all,

I'd just lost both my parents.

Buck and Jean didn't really like any of Gordon's children except Sandra; when Sandra did what they approved of, which Sandra seldom did. Sandra ran away and got married 6 months after Daddy died. When Sandra eloped, that was all Buck and Jean could talk about. I hid out in my room after finishing my chores, Buck and Jean forgot all about me for a while. They were too busy with Sandra.

Although Jim and Barbara didn't get any beatings, their life wasn't easy. They had lots of chores to do, and lived in fear that what was happening to me could happen to them. Evil and fear oozed from the walls of that house, frustrated anger was felt in every room. Everyone living there was touched by it, and each of their lives was changed in some way. The inside of the house maintained a gloomy look. Plants died and flowers wilted, unhappiness hung in the air like smoke, settling on everything; the drapes, the furniture and even the hole my Dad had burned in the carpet.

Buck and Jean never showed us kindness or encouragement. We were ridiculed and put-down, never quite good enough. We were always the dirty, wild animals from the country, even though we never did any mischief now, we were too afraid.

Jim and Barbara stayed away from me, for fear of what might happen to them. I had no allies. It had been decided by Buck and Jean that I was bad. I no longer cried when getting my punishment. I showed neither fear nor remorse for my behavior. I was defiant and VERY angry. Buck said it was his duty as my guardian to break me, he couldn't let me continue with my attitude. He started to repeat over and over while punching and kicking me, "Cry toughie! Why don't you cry? I'll show you whose tough!"

All the while lashing out, punching, knocking me down and KICKING, KICKING, KICKING while I pulled myself into the fetal position and tried to protect my head. Cry? I thought, let him beat me to death, I'll never cry. Is it tears he wants to see? Never from these eyes!

During one such beating, Jim began to cry. Suddenly he leaped on Buck's back, throwing his arms around Buck's neck, hanging on, with tears streaming down his face as Buck kicked at me lying on the floor.

"Stop it!" Jim screamed, "Stop it! Leave her alone! I can't stand it anymore! I can't stand it anymore!"

Everything stopped, all that could be heard was Jim's sobbing, "I can't stand it anymore!" Jean spoke up, "Buck I think you better take Shirley upstairs, these other children don't need to see this, it upsets them."

Buck took me upstairs after that, and the beating took on a new viciousness, now there were no witnesses, it had become a private ritual between the two of us. As he beat me now, I saw a look come into his eyes, a look I would never forget, a look I'd never seen before, a look I didn't identify until many years later- - a look that said this man was in ecstasy.

Buck enjoyed every punch, kick and taunt he gave me. He was glad Jim had jumped on his back, now he could really get down to business. He liked it when I didn't cry. It was more exciting that way. I wouldn't cry, my anger wouldn't let me, and he'd beat me until he was tired. He was satisfied until the next time.

It was during this time Buck became impotent and could no longer perform his marital duty to his wife. After being upstairs with me, he was too tired and sexually drained to be with anyone. I fulfilled all his fantasies.

He never told Jean about his pleasure, but she sensed that his impotence had to do with me. Jean became resentful, calling me names and accusing me of things I'd never heard of before, much less done them.

"You little slut," Jean would start in after I got home from school, "What took you so long? You're 10 minutes late! You were probably letting some boy feel you up! Buck! Come here, I think we should take Shirley to the doctor and have her checked out for disease. She didn't come right home after school and there's no telling what this little slut's been doing!"

Buck turned and looked at me, a cigarette dangling from his mouth, a sneer on his lips. "What have I told you about not coming right home from school? I guess you'll never learn - - I get tired of doing this," that gleam comes into his eyes, "but it's my duty as your guardian to see you're brought up right!" He says this as he walks behind me, headed for the stairs.

"Buck! Don't be too hard on her." We hear Jean call as we climb the stairs. I had just turned 13.

*****

Gordon's children had always gone to Catholic schools. Jim was sent to the public high school when he graduated from the 8th grade. Buck and Jean said they couldn't afford to continue his Catholic education, and anyway, he was a boy, he could handle it.

I was going to graduate from the 8th grade in a few months and Jean began to say things: "I really don't think we need to send Shirley to Bishop Ward High, we could save a lot of money, that would only be wasted on her. She always gets poor grade cards, she's not very smart. I can't see what advantage there would be to send her to Catholic school. It hasn't done her any good so far."

Buck and Jean acted like I was unworthy to get a Catholic education, but they really wanted to stop paying tuition. They'd already put Jim in public school, and now with me in public school, they would only have to pay tuition for Barbara who was ten years old. The only money they ever spent on us was for tuition at Catholic school, because Jean had to keep up appearances with Monsignor Spurlock, who was head of Blessed Sacrament Church and School. Once we graduated, he didn't know where we went to school, but we had to finish Blessed Sacrament.

I was secretly glad I was going to public school. I hated all the nuns with their talk of sinning and damnation. I knew all about hell, I already lived there. And as far as punishment for my sins, I was being punished right here on earth. I hated all the kids at Catholic school. They were all such goody two-shoes, prancing around in front of the nuns, seeing who could be the most pious. And I hated those damn uniforms. I wanted to wear real clothes.

I watched the kids from public school walk home; the boys with leather jackets, tee shirts with the sleeves rolled up, ducktail hairdos and cigarettes sitting snugly behind their ears. Most of the girls wore ponytails and bobby sox. They wore pedal pushers and poodle skirts and sweaters stretched tightly over their firm, budding breasts. These kids were always laughing and joking, something I never did. I wanted to know these kids. I wanted to be a part of their group. I was lonely and I only wanted someone to care about me. I longed for a friend I could talk to, someone I could laugh with, someone to share secrets with. But I knew I could never have a friend, Buck and Jean would never allow it.

I had started my period and was wearing a bra. I was turning into an attractive brunette just like my mother. But I thought I was ugly. Jean had told me enough times how plain I was. I believed her, and carried myself that way; drooping shoulders, head hanging down with hair in my eyes. The summer after I graduated from the 8th grade, I met a boy who was visiting the boy next door. He like me and invited me to come to Sunday Bible School at his father's church. His father was the pastor of a large Episcopalian Church. Everyone in my family was shocked by this boy's attention, but no one was as shocked as I was.

Jean said, "Who would ever have thought a nice boy like Ronnie Wilson would invite Shirley anywhere! Well, this won't last, as soon as he gets to know her he'll be gone. I'm just surprised he likes her at all, she's so plain. He could have any girl he wanted, he probably feels sorry for her."

Buck said: "He's only after one thing, that's why he likes Shirley."

I didn't know what that "one thing" was. No one had ever sat me down and told me about the birds and the bees. And sex was never discussed at the Catholic School. But whatever it was, he could sure have it! I was starving for affection.

For the first time since living with Buck and Jean, I was allowed to go somewhere alone. After all, Ronnie's dad was an influential pastor in the community - - just the kind of people Jean wanted to know.

I went to the Bible School and I had a wonderful time. Ronnie began calling me, but I was too needy for affection, and he soon quit. As far as that one thing Buck said he wanted, Ronnie never tried.

"I told you," Jean said, "Boys like that, don't go out with girls like you. You didn't let him do anything, did you? Once boys get what they want, they're gone. That's probably what happened, you've acted like a slut and disgraced this family."

I was still a virgin, no boy had ever kissed my lips, never touched my breasts, and no one ever told me about sex. All I knew were the remarks Buck and Jean made to me, which I didn't fully understand. I knew the feelings my developing body gave me and I figured this was all part of the natural badness I possessed.

I thought less and less about my parents coming back - - it was obvious they didn't want me either.

*****

Jean sent us to our rooms everyday for 2 or 3 hours. Usually this happened in the afternoon and we were allowed to come out at dinnertime. We could do whatever we wanted at this time, provided we did it silently. We could sleep, we could play (silently), but Jean encouraged all the children to read. She provided us with all the popular children's books: "The Bobbsey Twins", "Cherry Ames-Nurse" and "The Nancy Drew Mysteries". She gave Jim a collection of "Tom Swift".

I couldn't wait to go to my room and read. I knew when I went to my room and opened my book, I'd be gone - - gone from Kansas City - - gone from 28th Street - - gone from Buck and Jean's house. I would enter another world, away from this house. I traveled all over the world in these books, becoming the heroine; having dangerous adventures and passionate romances.

In the summer of my 13th year, I yearned to read the books Jean kept in the bookcase, the books I wasn't allowed to read because I was too young.

It was my job to keep these bookcases dusted and the glass doors clean. Buck and Jean never checked to see if my chores were done right; they knew I always did a meticulously through job in all my chores.

These bookcases were seldom opened and looked at except by me, while cleaning them. On the top shelf were the encyclopedias with shiny gold lettering. After that were the books in all different colors and sizes. Books about everything and everyone. I held these books lovingly and cleaned them gently. I longed to enter their world and live their adventures.

If I were to arrange these books so no one could tell that one of them was missing, maybe I could sneak it to my room and read it, I thought as I sat on the floor dusting the books. After all, the worst they can do is punish me, and they were going to do that anyway.

Once I'd made my decision, I had to wait a few days before I had a chance to get a book. It was summertime and one day, while everyone was out in the yard and I was cleaning the bookcases, I grabbed a book, ran upstairs and hid it, and was back down again before anyone came in the house.

I was eager to be sent to my room that day. I couldn't wait to see what I was too young to read! Taking the book had been so exciting! All morning my heart raced and I could hear it beating in my ears, afraid I'd be found out!

Finally it was time to go to my room. I went upstairs and waited a few minutes before getting out the book. Buck and Jean never bothered us during this time, as long as we were silent. I knew I was safe now, as long as they didn't discover the book was gone.

I took the book out and looked at it, it was a fat, black book with gold letters that read "Désirée" by Annemarie Selinko. I opened the book and began to read.

In the summer of my 13th year, I found the first friend, who never disappointed- - my books. After that, it became easy to get the books. No one ever discovered them missing. Finishing one book, for I only took one book at a time, I'd replace it and take another.

I longed to be away from this place, and reading was the only escape I had. The only thing Jean ever did for me was to introduce me to the pleasures of reading a good book.

*****

In the summer of my 13th year, the summer before I entered public school, many changes occurred within me. I never stopped to examine these changes, I didn't think about it, they just happened. I began to walk differently, a slow, loose sensual walk; the way I talked changed, defiant and angry. Boys were looking at me now, older boys- - boys 16 and 17. I never dared to give any of them my telephone number, but sometimes when I thought it was safe, I would stop and talk to the boys in the neighborhood. Most of the time I just looked at them.

When getting punished, I would no longer fall into the fetal position, but kept getting up and trying to fight back. I would scream at Buck, "Keep your hands off of me! Leave me alone!"

Buck just snickered, he really enjoyed me fighting back, and it was more fun that way. "Wanna fight, toughie?" he'd say. "Think you can lick me?" he'd punch me on the side of my head, knocking me down. All the while he stood in a boxer's stance, hands curled into fist, a cigarette dangling from his lips and softly laughed, "Get up, toughie, get up and fight!"

*****

That autumn, I entered public school for the first time. It was totally different from Catholic School. The kids were friendly. There was no talk of heaven or hell. The girls would come up and introduce themselves, wanting to know who I was and where I came from.

"Hi! You're a new girl, aren't you? What's your name? I'm Roxy."

"Hello, my name is Shirley."

"Did you just move here?" Roxy asked.

"No, I've been going to the Catholic School until this year."

"No kidding!" Roxy replied, "What was that like? Do those nuns really beat you with switches?" Roxy laughed.

"Only when you're real bad, mostly they make you stand in the wastebasket, in front of the whole class." I looked at Roxy. She was laughing, but not at me. We began to laugh together.

Roxy stayed by my side between classes and we ate lunch together. Roxy pointed out different people to me - - filling me in on what was going on.

Over there, that girl with the blonde hair and pink sweater, talking to those boys, that's Linda Carlson, and that's her friend Molly with the red hair. Stay away from them, they think all the girls want their boyfriends, they'll give you nothing but trouble," Roxy would report.

"See that guy going through the cafeteria line with the blue shirt? That's Terry Ross, he's running for class president. He's a mister-know-it-all, but he's a pretty nice guy," Roxy chattered away.

Roxy lived just one block from me, less than that if you cut through the houses. We exchanged phone numbers and walked the ten blocks home together that first day.

Half-way home, there was a group of boys talking in the parking lot of a hamburger stand, one of them was watching me.

"Who are those boys, Roxy? Do you know them?" I asked.

"Yeah," Roxy replied, "Those guys are just hoods, they seldom go to school, usually they play hooky. When they do come to school, they always start trouble. Roxy looked over at the boys, "And that one looking at you, that's Johnny Bill Barton. He and his little brother don't have a dad, there mom works all the time, and they usually play hooky at his house. Those kids are just waiting until they're old enough to drop out of school, they're NOWHERE."

I took all this in while watching Johnny Bill Barton watch me. His eyes followed me until I turned the block and passed out of sight.

That night Roxy called. Immediately, Buck and Jean wanted to know...who was it?...Where did she know her from?...Where did she live?...Was she Catholic?...Was she a nice girl?...Where did her father work?

"I don't think you should associate with her," Buck and Jean finally decided.

The next day, I went to school, but I didn't tell Roxy what Buck and Jean had instructed.

"You tell that girl not to call here, anymore," Jean called after me as I went down the front steps, headed for school.

As I approached the school, there he was. Johnny Bill Barton, standing on the sidewalk, watching me.

"Hey, you! New girl! What's you're name?" He called out when I walked by.

The other guys in Johnny Bill's group began to smile. Johnny Bill thought he was a ladies man. He liked to show off for the other fellows and demonstrate his "smooth moves."

I stopped in front of Johnny Bill, feeling shy and embarrassed with everyone looking at me. I looked at the ground, "My name is Shirley."

"Well, listen Shirley, me and a couple of my friends are going to my house, we thought we'd have a party. Why don't you come alone?"

"Right now?" I asked him and he nodded his head. "I've got to go to school, maybe some other time." I started for the school and saw Roxy running down to meet me.

How daring! I thought, what an adventure that would be- - skipping school! I had never dared think of anything like that before, just the thought of it sent waves of heat up and down my thighs, and it made me feel light-headed.

That afternoon when school let out, there was Johnny Bill, halfway down the block, waiting for me.

Roxy said, "Don't talk to that creep! If you do, I'm not walking with you!"

When we got to where Johnny Bill was standing, I stopped and Roxy walked on, "I'll see you LATER!" she called over her shoulder.

Johnny Bill looked me up and down and smiled, grabbed my books from my hands and said, "Let me walk home with you, OK?"

"Okay," I said.

We walked toward my house slowly. Johnny Bill did most of the talking. I was shy around people, and after the Ronnie Wilson episode, I was afraid I'd say the wrong thing. I like Johnny Bill, he was cute and he was nice to me and I didn't want to do anything to make him quit liking me.

Johnny Bill talked about his mom and his little brother. He talked angrily about his no-good dad who beat his mother and ran off.

When we got to my street, I stopped and reached for my books, "I'll take my books now, I just live down the street, you don't have to walk me all the way."

Johnny Bill held the books out of my reach, putting them behind his back, "Why? You don't want me to know where you live? Are you ashamed of me?" he said with a hurt note in his voice.

I turned down the street, and Johnny Bill followed me, talking his head off. I was praying no one would be outside to see me. I dreaded what might happen to me. Most of all, I dreaded what Buck and Jean might say to me in front of Johnny Bill. I didn't want Johnny Bill to see Buck and Jean.

As the house came into view, there was Jean, standing on the porch, with her arms crossed in front of her, watching Johnny Bill and I come down the street.

I snatched my books from Johnny Bill's hands, dashed up the front steps and was in the front door before Johnny could blink his eyes.

"Hey" he hollered "What's the matter with you?" He started up the front steps, Jean shouted from the porch, "You better get out of here boy! Don't come sniffing around here again."

I watched from the window as Johnny Bill turned around and left.

Jean came right into the house, "You wait until Buck gets home and I tell him about THIS! I was worried sick, you were late, and you come sashaying down the street like a slut with some greasy-haired boy AND he's carrying your books! Well, I know what you've been up to! You've always been a little slut, letting boys do what they want. You wait until Buck gets home! I won't have any sluts living in this house, young lady! Go to your room until I call you."

I didn't say anything. I went to my room and waited for Buck to get home. All I could think was how could Jean yell at Johnny Bill like that? I'm so embarrassed! How can I go to school and face him tomorrow?

When Buck got home, he came upstairs to my room, "I hear a boy walked you home today?"

"Yes!" I screamed at him, "Yes, and he likes me, too!"

Buck punched me in the stomach. "What have I told you about talking back to me?" And so it began, again.

After my punishment, Buck brought me downstairs while he and Jean discussed me as if I weren't there.

"Buck, I think we should take her to a doctor, she could be pregnant." Buck replies, "It's too late now to do anything about it."

The next day I hated to face Johnny Bill. What would I say to him? I didn't have long to wait. There he was, at the end of the block, out of view of the house, waiting for me. At that moment, I loved Johnny Bill Barton with all my heart. "Hey," he said, "Got it pretty rough at home, huh?"

"A little" I said shyly.

"How'd you get those bruises on your face?" he asked.

I began to cry, and for the first time I told someone what was going on at home.

*****

"Listen," Johnny Bill began, "You're already late for school, why don't we go by my house, we can talk there. If we stay out here on the street, the truant officer might come by and take us in. What do you say?"

"Sure," I said with a new recklessness in my voice, "Lead the way."

Johnny Bill's house was only a few blocks from the school. It was a shabby one-story house, with a sagging porch roof. The house needed a new coat of paint, the yard was over-grown with weeds, and an old broken down sofa sat on the front porch. We entered the house from the kitchen, dirty dishes on the table, pots and pans piled high in the sink. There were three other kids there, Johnny Bill's brother, Bobby, Bobby's friend Ted, and Ted's girlfriend, Pam.

Johnny Bill took my hand and led me to the basement and we talked all morning. I told him about my parents dying (I didn't tell him they were coming back) and about my life with Buck and Jean. When I told him how they said I was bad, Johnny Bill laughed, "You? Bad? Why I bet you've never done anything bad in your life!"

He kept a pack of Winston's rolled up in his tee-shirt sleeve. He took a cigarette out and lit it. "Ever smoked a cigarette?" he asked.

"A couple of times, Jean would give me a cigarette, she says it calms you down."

I took the burning cigarette Johnny held out to me, I puffed on it and began to cough and choke.

"Not like that!" Johnny Bill laughed, "You're not inhaling." and he showed me how. I tried again, and again I coughed and choked. "It takes a while to get used to." Then he smiled at me, I smiled back and he leaned over and kissed me. This was my first kiss, I was frightened, and yet I liked it, it made me tingle all over. He kissed me again, this time reaching out and caressing my breast. Feeling totally confused and afraid, I jumped up. "Please don't do that, it's wrong." I held my arms over my breast, hiding them, feeling ashamed.

"There's nothing to be afraid of, you'll feel good, I promise." he told me in a husky voice, reaching for my hand.

"Just give me a little time, I'm not ready yet. I think we should go upstairs and see what everyone's doing." Johnny Bill followed me upstairs. When we got to the kitchen, Bobby, Ted and Pam were holding a Kotex to their noses and passing it around. When the Kotex got to Bobby, he pulled out a tube of airplane glue, just like the glue Jim used to put his model airplanes together, squeezed some of the glue onto the Kotex and held it to his face.

"What are they doing?" I asked Johnny Bill.

"They're getting high. Wanna try it?"

"No, I don't think so," I never did like the smell of airplane glue, it always gave me a headache, and putting it on a Kotex made me feel very uncomfortable. I went outside and sat on the sagging sofa, on the sagging porch.

Johnny Bill and I talked and I practiced smoking cigarettes. Pretty soon I saw the kids walking home from school. "I have to go now, I don't want to be late and get in trouble."

"OK," Johnny Bill said, "I'll see ya tomorrow."

All the way home I worried that Buck and Jean had found out I skipped school. Maybe the school called? The Catholic School would call. I knew that. I entered the house, waiting for the explosion, but nothing happened. Everything was like normal, Jean sitting in the living room in her slip, her poodle on her lap, sipping on a cup of coffee.

"How was school to day? Did you see your little boyfriend?" She was laughing and petting her dog. I got frightened. Did Jean know?

"No," I lied, "I didn't see him, he wasn't at school today."

"Well, he didn't look like a very nice boy. It's best you don't associate yourself with him." Jean turned away from me and focused all her attention on the poodle sitting in her lap, petting cooing and kissing at the dog. I knew I'd been dismissed, so I went to my room. I lay on the bed and thought about Johnny Bill.

The next day was Friday. On the way to school, there was Johnny Bill by the hamburger stand, looking up the street, watching for me. "Hey." he ran to meet me, "Coming by my house today?"

I knew I'd got away with skipping school yesterday, but I was afraid to press my luck. Anyway, being alone with Johnny Bill made me nervous. I really like him, but it was a sin to let a boy touch your body. Heck! It was a sin to touch your own body! "No, I better not, not two days in a row." He seemed disappointed.

"OK, maybe I'll see ya after school."

When I turned and waved at Johnny Bill, heading for the school, I didn't know I would never see him again. I didn't know this would be the last time I'd ever see the face of the boy who kissed me for the first time, the first person I ever told about Buck and Jean.

*****

When school let out that day, Roxy and I headed home together. Although Roxy was a little peeved with me for walking home with that "hood", she liked me and was forgiving.

Johnny Bill was nowhere around, and I felt a sinking feeling all the way home. I looked for him but he didn't show. Maybe I should have gone with him today? Maybe I should let him touch my breast?

When we got to Roxy's street she asked me to come to her house the next day which was Saturday. "I don't know," I replied, "I've got a lot of things to do tomorrow. Maybe."

All that night, I thought about Johnny Bill. Why didn't he come today? The next day I started my Saturday chore, which was laundry. After only four days at the public school, my whole life had changed, a whole new world had opened up to me. I couldn't keep my mind on my chores. I wanted out of that house. I wanted to be with other kids my own age.

I went to the basement, where the washing machine was, and poured all the detergent down the floor drain, then I returned upstairs and announced. "I've run out of detergent, I don't have any for the next load."

Jean stopped petting the dog long enough to look at me suspiciously, "I thought I just bought a box of detergent. Are you sure? Did you look real good? You better go down and look again."

I went downstairs and stayed long enough to make it appear I'd been searching. When I returned, I brought the empty box with me. I was afraid, I'd never done anything like this before, but I couldn't turn back now. I had to go ahead and play it out. "I couldn't find any detergent, and I've used everything in this box." I held the empty box out for Jean to see.

"Well, I guess we'll have to get some detergent." Jean said. I put a look on my face, frowning as if I didn't want to go. I knew Jean would make me to go the store, if she thought I didn't want to. "You might as well stop scowling, and go to Jack's market. Tell him to put it on my bill."

I threw the empty box in the trash and headed out the door. When I knew I was out of Jean's sight, I cut through the houses and went straight to Roxy's house. When I got there, Roxy was glad to see me, and we went to her room and talked all day.

"You'll never guess what happened!" Roxy began, "You know that boy that likes you? Johnny Bill Barton? Well, yesterday the truant officer went to his house and they took him, his brother and some other kids to juvenile detention. They're probably gonna send him away. This isn't the first time he's been in trouble."

I didn't say anything, I didn't ask Roxy any questions, and I didn't tell Roxy I had skipped school with Johnny Bill. Now I knew why he hadn't been there, and although I hated to hear he was in detention, I felt better.

Around 5 o'clock, Roxy's mother knocked on her door. "Roxy, Shirley's uncle is here, and he wants Shirley to come home now." I froze. Terror filled my whole body. Of course he knew where Roxy lived! Hadn't they questioned me endlessly that night Roxy had called? I got up to leave, the front door was open and Buck stood on the front porch grinning at me, "Didn't think I'd find ya, did you? There's no where you can go where I won't find you! Come on, let's go."

On the short walk home, Buck was chuckling under his breath, "You've done it this time! You wait until I get you home. You think you can get out of your chores, lying about going to the store! I'll show you!" I entered the house and went straight upstairs and Buck followed. I knew what was going to happen. Why try to avoid it?

*****

That night in bed, anger boiled inside me. I couldn't go to sleep, the house was quiet. I couldn't stand to be there one more minute! I eased out of bed so I wouldn't wake Barbara, and got dressed. I climbed out the window, onto the back porch roof, slid down the sloping roof and jumped to the ground. I crouched there a few seconds, breathing hard from excitement, waiting to see if anyone had heard me. Nothing. Just silence. I jumped up and ran down the alley. My heart was singing, I'm free! I'm free!

I didn't know what I was doing or where I was going. As long as it was away from that house, I didn't care. I walked the city streets that night and no one bothered me. While walking down Minnesota Avenue, a business district, at 2 o'clock in the morning, with my shoes in my hand, I was picked up by the police and taken back to Buck and Jean's house.

The officers came in the house and talked to Buck and Jean, but mostly they talked to me. One officer was young, he didn't look like he shaved yet, and the other officer was older with a sprinkling of gray hair. The older officer did all the talking. "Shirley, you shouldn't be out walking the streets this time of night. It's very dangerous, all kinds of things can happen to a young girl."

"I can take care of myself!" I replied in a defiant manner. I was angry with the police officers, I didn't want to come here, but they'd brought me anyway.

"Why did you run away?" the officer asked. Buck and Jean looked at each other, then Jean turned to the officer, totally ignoring me. "We've done everything we can for Shirley. We don't know why she acts the way she does, we've sent her..." the policeman stopped her.

"I'm sure you have, Mrs. Comte, but I'd like Shirley to answer that question. Well, why did you run away?"

Jean wasn't used to being cut off like that, she narrowed her eyes at the officer, but she didn't say anything. She turned that hateful glaze to me.

I was afraid, I knew this policeman was going to leave me here with Buck and Jean. I didn't want him to ask me any questions. "I ran away because I wanted to."

The officer sighed, "Well if you keep running away, they'll put you in the detention center, and they'll lock you up in a reform school. I know you wouldn't like that. You have a nice home with your aunt and uncle. You don't wanna be locked up, do you?"

Reform school? I had no idea what that was, I'd never heard the word before. Reform school? Send me away? Is it possible there's an escape from this hell? I raised my head and looked the officer right in the eyes, gone was the anger and defiance from my voice, replaced with passionate curiosity. "What's that? What's reform school?"

"That's where they'll lock you up, and keep you away from your family until they think you're ready to come home. You don't wanna go to a place like that, but that's where they'll send you, if you keep running away."

I couldn't believe my ears! There WAS an escape- - I could get sent away- - finally, there was hope. I had made up my mind, before the policemen left the house, I would run away everyday. Every chance I got, until they sent me away to reform school. After the two officers left, I waited for Buck to take me upstairs, but nothing happened.

*****

After I learned there was the possibility of escape, there was no way they could keep me home. They couldn't let me go anywhere, because I wouldn't come back. I ran away everyday. I found out where the "bad" kids hung out, and would treat everybody with the money I'd steal from Jean's purse.

After a week had passed, they quit taking me to Buck and Jean's but would take me to the juvenile detention center- - Kaw View. No one stayed at Kaw View very long, it was somewhere to keep you until you either went home, or went to reform school.

They put me in a room with a single bed, toilet and sink. There were no chairs, there wasn't enough room. The walls were cinder block and the door was metal. Everything was painted a dull, dirty pink and the door was locked.

There was a girls' wing and a boys' wing, and a rec room where everyone could get together if they weren't confined to isolation. It wasn't a great place, you were locked in and could only look at the outside from a window. But you could read or talk to the other kids and no one beat the hell out of you.

After a few days at Kaw View, Buck and Jean would come and get me, and the running away would start all over again. Buck stopped punishing me. Buck and Jean didn't like the juvenile system poking their noses into their life. They played the role of law-abiding, God-fearing people, who were trying to do the right thing for their orphaned nieces and nephew. It was a role they played very convincingly.

Buck had been given an award for being one of the best airline mechanics in the world. Jean belonged to several social clubs, and they both worried their dirty little secret would be found out.

Finally, after a month of running away, I was ordered to appear before the juvenile court Judge- - Joe Swinehart, who said, "I don't want to send this girl to the Girls Industrial School. She hasn't done anything but run away, but before I make a decision, I'd like her to have a psychiatric evaluation."

Before my appointment with the child psychologist, Buck and Jean talked to him. They told him I had "spells" and that I made up stories. They didn't know what to do with me!

I found that my angry, defiant attitude had gotten me further than I'd ever imagined and I continued to display this all the time. I wore this attitude like a suit of armor.

They took me to see the psychologist. He had a fancy office on the Country Club Plaza. There were lots of framed certificates on the wall. He sat behind a huge desk in a swivel chair, swinging slowly back and forth.

I told him everything, but I did so in an angry manner. The conclusion was that I had "spells" and made up stories. I was sent to the House of Good Shephard, a home for wayward Catholic girls.

*****

I told anyone who would listen about life at Buck and Jean's but most people wouldn't listen, and those who did, didn't believe me.

"How can you say those things about your aunt and uncle? You don't appreciate anything!"

I enjoyed being in the home for wayward girls, I'd rather be bad and locked up, than good and at Buck and Jean's, I thought.

The home was in a stone building, four stories high. The place was locked and the girls were not allowed to go out. I slept in a large dorm with about 20 girls. Every girl was assigned a clean-up chore to do, and all girls attended classes in the building. Mass was served every morning in the chapel.

I had never met girls like these before- - so bold and daring. Many of them had boyfriends on the outside, and some of them were pregnant, all of them were older than me. I wanted to be like these girls.

I had been at the House of Good Shephard for only two weeks, and already I'd been involved in a couple of incidents and punished. But punishment here wasn't the same as at Buck and Jean's.

Some of us girls had tp'd the dorm and weren't allowed to watch TV for a few days. I also helped a girl run away while doing kitchen duty, but the girl was caught right away and we were both confined to the dorm.

One evening three girls and I were in the library on the third floor. The building had bars on the windows on the first and second floor, and on the basement windows. The basement windows were partially underground, there was a hole at each basement window and an iron railing surrounding the hole. On the third and fourth floor, there were no bars, the windows slid open easily. One of the girls started to speak, "I'd sure like to get out of this place. If I could get out of here, I'd call my boyfriend, he'd come get me."

Then another girl spoke up, Athere's a box of jump ropes here, we could tie these together, tie them to the radiator and climb out the window."

Everyone agreed it was a great idea, and we all became excited about the adventure. I was caught up in the moment, it never occurred to me that I had nowhere to go if I ran away, no one would be happy to see me. If these girls wanted to run away, well, I was going too!

We busied ourselves tying the jump ropes together. At last it reached the ground, 3 1/2 stories down. The four of us stood at the window and looked down, "Well, who's going first?" Someone asked.

"I'll go, but I don't want to be first," someone else said. They all hesitated and looked at each other. Finally, I said, "I'll go first, I'm not afraid."

I climbed onto the window ledge. I lightly took hold of the jump rope and swung my body out the window. As soon as I went out the window, I lost my grip on the rope, and fell 3 1/2 floors, landing on the iron railing that surrounded the hole in front of the basement window. I didn't know how to climb down a rope!

This wasn't like in my dreams, where you fall and begin to float. I was on the ground before I realized what happened. I hit the railing so hard with my left side I bent it. I couldn't breathe. I rolled off the railing and sat on the ground, trying to get my breath. I looked up at the window and saw all three girls staring down at me.

Then another girl started out the window. She hung on tightly, and made it safely down. When she jumped to the ground, the girls in the window pulled the rope up and closed the window.

"They're not coming," the girl said "They got scared when they saw you fall. Come on, let's get out of here."

I got up, I could barely breathe, there was a stabbing pain in my side but I followed the other girl.

We went to a restaurant, and told the cashier we needed to call our parents, we were stranded and needed a ride home. The other girl called her boyfriend but he wasn't there. "Do you know anyone that will give us a ride?" She asked me.

I didn't really know anyone very well. Certainly, no one who would give me a ride after running away from The House of Good Shephard, but I couldn't admit this to the other girl. I had the telephone number of a boy I'd met while running away. His name was Terry, so I called him.

He was home, and said he'd be right there to give us a ride. He was an older boy, almost eighteen and he had his own car. We went across the street to the cemetery and rested against the tombstones, waiting for Terry to show up.

I couldn't breathe very well, and when I spoke, it hurt my side. I turned to the other girl, "My side really hurts, and I can hardly breathe. Do you think I'm OK?"

"Sure," the other girl said, "You just got the wind knocked out of you. You'll be okay in a little while."

It took Terry almost an hour to get to the cemetery, he'd stopped and asked his friend Bill to ride along with him, he hoped we didn't mind. The other girl told them where she wanted to go, and exactly how to get there. When she climbed out of the car, she went off without so much as a backward glance at me.

"Where do ya wanna go?" Terry asked me.

"I don't know where to go, but I don't feel very good. I can hardly breathe."

"You know, I always kinda liked you," he winked at Bill. "Why don't we go make out?"

"No," I gasped, "Why don't you take me to 18th and Quindaro, I can make it from there."

"OK, I'll take you to 18th and Quindaro."

At about this time, Bill reaches over and pinches my nipple. "Stop it," I pushed his hand away. He reached for my nipple again. "What are you doing? I don't even know you!"

"Yeah" Terry leers, "but you know me."

Terry didn't go to 18th and Quindaro, not right then. He drove down by the river and over the railroad tracks, to a deserted area called Bell Crossing. He parked the car in the high grass and said to Bill, Hey man, why don't you take a walk and let me and Shirley talk."

Bill got out of the car and disappeared into the night. "OK," Terry turns to me, "Why don't you take them clothes off?"

"No" I sobbed, I was frightened now. He had the same look in his eyes, the same look Buck gets when he punishes me. "Please, Terry I don't feel good."

Terry ignored my plea, he began ripping at my blouse and tugging at my skirt, all the while fumbling with the zipper on his pants. I tried to fight him back but I couldn't breathe. My side hurt, and my strength was gone. Tears streamed down my face, but I couldn't fight anymore.

"Please, don't..."

Terry pushed me down in the seat and took my virginity. Then Bill got in and fucked me next. They took me to 18th and Quindaro, laughing and patting each other on the back. "She was a virgin, man. I thought I was gonna break my dick trying to get in." laughing, they drove off into the night.

I sat down at the bus stop, I was tired, my blouse was torn, I was dirty and I couldn't breathe very well. What should I do? I thought. I had no one I could call except Buck and Jean, and I'd rather die than do that. I knew it was late, there were very few cars on the street. At that moment, I felt I was the only person left on the planet, this made me feel peaceful. I lay down on the bench and went to sleep.

I had just dozed off, when a man touched my shoulder, "Hey, what're you doing here. You don't look so well, want me to take you home?"

"I don't have a home," I replied.

"Well, why don't you come to my house until we can figure out something."

The man had pulled over when spotting me at the bus stop. He put me in his car and took me to his house. "How old are you?" he asked me.

"I'm eighteen, and I don't have anywhere to go, my parents put me out," I lied to him. "Well, you can sleep in here for tonight," he opened a door to a disheveled TV room, and pointed to a sofa. The pain in my side was getting worse, I sat on the sofa and went right to sleep.

Later that night, the man woke me up, pulling and tugging at my clothes, just like Terry had done.

"Please, please, not again!" I screamed at him, then I couldn't breathe after screaming, and began gasping for air- - my eyes grew huge trying to pull some air into my body and the man moved away, "You better call somebody, you're not well." he said.

The next morning the man asked again, "How old are you?"

"I told you already, I'm eighteen," I could tell he didn't believe me. "Honest, I'm really eighteen," I added, trying to sound sincere.

"I think you should call somebody. Call your parents. I don't think you should be here."

"I've already told you, my parents put me out."

"Well, you better call somebody, and have this mess straightened out by the time I get home from work." and he left for the day.

All day I worried about what I should do. I have no one I can call. I can barely breathe. What should I do?

That evening, the man questioned me again, and this time I told him the truth. I was thirteen years old, I'd run away from a girls home and hurt myself, how Terry and Bill fucked me without any regard for my feelings. I told him about Buck and Jean and how I couldn't call them. "Won't you help me?" I asked.

"I don't know, I'll have to think about it."

Again that night, the man came pulling and tugging at my clothes. This time I let him do what he wanted, hoping he would help me. The next morning, he woke me up, "You better get up, I've called your aunt and uncle. They're on the way here now." As soon as he finished speaking there was a knock at the door.

I learned a valuable lesson that day, one I'd never forget. Just because you give a guy what he wants, doesn't mean he'll give you what you want.

*****

It was a good thing the man had called Buck and Jean. They took me to the hospital emergency room and after being looked over by the doctors and x-rayed, they discovered I had three broken ribs. One of the ribs had punctured my lung, and my lung collapsed. The lung had filled with blood and fluids and they inserted a thin rubber hose into my side, just below my breast. The rubber hose was connected to a gallon jug, and every hour the nurse would come in and put Vaseline on the hose, and siphon the fluids from my lung into the jug. The doctors said I probably wouldn't have lived another day without medical attention.

I stayed in the hospital for 3 1/2 weeks. One week for every floor I'd fallen. While staying in the hospital, and being examined from head to toe, they discovered I had gonorrhea. They didn't tell me. They told Buck and Jean. It didn't take them very long to confront me about it. "She's almost dead, and still she can manage to get a disease."

"I was raped." I told them.

"Well, that's a likely story. Just something I'd expect you to say."

The House of Good Shephard didn't want me back at their institution, and I was ordered by Judge Swinehart to be sent to the reformatory in Beloit, KS., the Girls Industrial School. After being released from the hospital, I was again sent to Kaw View until arrangements could be made to transport me the 300 miles to Beloit.

Within five days of returning to Kaw View, arrangements had been made, all the papers signed, and I was now a ward of the State. No longer were Buck and Jean my guardians, no longer were they executors of my estate. I was under the care of the State of Kansas and on my way to a State Institution, not a Catholic home.

We left early in the morning because it was a long ride. The driver was an older, heavy-set man, and the female chaperone provided for all female inmates being transported, could have been his sister. They pulled up in a late model, dark blue Ford with four-doors. They put me in the back seat, and they sat up front and chatted during the whole trip. They only talked to me when they wanted to stop and eat, then they asked me if I was hungry. For hundreds of miles I wondered what reform school would be like. The back doors of the car had no door handles or locks. You could only open them from the outside. I looked out at the flat, lonesome prairie of Kansas, wondering what was ahead for me.

The Girl's School was right next to the highway, about ten miles before you get to Beloit. "Well, here you are," the driver announced, "here's your new home!"

I was surprised. I didn't know what to think. It wasn't anything like I expected. There were no walls, there were no fences, but a long circular drive, with five or six buildings, a couple of the buildings were very old, made of stone, but the other buildings were low, long, modern brick buildings. The lawn was well kept and at the end of the drive was a flagpole with the State flag of Kansas and the American flag floating in the dry prairie breeze. I saw girls, alone, and in groups, walking from one building to another. It looked like a college campus!

The school had no fences, because they didn't need them. If the girls ran away, there was nowhere to hide on the flat Kansas prairie. Everyone in the little town of Beloit knew they were given a cash reward for every runaway they turned in. Unless the girls could plot a scheme with someone on the outside, to pick them up on the highway, it was pretty hard to get away. To form a plot with someone on the outside was also very difficult as all in-coming and out-going mail was read, and all telephone calls were monitored. Although it looked like a college campus it WAS the State reformatory for girls and the girls knew they were locked up. I was the youngest girl on campus (it was always referred to as a campus and not a reformatory.) Most of the girls were 15 or 16, some were 17. They didn't keep you after you turned 18, they either sent you home or to the women's prison. I was the only one there who was 13.

Immediately upon arriving there, all girls were taken to the infirmary. There, she was stripped, examined for contraband and put into the shower. She was given a foul smelling soap that kills lice on the body and in the hair. After the shower, she was given a blood test and a pelvic exam by a doctor. Then the new girl is locked in a small room for 4 or 5 days until the results from the test came back. This was done to prevent the outbreak of a disease among the school population. Although the new girl wasn't allowed to leave the room, they did everything to keep her occupied during her isolation. She could write letters, do crosswords or needlework. Of course, I read books. In my four days in isolation, I read "Rebecca" by Dauphne DuMaurier. There were horror stories about how girls reacted to being locked up for 4 days, I didn't mind at all.

The girls lived in what they called cottages. Each cottage consisted of about 25 or 30 girls and a housemother. There were 4 cottages at the time I arrived on campus in 1962. Girls were assigned to the cottages according to the results of the psychological testing and severity of the crime committed. The only crime I ever committed, was running away from home, so I was sent to ADII, "D stood for administration building, which is where the cottage was located. Girls assigned to ADII were usually the younger, shyer girls. Their behavior was less aggressive.

The girls in ADI were more aggressive, it was a livelier group. The housemother of ADI was a legend at the school. A short, club-footed woman who wore her black hair pulled severely back in a tight bun, she would take you "off privileges" (rec time, off campus, excursions, cigarettes, etc.) for any minor offense. Her name was Gladys Hastings. No one wanted to be in ADI under her strict rule.

Shadyside cottage was where all the really bad girls stayed. These girls were very aggressive in manner and speech. Shadyside was one of the old stone buildings sitting off by itself under a group of trees. The girls in Shadyside had fewer privileges than the girls in the other cottages. Most of them didn't go to school, but worked in the kitchen or the large, industrial-sized laundry.

The fourth cottage, Grandview, was for the girls getting ready to go home. A new girl was NEVER sent to Grandview. This cottage was small, only 10 to 12 girls lived there. It looked like a large, private-family, ranch-style house. The girls in Grandview didn't mingle with the other girls, they had their own kitchen and dining room, and many of them had jobs in the little town of Beloit. These girls were being prepared to reenter society. Although you could be sent home without going to Grandview first, it didn't happen very often.

The campus woke up early, and every single girl had a clean-up chore to do; dusting, buffing, bathroom sinks, toilets, showers, until the whole cottage was spotless. After clean up, the girls walked single-file to the old stone building where the kitchen and cafeteria were located.

After breakfast the girls went either to the modern school building or to the laundry. The school provided Reading, Writing, and Arithmetic but there were many classes in handcrafts; hook rugs, crocheting, knitting, sewing, cooking and even a cosmetology course.

Just before lunch, the girls would return to their cottages for a head count and walk single-file to the cafeteria.

When school was out in the afternoon, the girls would mingle on the grounds. There were lots of picnic tables, swings, slides and teeter-totters for the girls to play on.

Returning to the cottages for head count just before dinner, again they walked single-file to the cafeteria. After dinner, the girls returned to their cottage for the night. They could watch TV or socialize in the rec room until "lights out". The school always tried to provide the girls with things to keep their minds occupied. There were board games to play and cases of books to read. Many of the girls spent their time knitting or crocheting and the school made sure they had the material they needed.

The girls were allowed to have 3 cigarettes a day; one after lunch, one after dinner and the last just before "lights out". Smoking was usually the first privilege to be taken away when a girl broke the rules.

Every Saturday the girls boarded a bus, (unless she was "off privileges" or in Shadyside) and went to the movie theater in Beloit. In the summer they went to the town's public swimming pool instead. They always went in the mornings, and everyone in the town of Beloit knew the girls school had reserved these businesses on Saturday mornings. The people in town didn't mind having the girls school in their town. The girls were young, they brought visitors who spent money in the town, it provided jobs for the local people and if they spotted a run away, and they could pick up a little cash when they turned her in.

Sunday was spent going to chapel, writing letters home or having family visits. Usually visitors sat at the picnic tables on the well-kept grounds, unless it was winter, and everyone could look out the windows and see who had company. Some girls were allowed to go into the town of Beloit with their families and shop or have lunch.

I was happy at the Girl's Industrial School. Six months had passed since I first arrived, and I had learned many things. I could knit and crotchet anything, I learned to embroider and I could make my own clothes. Most important, no one had hit me for that six months. I was 300 miles from Buck and Jean and that suited me fine.

I had thought the girls at the House of Good Shephard were daring, but after being at the GIS, I realized how meek the Catholic girls really were. Many of the girls frightened me, but being in ADII wasn't so bad. As long as I could avoid the aggressive girls at school and in the lunchroom, being in the cottage was pretty safe.

I talked to a few girls, but formed no close friendships. I spent most of my time reading, knitting and crocheting, keeping to myself. One morning the housemother, Mrs. Johnson stopped in front of me while doing the head count, "You have an appointment this afternoon at 1 o'clock. You're to go to Dr. Robinson's office. Don't forget."

"Okay, I'll be there, do you know why he wants to see me?"

"He'll tell you everything when you see him this afternoon."

There were a few counselors and child psychologist at the school, but Dr. Robinson was the head psychiatrist and he held few interviews. All morning I worried about what he wanted. When I arrived at his office exactly 1 o'clock, I knocked softly on the door.

"Come in, come in and sit down, Shirley." Dr. Robinson called out to me.

When I entered the room, I saw my counselor, my housemother, one of my teachers from school and Dr. Robinson sitting at a long table. I sat down in a chair facing them. Dr. Robinson did all the talking.

"How are you doing, Shirley?"

"OK" I answered.

"How's school going?"

"OK" I wondered what this was leading to. All of them were smiling at me.

"I won't keep you in suspense any longer. Shirley you never break any rules or lose your privileges, and you get along well with the other girls and respect your housemothers. You should never have been sent here in the first place, we've decided there's nothing we can do for you here, we're going to send you home next week."

I had never told any of the counselors at GIS about my life at Buck and Jean's, since no one at the House of Good Shephard had believed me, I felt it was useless. Everyone at the table was grinning at me. This is what all the girls wanted, to go home, all except me.

"I don't think I'm ready to go home yet," I told Dr. Robinson.

"Shirley, you should never have been sent here, this is no place for you. You'd be better off with your aunt and uncle then here with these girls."

I just looked at them, they were still grinning at me.

"Don't you have anything to say? Aren't you happy?"

The rest of the interview was a blur, I agreed to everything they said and left the office. I headed towards the school, then I stopped, panic surged through me, the shock was wearing off, all I could think was I can't go back to Buck and Jean. I've got to figure out a way to stay here.

I looked out past the campus to the lone Kansas prairie. If I'm bad, I thought, if I break some rules, they'll let me stay here. I knew then I could no longer live here quietly, in order to stay, I'd have to be more like the other girls in my attitude. After all, being angry had got me here; staying angry would keep me here.

Slowly, with deliberate steps, I WALKED off the campus, walked along the road leading to the highway. They picked me up within an hour and put me in isolation. They said I RAN away, but I hadn't run anywhere, I walked all the way, waiting for them to pick me up and bring me back, wondering what took them so long.

*****

I was placed in isolation for a week, and released back into the cottage. I lost all off campus privileges and, of course, I wouldn't be allowed to go home.

Dr. Robinson talked to Buck and Jean a few times, but Buck and Jean had never come to visit me, and wrote only rarely, to keep up appearances for the school. The role they played was very important to them. They cared nothing about me, but they did care what people thought about them.

"I don't know why Shirley acts that way. Ever since her parents died she hasn't acted normal. She would have these spells and run away from home all the time." Jean told Dr. Robinson in a syrupy voice with a heavy Southern accent.

Jean was secretly glad I wasn't coming home, Buck was disappointed.

*****

During the week in isolation, I had lots of time to think. The nuns at the House of Good Shephard had made me feel ashamed when I told them about life at Buck and Jean's, they said I didn't appreciate anything and it was my own fault. Maybe it was my fault, I thought, maybe there's something about me, something everyone can see, that disgust them. Is it the way I look?

I didn't tell the counselors at GIS that I didn't want to go home, I didn't want them to know what had happened at Buck and Jean's. So far, everyone at GIS had been fair with me. When I first arrived I received a scrubbing down in the showers with a hard-bristle brush, but all new girls had pranks pulled on them. I had never been singled out for ridicule, and I didn't want to tell them about my past. They probably wouldn't believe me anyway.

During my first 6 months in the reformatory, I had kept to myself, no one bothered me and I was peaceful and happy. All that changed after my talk with Dr. Robinson. I was going to have to do things I didn't want to do, if I wanted to stay here. WHY? Why do I have to live like this? Anger boiling inside me, I returned to ADII.

Some of the rules at GIS were:
NO RUNNING AWAY
NO PIERCING OF EARS
NO TATTOOING (done with shoe polish, since the girls weren't allowed ink of any kind)

NO SCRATCHING ON THE BODY WITH NEEDLES OR PINS
NO TALKING IN THE LINE TO CAFETERIA OR AFTER LIGHTS OUT
NO PASSING OF NOTES BETWEEN THE GIRLS
NO INVOLVEMENT IN GIRL BUSINESS

Two girls involved in a love relationship was called "girl business", usually refereed to as just GB. The words lesbian or homosexual were never used, either by the staff or the girls, it was always GB. Most of these relationships were harmless, platonic affairs, two girls reaching out for a close friendship, but not all of them. Some of the girls were involved in very heavy homosexual affairs, and this was strictly against the rules.

Rules against GB were strongly enforced by all the staff, but that didn't stop it. GB was a fact of life at GIS.

After I returned to the cottage I began to break the rules, little ones at first. I'd lose cigarettes or rec time, but I knew every time I lost a privilege, it was another mark against me (or another mark for me!).

I pierced my ears and was off privileges. My ears got infected so I let them close up and heal, then pierced them again. And again, I was "off privileges." I tattooed on my arm, on the inside of my knee and on my ankle. I scratched LOVE on one arm and HATE on the other and was sent to isolation until it healed.

Girls were allowed to go home for a five-day pass after they'd been at the school six months. This was the ultimate privilege, but I was never even considered for a pass because of my behavior. I began to enjoy the excitement of breaking the rules. I didn't get involved in GB. The thought of touching another girl that way made me uncomfortable. None of the girls approached me in that manner, and I approached none of the girls.

The restrooms of the school were locked and only opened at certain times. One day I had to pee, I had to pee real bad. I went to the office and asked them to unlock the restroom. "No, you'll just have to wait until next hour," the teacher told me. I pulled down my pants and urinated in the hall, in front of the bathroom door. That was the end of my education. I was kicked out of school and assigned to the laundry.

It was a big laundry located in the basement of the administration building. All the clothes were washed and starched, then thrown damp into a large basket, the girls ironed these clothes until dry, there were no dryers that I can remember. The sheets and flat items were put through a mangler, but the clothes were done at an ironing board. There were about 15 ironing boards on the south wall of the laundry. We did the laundry for the whole campus, including the staff.

I had been at GIS for 18 months, I was 15. Four girls and myself were "off privileges" for talking on the way to the cafeteria. When we returned to the cottage, we gathered in one of the girls room.

"I'm tired of always losing privileges" one girl began, "I'd like to give them something to take me off privileges for."

"Yeah, me too." said another. "I wonder what they'd do if we barricaded ourselves in this room and refused to come out?"

"They'd probably have the maintenance men take the door off." someone replied.

We became excited by our talk, our bodies were pumping adrenalin. We pushed all the furniture (a dresser and bed) against the door and refused to come out. The staff didn't try to take us out, they just waited. We had no food or a bathroom, they knew we'd come out eventually. We relieved our bowels in shoeboxes and threw it out the window. We stayed in the room 2 days, when hunger forced us out. We were all sent to isolation for two weeks, and when released, I was sent to ADI whose housemother was the dreaded, club-footed Miss Hastings.

*****

Gladys Hastings looked mean. Hobbing along, with a permanent scowl on her face, she tolerated no nonsense. She lived on campus and working at the school was her whole life. She took her responsibility seriously and ran a tight ship.

I knew being sent to ADI was a demotion and I was glad, but I was worried about Miss Hastings. Once in the cottage, the strangest thing happened. Miss Hastings liked me. Miss Hastings, who never favored anyone, would bring me candy bars and books and showed me special favoritism. She brought me her own books to read, books not available in the girl's library.

At first I was surprised and didn't trust this show of affection, but it didn't take me long to come around. I grew to love Miss Hastings. I cared what Miss Hastings thought and I wanted her to be proud of me and so I began to change my bad behavior.

Gladys Hastings saw herself in me. Short, club-footed, she understood my feelings of being ugly and unloved. Poor little girl, Gladys thought to herself, no one ever comes to see her, she rarely gets a letter. She reached out to me and tried to show me there was someone who cared.

At about this time, a new psychologist joined the staff at GIS. He wasn't long out of college and lived on campus with his wife and new baby. The new psychologist's name was Denis Shumate, and I was scheduled to see him.

Denis Shumate took an interest in me, and I went to see him 3 times a week. "What is it with this girl," Shumate thought, "She didn't do anything to get sent here, but does everything to stay."

He picked my brain three times a week until he broke me down. When I revealed that I thought I was dumb, he looked at me, shocked, "Our testing here at the school shows you have an IQ of 140. That's not dumb! That's very high!"

When I told him I thought I was ugly, he got angry, "How can you say that? You're the prettiest girl on this campus!"

When I cried and told him about Buck and Jean, and how no one believed me, he put his hand under his chin and gazed straight into my eyes, "I believe you, Shirley."

"You're just saying that to make me feel better!" I sobbed.

"No, I believe you, and I'll prove it to you. I'll call your aunt and uncle right now, and you can listen."

And that's just what Denis Shumate did. He got the phone number from my file and dialed. Jean answered the phone, Buck was at work. Mr. Shumate introduced himself as my new psychologist, "I thought you could help me understand Shirley a little better, Mrs. Comte. She doesn't seem to want to go home, and I thought you might know why?"

Jean assumed her usual, syrupy-sweet role. "Why, Mr. Shumate, we've discussed this with her other psychologist at the school. It should all be in Shirley's records, I don't think I can add anything else."

"I don't have her records with me, and I'd like to hear it from you." Denis Shumate winked at me.

"Well, as you know," Jean began, "Shirley was orphaned and my husband and I took her and her brother and sisters in. We tried to provide a good home for them, but Shirley would have these spells and run away. We don't know why she did it, we felt it had something to do with her parents dying."

"Mrs. Comte, Shirley tells me her uncle would beat her. Is this true?"

Jean gasped, "Well, didn't they tell you she makes up stories? Surely you don't believe that wild story?" Jean laughed nervously.

"As a matter of fact, yes, I do believe it. I believe every thing she's told me. I believe you and your husband treated her so badly, she'd do anything not to come back."

Jean wasn't used to people not believing her. She lost all her genteel manner and shouted at Denis Shumate. "Who do you think you are? Questioning me about something that little liar has said. Maybe you shouldn't be working there with those girls. I'm going to report you to the Superintendent of the school!" and she hung up the phone.

Mr. Shumate returned the phone to the cradle and turned to me, "She really got mad, she hung up on me! I thought she was going to bite my head off!" he laughed, "I guess the truth hurts!' We laughed together and the healing began.

*****

Once it was known (and believed) why I didn't want to go home, there was no reason for me to act up. Mr. Shumate promised he wouldn't let them hurt me again, and I believed him.

Denis Shumate was a big man, he'd played football in college. He was in his early twenties and full of ambition. He really cared about the girls and wanted to make a difference in their lives.

I adored him, in a foolish school girl way. He said it wasn't my fault that Buck had beat me. I wasn't bad, Buck was the bad one. He praised me and encouraged me in everything. Having Denis Shumate and Gladys Hastings behind me sowed the seeds for a long and painful healing.

I never told Mr. Shumate my parents were coming home someday. I never thought about my Mom and Dad anymore. They hadn't been a part of my life for many years. Their faces faded in my memory. When I told someone my parents were dead, I never stopped to think just what dead meant. I refused to think about these things; I hadn't grieved for my parents.

I didn't think of these things consciously, but at night, when I went to sleep, when I had no control of what I thought, I would dream of my Mom and Dad. We would all be walking in a wheat field, the whole family, and one by one, everyone would disappear into the field but me. I would run through the golden field, looking for everyone. I knew from the light in the sky it was dusk, and darkness was rapidly approaching. Sometimes I dreamed we were all together again, in the country, playing with the Dolan kids. Only in my dreams, did I think of my parents, because ALWAYS in my dreams they were alive.

*****

Another year passed and I was 16. I was turning into a woman. I was small-boned with small even teeth. My face was round with dark, almond-shaped eyes and thin lips. I didn't realize I moved my body in a sensual way, it was something I did naturally. The girls began to make fun of the way I walked and called me "rubber butt." When I tried to change the way I walked, I couldn't do it. I had to think about walking differently and as soon as I realized, I returned to the "rubber butt" walk and soon accepted it as my own unique walk.

One day Mr. Shumate began talking about my future, "You can't stay here forever, Shirley. Someday you'll have to go home. I know you don't want to go, but you're older now, it's been almost 3 years since you've been home. Maybe it'll be different this time."

Panic filled my every pore. "But, Mr. Shumate, you promised you wouldn't let them hurt me anymore! I DON'T WANT TO GO TO BUCK AND JEAN'S!"

"Honestly, Shirley, I want what's best for you. I'm worried about you, I think you're becoming institutionalized. Everything here at the school is planned for you, you don't have to make any decisions for yourself, just follow the rules."

"These years in your life are very important in your development as a woman. I want you to get out of here someday and lead a happy, successful life. I'm afraid if you stay here much longer, you won't be good for anything but a convent, or a prison, and I'm sure you wouldn't be happy in either place. You're too smart and too pretty to throw your life away in some institution."

"Why don't you go home for a five day pass? Try it and see what happens. Maybe your aunt and uncle are sorry about what's happened and will treat you better. What can happen in five days? Would you try it for me?" I couldn't refuse him anything he asked.

I had made friends with a Negro girl named Joyce. Joyce had brown skin with copper hi-lights and she always wore frosted pink lipstick. She reminded me of Tina Turner. Joyce was always laughing, and I liked being around her.

Joyce was an expert on boys and constantly talked about her fast life on the outside. Joyce always talked about love and romance, something I only knew from books. Joyce was from Kansas City.

When I told Joyce I'd be going home on a pass, she gave me all her friends phone numbers, with messages to give each one.

I began to wonder what it would be like on the outside. Maybe it will be different, just like Mr. Shumate said. I wanted to begin my life, I felt I was waiting for something to happen. Maybe Mr. Shumate's right, maybe I do need to get out of here. Nothing is ever going to happen here. I started to look forward to my home pass. I pushed my fears into the back of my mind. And with Joyce ALL excited about getting her messages out, it had become an adventure.

I left early in the morning, before the other girls got up, and was taken to the Greyhound station in Beloit. From there, I took the bus to Kansas City, stopping at every little farm community on the way. It was about a ten hour ride, and I didn't arrive in Kansas City until evening.

I watched the farm towns go by, one after another. The closer I got to Kansas City, the closer I got to Buck and Jean's house, the more I began to worry, what if Mr. Shumate is wrong?

What would happen if Buck hit me? What would I do? I'm not the same girl I was 3 years ago.

The bus was delayed for over an hour in Topeka, and by the time it rolled into the tiny bus depot in Kansas City, KS., the station was closed. No one was there to meet me, and I had to wait on the sidewalk in front of the station door. I looked up and down State Avenue, there were very few cars on the street, and a hobo wobbling drunkenly down the block.

I should just leave right now and not go to Buck and Jean's. I thought about this for a few minutes, but discarded the idea. Where would I go? I didn't know anyone, and Mr. Shumate was counting on me to give it a try. I didn't want to disappoint him. I looked in my purse for a dime and called Buck and Jean.

"Hello" Jean's sickeningly, phony voice came over the wire.

"This is Shirley. I'm at the bus station."

"Buck! Shirley's here, why don't you go to the station and pick her up, Buck will be right there," and she hung up.

I hadn't seen Buck and Jean in 3 years. I knew they cared nothing about me, but there was always that hope that maybe they would change and love me. This was the only family I had, why couldn't I be a part of it? Why couldn't we be happy like Beaver Cleaver?

Buck pulled up in front of the station with a cigarette dangling from his lips, sneering as usual, he hadn't changed. "Look how you've grown! Boys will be following you like a dog in heat!"

Oh boy! I thought, this is a great welcome after three years!

Buck started asking questions about the school and I answered in as few words as possible. The air between us crackled with tension. He was leering at me with every word he spoke, looking my body over from head to toe with that familiar look in his eyes, and I hated him for it. The atmosphere around us was ready to explode at any moment and we both knew it.

The house was only ten minutes from the bus depot, but it felt like hours. Why did I come back? When we got to the house, I bolted from the car and ran into the house.

There was Jean with the dog on her lap and Barbara sitting off by herself, sort of hiding in the dining room.

"Where's Jim?" I asked Jean.

"Jim moved in with Sandra and her husband after he graduated from high school."

"Oh" was all I could say. I didn't know Jim had moved, but I wasn't surprised. Barbara was the only one left at Buck and Jean's, but it was almost as if she wasn't there. Barbara rarely spoke, only when someone spoke to her. She worked very hard at not drawing attention to herself, and she was very good at it, I hardly noticed her at all.

During my three years in reform school, my personality had changed. My name was rarely called for mail, I never had weekend visits from family who loved me, like the other girls. I had grown to accept the fact that no one cared about me, and thought it was my fault. Miss Hastings and Mr. Shumate said they cared, but they only entered my life recently, and once I left the school, I knew I'd never see them again. They weren't my family, they were just doing their job. I wanted a loving family, people who cared about me.

I adopted the "I DON'T CARE" attitude (although I really did care). I was obnoxious and angry with strangers for no reason, "What are you looking at?" I'd growl at people. I didn't like for anyone to stare at me. I took on the tough girl image that I'd learned from the other girls at GIS. I wasn't always pleasant to be around, and I DIDN'T CARE! If no one loved me, well, I'd get along just fine by myself. This was the girl who came home for a 5 day pass. I wasn't the same girl who left 3 years before.

The first night went smoothly enough. No one showed any great happiness to see me, but it was late and we all went right to bed. I tried to talk to Barbara, but Barbara didn't have much to say. She avoided me as much as possible. Barbara acted like she was afraid of me.

The next day Buck went to work and I sat in the yard reading most of the day. Jim and Sandra called and invited me to come to Sandra's house during my visit. "I don't know" Jean told Sandra, "you live across the state line in Missouri. I don't think she can go out of state."

Later that day, Jean started questioning me about the reform school and my life there. "What about this Mr. Shumate?" she narrowed her eyes at me, "Has he ever tried anything with you?"

I became instantly angry. How dare you try to cheapen the only good relationship I had since my parents died? "What do you mean, has he tried anything?" I spoke slowly, calmly, but there was a hint of threat in my voice and I looked Jean dead in the eyes.

"Oh, you know what I mean. Has he ever tried to touch you?"

I was raging now. I stood up and leaned over Jean sitting in the chair, Jean sat back, fear on her face.

"No, I don't know what you mean, and don't you ever say anything about him again, you, you bitch!" I was still in control of myself, I appeared deadly.

"GET AWAY FROM ME!" Jean yelled, "Get away!"

I left the room and went outside. Jean didn't tell Buck what had happened, and I didn't stop to wonder why. Three more days and I can leave, I thought.

That evening after dinner, I began to call Joyce's friends. Of course, Buck and Jean had to know who I was calling, so I told them.

"Who's friends? Not that nigger gals friends?" Buck sneered at me.

"I don't know why, with all the girls at that school, you gotta pick a nigger."

"Stop calling my friend a nigger. You don't even know Joyce!"

"Where I'm from," Jean cuts in, "We always called them Negras."

"Next thing you know, she'll have some big, black buck for a boyfriend." this was from Buck.

"So what if I do! If I want a Negro boyfriend, so what! Negroes are just like everybody else!" (In 1965, black people were referred to as Negro, not Black or "fro-'merican, that came later.)

46

Buck approached me "You ain't so big that I can't take you upstairs."

I had been standing by the phone and I turned to face him, "We don't have to go upstairs, why don't you go ahead and try, old man."

"I'll show you who's an old man!" He started to remove his thick leather belt.

Jean was afraid, I had frightened her that afternoon, and now this! They might kill each other! Jean thought to herself. She certainly couldn't send Shirley back to the girls school all beat up! Jean spoke, "Buck, leave her alone. She's nothing but a troublemaker. I'll call Sandra and she can stay there until her pass is over." Buck never did anything without Jean's okay. He was disappointed, he was all excited but he backed off mumbling under his breath to me that he'd show me who was old!

The next afternoon, Sandra came and took me out of that hellhole. Un''''til she arrived, I stayed out of everyone's way. I didn't like these confrontations, it scared me, I didn't know where they might lead. All I knew was that I had to stand up for myself. I just HAD to. I couldn't let Buck see my fear.

Sandra lived in a lovely, new house in Grandview, MO., a suburb of Kansas City. Sandra had two small daughters ages 3 and 2. Sandra was the big sister I had never known. Sandra talked away like they'd been friends for years. When we arrived, Jim was so-o-o happy to see me. This surprised me, I thought they didn't care anything about me.

We talked long into the night, we spoke of things we'd never discussed before. Jim told of the horror he went through watching Buck beat me. He had his own hellish stories to tell, they didn't beat him, but his life wasn't pleasant. "I knew for years, I was leaving as soon as I was old enough. Whenever I got angry, Buck would always challenge me to a fight. You don't like it?' he'd say, "You wanna try and do something about it? Come on, think you can whip me?" Well, I practiced every chance I got, I lifted weights, I practiced karate kicks, I was getting myself ready. One day, just before I graduated, he took all the money I'd made at Jack's Market that week. ALL OF IT! I needed that money so I could take my girl, Naomi, to the prom. He could have let me keep some of it! When he asked if I wanted to do something about it, this time, I was ready to take him on. Okay' Buck says, "Go pack your clothes, it's time for you to move.' He doesn't want to fight someone who'll fight him back!"

Sandra told her stories of life there, how they had always accused her of fooling with boys. When she was 14, Buck began to try and sexually molest her. This was why she ran away and got married. We started to discuss Barbara. She was all alone with Buck and Jean. God only knew what kind of games they played with her.

We talked until we were tired. I couldn't remember the last time I felt this good! This was my sister and this was my brother, this was my family and they loved me!

Sandra looked at Jim, "Should I tell her?"

"That's up to you, Sandra. She has a right to know." Jim replied.

"Tell me what?" I wanted to know.

"Well," Sandra began, "Jean is not who she says she is. She's much closer to us than an aunt."

"She's our grandmother, isn't she?" I stated. I had never questioned the fact that Jean was our aunt. When I said these words, not only did I surprise Sandra and Jim, I surprised myself.

"How did you know?" Jim asked me.

"I don't know how I knew. I didn't know. But when Sandra said she was much closer to us than an aunt it just came out." We all laughed and started humming the theme song from the "Twilight Zone."

*****

When Sandra ran away and got married, they went to Memphis, Jean's home town. She and her husband, Sonny, rented a place from an old woman who knew the Sandy family, and she knew the Cole's, Jean's family.

Her real name wasn't Jean, it was Mabel, but she had changed her name. She had married Clarence Gordon Sandy, and they had a son named Clarence Gordon Sandy, Jr., my father. Mabel and Clarence left Gordon in Memphis with the Sandy sisters, and they raised him. They traveled around from place to place but the marriage didn't work out. Jean married Buck who she'd met in Texas. She didn't tell Buck she'd been married before, and he didn't know she was old enough to have a teenage son.

She moved to Kansas City to get away from anyone who could tell Buck her secret. She wasn't happy when her son, Gordon, came to

Kansas City, but what could she do? And if that wasn't bad enough, he told Virginia! When Jean had looked at her son in his coffin, she didn't claim him, she didn't grieve for him, she was relieved he was dead. Ever since she's married Buck, Gordon had maliciously held the secret over her head, tormenting her, always threatening to tell, but in the end, he never did.

"Did you tell her you knew?" I asked Sandra.

"Yes, I did, but she denied everything, said it was all lies, and said the Sandy's never liked her anyway. I told her the Sandy's didn't tell me. She's gone through all this, I doubt if she's going to confess now."

"WOW I thought, Ashe's my grandmother, and she let Buck treat me that way! WOW!"

I spent the rest of my pass at Sandra's and had a wonderful time. We all promised to keep in touch with each other. I was scheduled to catch the bus early in the morning to Beloit, so Buck and Jean came to get me the night before.

The silence lay heavy in the car, it seemed to make everyone jumpy. Jean started to ask about Sandra and Jim, wanting to know how they are doing. Talking as if nothing were wrong with our family.

She's so phony, I thought, look at her, playing the Southern Belle. She's my father's mother, she should have looked out for me, she should have loved me. I had always yearned for Jean to accept and love me, and it was a heaviness in my heart that I couldn't please her.

As I looked at Jean now, I felt a load being lifted from my shoulders. I looked at Jean and I felt pity. It didn't matter to me anymore if Jean liked me or not, after all, who was Jean? Someone who's real name was Mabel, someone who had deserted her son and allowed her grandchildren to be mistreated, someone whose whole life was a lie, and for what? For Buck!

I swore a I looked at Jean that I'd never be like her. I'd never lie about who I am. And I never did.

*****

When we got to the house, I went to my room and kept to myself. I didn't feel like having another episode with Buck and Jean. I felt too good after being with Sandra and Jim, and I didn't want to spoil it.

Early the next morning, Jean took me to the Greyhound station, told me good-bye and left. She never got out of the car. I went into the station and waited for my bus to leave. All morning on the ride back to GIS, I thought of Jean and her secret.

There was an hour lay-over in Manhattan, KS. Manhattan was a college town, K-State was there, but if was also a soldier's town because Fort Riley was only a mile away.

I was waiting for my bus to leave, when a light-brown Negro in a solder's uniform sat down next to me. "Hey, you've gotta be the best lookin' thing I've seen in a long time. I think I'm in love!"

No one had ever spoken to me like this before, I was startled. "You're just kidding," I said to the man, smiling at him.

"Don't you believe in love at first sight? I saw you sitting here, and I said that's the girl for me! What's your name? My name is Lee."

"I'm Shirley. What are you doing at the bus station? Are you headed somewhere?"

"No, I'm not going anywhere. I'm stationed at Fort Riley, and something told me to come over to the bus station today and There you were! Come on, let's go somewhere and get a beer."

"Oh no," I told him, "I can't do that, I have to be on that bus in fifteen minutes."

"You can always catch another bus. If you leave now, I'll never see you again. You'll be passing up a chance for love. Come on, we'll get married tomorrow!"

I was totally swept away with his words. This is like something right out of a book! He was charming, handsome and he was in love with me! I didn't even think about what I was doing. "Okay, let's go," I said. All I had was the clothes on my back, my luggage was on the bus.

His car was in the lot at the station. He stopped to get some beer and we rode around Fort Riley. He was from Grand Rapids, Michigan. He talked all afternoon of his plans to marry me and take me home with him when he got out of the army. He drove to Junction City, 20 miles from Manhattan, and rented a motel room. He said he wanted to make love to me, and I let him.

My first experiences with sex were unpleasant and forced, I thought it would be different this time, but it was a disappointment. I didn't hear any bells ringing or feel any tingling sensations, like I read about in books. He jumped on, pumped roughly away for a few minutes then rolled off. I couldn't see what all the fuss was about. If this is what all the boys wanted, I didn't think it was such a big deal!

Before the sun came up, Lee woke me, "I've gotta be on base at 8 o'clock. Why don't we get some breakfast? I saw a little diner across the street when we checked in yesterday."

I got dressed and we walked across the street to the diner and sat down at a table. It was a small café, with a counter and four tables. A tall, skinny waitress, about 40 years old, leaned behind the counter talking to the morning regulars.

We sat at the table for about 10 minutes, waiting for a menu. Finally the waitress strolled over, "I can't serve you two, you'll have to leave."

"Why?" I asked, "What's the problem?"

"Come on, let's go." Lee said, rising from the table.

"No! Wait, why can't you serve us?" I turned to the waitress.

"Negroes and whites can't sit together in here, if you want breakfast, you'll have to sit at separate tables."

I wanted to stay and argue with the waitress but Lee was already headed out the door. "Come on, let's get out of here, I've lost my appetite." He took my hand and pulled me out the door.

This was my first experience with racism, except for Buck's remarks on my home pass, I'd never dealt with racism before. When I grew up in the country and went to Catholic School, I hadn't met any Negroes. The subject of Negroes had never come up in my life until now. No one told me I was supposed to hate them. Being treated this way in the restaurant shocked and angered me.

"I gotta get on base. I'll pay for the room for another day and I'll be here at 1 o'clock to pick you up." Lee kissed me and he was gone.

I watched TV in the room until someone knocked on the door.

"Who is it?" I called.

"It's the management. Are you staying another day?" I opened the door. "My husband has already taken care of today's rent." It made me feel grown up to say this to the man.

"Nobody's paid for this room for today. Check out time is noon, either pay the rent or leave," he turned and headed back to the office.

"Wait!" I called after him "There must be some mistake! He'll be here at 1 o'clock, he'll straighten it out then."

"Check out time is noon, either pay the rent or wait for him outside." And that's what I did.

I sat on the steps in front of the motel, waiting for Lee who loved me and wanted to marry me. 1 o'clock came and went...two o'clock...three o'clock...four o'clock, I sat and waited. "Something must have happened, I thought, he loves me, he told me he loved me, he has to come back!"

It was 8 o'clock, I'd been waiting all afternoon for Lee to show up, and now it was dark. Panic filled me, what would I do? I had no money, I had no food. Where was Lee?

A skinny, dark-skinned Negro man came up the street, watching me. He was older, late thirties, really old to me, I was only 16.

"I live down the block, and I've been watching you all day from my window. You musta been sittin' here ten hours. What are you doin'? You got somewhere to go?"

"I'm waiting on my fiancé to pick me up." I liked saying this.

"When is he suppose to be here?" the man asked.

"He was supposed to be here at 1 o'clock. Something must have happened to him."

The man laughed, "I don't think he's comin'. Say, how old are you, anyway?"

"I'm nineteen." I lied.

"Why don't you come down to my place? You must be hungry. Got any money?"

"No, I don't have any money, and I AM hungry, but I cant leave here, what if my fiancée comes and I'm not here?"

"Well, I don't think he's comin', but you can watch from my window, you can see the motel real well, if you're worried about it. It's not safe for you to be sitting in front of this motel at night."

I was tired and hungry, and I followed the man to his apartment. His name was Robert, he was from Detroit, but when he retired from the army he settled in Junction City. He said he had business interests there.

All the first night I sat in the window, watching for Lee. Lee had no intention of coming back, but I didn't know that. Lee had smooth talked my pants off, got what he wanted...a day's entertainment, and was gone. I wasn't wise in the ways of men, I thought he loved me!

Robert was nice to me. He bought me some clothes, fed me, gave me a place to stay. He laughed a lot and liked to talk. Every day he left for a few hours to "take care of business," but he spent most of his time with me.

He wanted to fuck me, and I let him. After all, it was easier to let him do it than argue. But when he asked me to lick his penis, I flatly refused. "Heavens no," I was shocked. "I'd never put one of those in my mouth! How nasty!"

Robert was much older than me and I didn't feel any attraction to him. I was still looking for Lee, everywhere I went I was hoping to see him. Robert wasn't a smooth talker like Lee. He was older, more serious, and a lot more honest.

I'd been staying at Robert's 3 weeks, when a friend of his came by while he was out "takin' care of business." Robert never had any friends come by before and I was surprised.

"Robert here?" the man asked, smiling from ear to ear.

"Not right now, he's gone, I don't know when he'll be back."

The man stepped into the apartment, "I heard ol' Robert had some young thang stashed over here. I guess they were right. Where'd you come from?"

I told him I'd been waiting for my fiance when I met Robert. "You say his name is Lee from Michigan?" he grinned even bigger, "I know him, I know where he's at right now. I just left him at a card game."

"Really?" I said, "You've gotta take me there!"

The strange man and I left walking and after a few blocks, we walked up the front steps of a run-down house and went inside.

"Well, where is he? There's no one here!"

"He musta just left" the man grinned at me, then he reached out and grabbed me. I tried to get away, but he kept coming, I knew what he wanted, and rather than get beat up, I let him fuck me.

After he was done, he laughed, "Ol' Robert thinks he's so slick, well I fucked his precious little white girl. HA-HA-HA."

I got dressed and walked back to Robert's, and he was waiting out front for me. The man called Robert and told him he'd fucked me. Robert was steaming mad.

He pulled me into the house, made me strip and take a bath, then he said, "I tried to be nice to you! You wanna act like a whore, I'll treat you like one!" He handled me roughly and fucked me hard. After he was done fucking me, he pushed me outside, totally naked and locked the door. I was crying. Is this a nightmare come true? Outside...naked...in broad daylight! I hid in the hedges along the front of the building. Finally, after an hour had passed, Robert opened the door and called me. When I ran into the house, he told me to get dressed, he wanted to talk.

"I shouldn't have got mad at you. It's not your fault, you don't know any better. PeeWee, that's the guy you fucked, has always wanted everything I've had. You're not the first girl of mine he's fucked. He blames me for losing his wife, he can't see it's his own fault. I just happen to be the one she came to. But I never thought YOU'D fall for PeeWee's mess!"

I told Robert how PeeWee had tricked me to the house and been forceful, so I just went ahead and did it. Robert looked at me, in a stern way, "You know, you shouldn't be here. I don't believe you're 19, you're probably about 15. You should be at home with your family. I'm going to buy you a bus ticket to Kansas City, I want you to go home, you'll be better off. Go home for awhile and maybe I'll send for you later." I didn't tell Robert I couldn't go home or that I'd run away from the reformatory. I didn't know what I was going to do when I got to KC, I tried to plead with him to let me stay, but he said, "No, it's best you go home."

*****

Robert put me on the bus and watched as the bus went down the road, headed for KC. All the way there, I thought about what I'd do when I arrived. I decided to call a girl who had been released from GIS only a couple of months ago, maybe she'd help me. She was a Negro girl named Colleen.

Colleen sent her brother to the depot to get me. All the people I had contact with were Negroes and although I didn't give it much thought, I was soon to learn that they did.

Her brother James showed up with another guy and when I got in the car, he began, "We can't take you to Colleen's, it wouldn't be safe since you're a runaway from GIS. I know another place."

It was dark and I couldn't see well, but I could see it was a shack with a rusted tin roof. There was no electricity and they burned candles for light. There were two other guys in the shack, drinking beer and talking. There were only two rooms in the shack; one room had two broken down love seats and the other room had a narrow unkempt twin size bed. James took me to the room with the bed, and pushed me down on the filthy mattress. "Okay, get those pants off!"

"Wait a minute!" I hollered at him, "What's going on? I'm getting tired of you guys always wanting to fuck all the time!"

James slapped me, then he reached into his pocket for a switchblade knife, CLICK, the blade was pointing at me! He laid on top of me with the knife at my throat, "OK, you fuckin' white bitch, take those pants off before I slit your throat!" James finished, he got up, fastened his pants and went to the other room, calling out before he entered, "Who's next?"

The four men raped me for what seemed like hours. Is this what it's all about? I thought, guys immediately go after one thing, were they all like this? Seems like it to me. They wanted it so bad, they were willing to kill you for it.

Some time later in the night another man appeared at the tin-roof shack, "Hey, what's goin' on here?" Leroy asked, "Who's this white girl?"

"She's some girl my sister Colleen met at GIS, she's a runaway. We got her up here fuckin' her, man. Wanna get your dick wet?"

"Look at this! She's crying! You guys oughta be ashamed for treating her this way! Hey white girl, get yourself together and come with me."

I wasn't sure I wanted to go with him, but I sure didn't want to stay where I was. Leroy, who was 24 years old, had a reputation as a bad ass. He'd just gotten out of Lansing Prison for attacking some people with a baseball bat and inciting a riot. He had done 3 years of a 5 year sentence. When Leroy said he was taking me out of there, none of the four other men dared oppose him.

"Take the white bitch, man. We're done anyway," they all laughed.

I left with Leroy. He liked to drink beer, one after another. He lived with his mother, he had his own entrance to the house and that's where he took me.

As soon as Leroy got up in the morning, he wanted a beer. He didn't have a job, and didn't want one. He spent his day trying to come up with beer money. He went from one person's house to another, looking for money, or maybe just a beer in the fridge.

On this day, Leroy made his rounds and took me along. Leroy ran into George at his cousin's house. George wanted to get a fifth of scotch, but he was only 18 and Kansas was a dry state. In order to get a bottle of scotch, he'd have to go the few blocks to Missouri but George wasn't old enough to buy it. Leroy was more than happy to get it for him, he knew he'd get a drink.

Leroy, George and I went to State Line Liquors and Leroy bought the Scotch and a six-pack of beer. We were all sitting in the front seat of Leroy's old car, riding around, sipping on the bottle. I had never drank before, except for a few sips, and I didn't like it very well, but Leroy and George sucked the bottle dry and started working on the beer. George started to touch me, rubbing my breast and thigh. "Hey, leave me alone!" I said, I was really getting tired of every male wanting to feel me up. "I'm getting tired of guys always touching me! I'm not a piece of meat, I'm a person."

"Yeah" Leroy slurred drunkenly, "Leave her alone, man."

George was drunk but so was Leroy. George didn't see the look in Leroy's eyes, he couldn't see anything. He didn't stop touching me. "Whata you care if I touch some white girl, huh? Come on, Leroy let me have her."

"I told you to leave her alone, George." Leroy didn't speak again, he drove to his house, jumped out of the car and ran into the house, when he came out he had a rifle in his hands. When Leroy ran into the house, George had gotten out of the car and was leaning against the automobile, facing the house. Leroy came running toward George, he pushed the barrel of the rifle into George's stomach and pulled the trigger. George crumpled to the ground and Leroy beat him about the head and shoulders with the butt of the gun. An ambulance pulled up with lights flashing.

I was still sitting in the front seat, and now I eased across the seat, away from the fight, got out of the car and ran as fast as I could away from there. My God! I thought, what happened? Did I really see that? What was that thing Leroy had in his hands? Was it a broomstick?

I ran for several blocks, when an old man said, "Over here." I went into the house to catch my breath. The man called the police and turned me in.

I was questioned by two detectives. One was white and the other was a big, Negro man named Boston Daniels (he later became the first black Chief of Police in KCK). This was the first time I met Boston

Daniels, who would later do me a great favor. "Why don't you tell us what happened? What happened between George and Leroy?"

"I don't know." I answered, "I didn't see anything."

"I know you saw something. You were right there. We have several witnesses who saw you run away."

"I told you, I didn't see anything." I said this with the angry attitude I'd learned, but these cops weren't impressed.

"If you didn't see anything, why'd you run?"

"I don't know, I just did!" I was afraid, I'd never been interrogated by detectives before. The only policemen I knew were the ones that picked me up when I ran away from Buck and Jean, and they were always nice.

We were in a small office with papers and Wanted Posters tacked on the walls. One detective sat behind the desk and Boston Daniels sat next to the desk, facing me. "Well, Shirley, we've got a dead boy and I wanna know why he's dead."

"Dead boy?" I echoed, "What dead boy? What are you talking about?"

"I'm talking about George Sharp...dead...and Leroy McKinley shot him, I wanna know what happened."

I couldn't speak, I looked from one detective to the other. They were both watching me, waiting. "I didn't know anybody was dead. I didn't see anything."

"Maybe you'd like to know what Leroy said? Wanna know what Leroy told us? He said you told him to kill George. He said you gave him the gun. He's trying to put this whole thing on you."

"I never told him to kill anyone! I didn't give him the gun, I didn't even know he had a gun."

I was easy for the detectives to break down. I told them what I'd seen, and was immediately sent back to GIS in Beloit.

*****

A new cottage had been built at GIS. A lone one-story building called Prairie Vista. The south wing of the cottage was the new isolation unit, and the north wing had rooms for ten girls. The ten girls who lived in Prairie Vista were the ones who couldn't adjust in the other cottages, for whatever reason. It was a new cottage and they were trying new ideas. The girls had group therapy meetings several times a week, this was something new at GIS.

I was placed in the new isolation unit after being returned to Beloit. Mr. Shumate didn't come to see me for a few days, and when he did show up, he was angry. "You managed to get yourself in a mess. What happened? Everyone thought you were dead. Your luggage was still on the bus, you got on the bus in KC. We thought someone had killed you!"

I told him what had happened, I told him about Lee. "Shirley," he had calmed down, he spoke softly to me, "I know you want somebody to love, but that's not the way. Men don't respect girls who are easy. Most men enjoy the chase. What you did was very dangerous, you didn't know that soldier, he could have done anything he wanted to you!"

I hung my head and wouldn't look at Mr. Shumate, I stared at the floor. I felt ashamed, he was disappointed with me. I didn't tell him why Robert had sent me back to KC, I didn't tell him what had happened in the tin-roof shack, I didn't say anything.

"What happened in KC? What happened between those men? How did you get involved in a mess like that?"

"I don't want to talk about it." I didn't want to think about Leroy and George, it involved that forbidden subject...death. I blocked George out of my mind, I didn't try to analyze what happened.

"You'll have to talk about it sometime, they'll want you to testify at the hearing. You were a witness to the shooting."

As it turned out, I didn't have to testify after all. I was afraid to go to court, so Mr. Shumate wrote a letter to the Judge, stating I was "psychologically unfit" to testify, I was still a minor, and I was excused as a witness.

I didn't go back to ADI with Miss Hastings, but was placed in the new, experimental cottage, Prairie Vista. Mr. Shumate knew I wasn't ready to live on the outside, and yet he knew I couldn't stay there forever. Since the disaster of my home visit, he also knew I couldn't live with Buck and Jean, so he began looking for alternative solutions. Where ever I went, he knew I would be on my own. He tried to prepare me to take care of myself.

First, he enrolled me in the cosmetology course. During the first part of the course, I did well, it was all textbook work. During the second part of the course, working on patrons, I had neither the patience, or the temperament to do other people's hair. I couldn't even do my own hair, so I dropped the course.

Next, he got me a job off the campus, working as a dishwasher in a Chinese Restaurant on the highway. I liked this job, I was in the kitchen, away from people. I only had to deal with the two brothers from Korea that owned the place.

The Korean brothers laughed a lot and were always bowing to each other. They were very polite, they didn't raise their voices. They told me what my duties were, and I was expected to do it. I was not the first girl from the reformatory to work there. Many girls had worked at the restaurant. Some had been sent home, and others had been fired because they didn't do the work to satisfy the Korean brothers.

I did everything they ask and took on more duties. The two brothers were always praising my work to the school. Mr. Shumate was pleased to see I could do so well in a job. I was 17 years old now, I'd been at GIS for over 4 years, longer than any other girl. Mr. Shumate sent me to Grandview cottage to live, to prepare me to go home. I refused to go to Buck and Jean's, and after finding this out, they said, "We don't want the little trouble maker, anyway." I had talked to Jean on the phone, I told her I knew her secret, I knew Jean was my grandmother. Jean didn't want to talk to me anymore, and she certainly didn't want me to talk to Buck.

Sandra and her husband were separated and he had the daughters in California. She was living with another man, and this just wasn't done in 1966. It wasn't done openly and society was very disapproving. Sandra was even fired from her job at the bank on "moral grounds." The State of Kansas would never release me to an adult that was living an immoral lifestyle.

Sandra rented another apartment and, although she and Bob still lived together, they had separate addresses. I was released from GIS into the custody of my older sister in the Spring of 1966. I was 17 years old and Mr. Shumate was worried about me. "I hope you'll be okay. Don't make any foolish decisions. I'm always here if you need me. You can call me anytime. It's a rough world, you already know that. But it can be a good world, too, and I hope you can find that out."

I was going to Missouri, there wouldn't be any meetings with the juvenile authorities every few weeks. I was leaving the State of Kansas, no probation, I was free.

*****

Sandra, her new lover, Bob and my brother drove to Beloit to get me. I watched them cruise down the long drive way in a brand new, white Ford convertible. I was so excited, I had made all kinds of plans! All the girls I would call, the girls that had already gone home. The girls I had grown up with in reform school.

It was 1966, young men were being drafted and sent to die in Viet Nam...there were love-ins and protest marches...The Motown Sound...The Beatles...bell-bottoms, mini-skirts and Twiggy...James Brown...discos and drugs...and Martin Luther King was preaching non-violence across the land. The Civil Rights Movement was in full swing. The country was in a turmoil.

All of my friends from Beloit were Negro girls (although now it was becoming more acceptable to say Black or Afro-American) except for Linda, another white girl from GIS that hung out with Blacks. The Blacks were militant and I liked this. After the episode at the café in Junction City, I became an outspoken advocate for Civil Rights.

Kansas City was very segregated in 1966. Blacks and Whites didn't go to school together, they didn't live in the same neighborhoods. And they never went to the same restaurants, bars or movie theaters. In Kansas City, the races were not supposed to mingle together. Whites didn't like it and Blacks didn't either.

Sandra and Bob went dancing every night. They'd met on the dance floor, and since they danced well together, they thought it was love. Bob thought he was the "grooviest" white boy in town. He could do the James Brown shuffle better than anyone.

I was always allowed in the clubs without ID, even though I was a minor. Sandra and Bob, who knew everyone at the bars, SWORE I was old enough. I also spent a lot of time with my old friends from GIS, especially Joyce. Joyce had gotten out of GIS not long after my home pass and now had a baby girl only a few months old.

It seemed like all the young girls I knew were having babies and I wanted one, too.

Joyce had introduced me to a guy named Willie, and I thought I was in love. I just wanted to be in love, be able to say I was in love. Willie never said he loved me, and he didn't want to be seen in the neighborhood with a white girl. He didn't tell me he felt that way, he was too "nice", he didn't want to hurt my feelings, but he always took me where no one could see us.

I wanted to have a baby, I read up on ovulation and the times when a woman is most likely to get pregnant. I counted up my days and told Willie, "On the 16, 17 and 18 of April are my peak fertility days. Make sure you get with me on one of those days."

"Oh no," Willie laughed it off like a bad joke, "You don't wanna do that! You don't want a baby! I don't want any babies. You have to take care of babies."

"I want a baby," I told him, "It'll be my baby, if you don't wanna do anything for this baby, that's fine with me. I'll never bother you for anything if that's what you want. I just want a baby!"

On the 17th of April, Willie and I got together in the back seat of a yellow 57 Chevy, I got pregnant for the first and last time. I had been out of reform school two weeks.

I still didn't care for sex very much. I had learned the hard way, not to be alone with a guy, unless I wanted to be alone with him. I enjoyed the kissing and fondling, but the act of sex itself I found distasteful. Joyce was always talking about orgasms, but I'd never had one while having sex with a man. I had masturbated, but of course I would never tell anyone, it was taboo (and a sin) to touch your own body. Sex was something I did because the guys expected me to.

The minute I got pregnant, I knew I was pregnant and I knew it would be a boy. Willie had already received his draft notice when I first met him. He was in boot camp when I found out for sure that I was pregnant. Willie was one of the lucky ones, Uncle Sam didn't send him to Viet Nam, instead he went to Germany. He hadn't wanted me to get pregnant, but now that I was, he made sure I understood, he didn't want any part of it. That was fine with me. I can handle this, I thought.

When I was 5 months pregnant, Sandra decided to try and reconcile with her husband in California. I couldn't remain living with Bob, (Bob didn't like me, I was a "nigger lover"). I moved in with my brother, Jim, who had a new wife, and she was pregnant, too. No one was happy about me being pregnant by a Black man. Abortions weren't legal in 1966, but I wouldn't have had one anyway. I wanted my baby, I had planned to have this baby, I had intentionally gotten pregnant.

Soon after Sandra got to California she discovered she was pregnant by Bob and when her husband threw her out she came back to Kansas City. Bob had gotten a bachelor pad in Kansas, he was enjoying his single life, but he took her back because she was having his baby.

My family sent me to Dr. Caruso, who made arrangements to have the baby "given up for adoption," to a professional Black couple. After all, it would be for the best. The doctor sent me to some lawyer he knew. It was decided I would have the baby, all the hospital and doctor bills would be taken care of. I would stay in the hospital after the birth of the baby, not say anything about giving it up, once released from the hospital, the lawyer's secretary would take the baby. Oh, it was all above-board and legal, they assured me. "Don't worry, we'll handle everything." the lawyer said.

I didn't want to give my baby away to some strangers, never knowing where he was, but I couldn't tell my family- - they wouldn't listen. My 18th birthday was rapidly approaching, and so was my due date.

I had my 18th birthday on January 5, 1967, I was no longer a minor, my family had no control. I went to see Dr. Caruso a week later. "Doctor, I've decided not to give my baby away. I never wanted to give him up, but my family doesn't want me to keep him. Now that I'm 18, I feel it's my decision to make. I hope you don't mind?"

"That's foolish," the doctor replied, "What are YOU going to do with a Negro baby? It'll ruin your life! And what about the baby? Don't you want him to have a chance in life?"

"I think the baby will be better off with its mother. I want to keep him, and that's that."

"You're a fool." the doctor growled at me.

I didn't tell my family about my decision. I had never intended to give my baby away, I only went along with it to keep down the arguing. I wanted this baby, like a child wants a toy. I didn't fully understand the responsibilities I was taking on. This baby wasn't really a person to me, but more like a doll that everyone said I couldn't have.

Living with Jim wasn't very pleasant. Jim was gone all the time, working as an auto mechanic and going to electronics school at night. He only came home to sleep. His wife, Delores, didn't seem to like me very well. Jim and his wife were both very disapproving of my situation, pregnant...by a Negro...not married. Jim and Delores had been married in the Catholic Church, their baby was blessed by the Sacrament of Marriage...my baby was not, and they took every opportunity to remind me of it.

I had no plans for the future, beyond what I was going to do that night. I lived for the moment, letting life lead me where it may, not once trying to take control.

More than anything, I wanted love, and hoped this baby would fulfill my dream. I was unsure of myself and tried to hide this by acting tough. I still assumed the "I don't care" attitude. I was angry, I never stopped to wonder why. It was just a part of me. I took my anger everywhere. I woke up angry and went to sleep angry.

I went for a visit to the doctor. I was due any day now. "Doctor, what hospital should I go to?"

"When you go into labor, call me, and I'll tell you where to go. I'll make all the arrangements."

So I left the details up to him.

On the night of January 24th, I started labor. At first I wasn't sure, I had always heard how awful the pain was, but this was more like menstrual cramps, so I waited. The pains were coming about every 45 minutes, so I woke Jim and Delores, called Dr. Caruso and went to the hospital.

The doctor told me to go to Trinity Lutheran. When we arrived, we approached the desk and told them who I was.

"Let me see," the receptionist said while shuffling through some papers. "I don't see your name anywhere. We're a private hospital, and in maternity cases we require a $200 deposit before the birth of the baby. You're not on the list. Who is your doctor?"

"Dr. Caruso, I just talked to him a few minutes ago, and he said to come here. He said you'd be expecting me." I was clutching my stomach now. The labor pains were getting more intense.

The nurse had a look of pity on her face. "Dr. Caruso is no longer on the staff at this hospital. He hasn't been here in a month."

"But I just talked to him! Why would he tell me to come here? I don't understand what's going on!" I turned to Jim and Delores.

"I can't admit you here without the deposit," the receptionist replied. "I know a young intern at General Hospital, he's a really good doctor. Why don't I call him and you can go over there."

I was afraid, I didn't want to go to General Hospital, my mother had died there, and fear always triggered my anger. "I'm going to call Dr. Caruso right now and find out what's going on!" I headed for the pay phone and dialed his number, but the doctor wouldn't take my calls, "He's out on an emergency," the voice on the other end of the line said, "Can I take a message?'

Maybe he's on his way here, I thought. While I was on the phone, Jim had been talking to the people at the front desk. He came over to me "It's okay now. They're going to let you have the baby here. I've told them about your money in the escrow account. They needn't worry, the bill will be paid. The Head of Obstetrics has agreed to deliver your baby. They have some papers for you to sign, then they'll take you to a room." Dependable, level-headed Jim, always nice to have around in an emergency.

I signed the papers and was admitted to the hospital. On January 25, 1967 at 8:57 a.m., I delivered a beautiful, healthy baby boy. It was an easy birth, the doctor said I was born to have children. I was given some kind of gas during the delivery, and I was completely out when they returned me to the room.

The babies were kept in a nursery, and brought around three times a day for feeding by the mothers. I was in a maternity ward with three other women. The nurses brought little blanket-wrapped bundles in pink and blue to all the new mothers, all except me. I waited, but when the nurses began to gather up the bundles and return them to the nursery, I stopped one of the nurses. "Where's my baby? Is he all right?"

"We're not supposed to bring your baby. Your brother said you were giving him up for adoption. A mother isn't allowed to see a baby she's giving up."

"What are you TALKING ABOUT?" I screamed at her. "I'm not GIVING HIM AWAY! I've signed no papers! I want to see my baby NOW!"

"I can't do that, I have my orders. Why don't you calm down" the nurse tried to take my arm but I pushed her away, "I'll call the doctor, and he'll straighten all this out, just calm down."

"I WANT TO SEE MY BABY!" I screamed at the top of my lungs with tears streaming down my face. Did they do it? I thought, did they accomplish what they had tried? Did they take my baby? Someone ran in the room and jabbed me with a long needle. I was out like a light bulb.

When I woke up, the nurse came in all smiles. "We'll be bringing your little boy in soon, you'll be happy to hear! It was a misunderstanding, it's all been taken care of. You'll be able to see him, but the doctor would like to talk to you first. I'll call him now and let him know you're awake."

An hour later, the nurse came back. "Your doctor is down in the father's waiting room, he wants to talk to you where it's private."

I entered the waiting room, the doctor watched me closely as I sat down across from him. I waited for him to begin. "You certainly look better than the last time I saw you." He smiled and I smiled back. "I wanted to talk to you before you saw your baby. I don't want you to be shocked."

"Why?" I asked, "Is something wrong? He's not deformed or anything, is he?" A thousand fears entered my mind in a matter of seconds.

"No" the doctor replied, "he's perfectly healthy, but he's Negro."

I began to laugh, relief flooded though me, "You think I didn't know that?" I said through my laughter.

*****

The nurse brought my baby in at feeding time. I had to feed him with a bottle. I had been given a shot to dry up my milk because they thought I was giving him up for adoption. He was a beautiful baby with rich brown skin like a South Seas Islander. He had long, wavy black hair that hung almost to his shoulder. I unwrapped him from his blankets, I counted his fingers, then I counted his toes. When I took off his diaper, I got worried. I'd never seen a male naked in the light before. I turned to the woman in the next bed. "Does my baby look deformed to you?" I held the baby out for the woman to see. The woman looked at the baby, then looked at me, a puzzled look on her face. "No, I can't see anything wrong, he looks fine to me. Why do you ask?"

"I always thought boys had 2 balls, but he's only got one!" I pointed to his testicles. The woman laughed, "He has two, but they're both in that sac." The woman found this very funny, and she laughed and laughed.

The typical hospital stay in 1967 was a week. All the patient's at

Trinity Lutheran Hospital were white, all, that is, except my baby. The nurse's pushed his cradle to the back of the nursery so the other patient's couldn't see him too well.

Everyday a woman from Birth Records, would come and tell me to pick a name for the baby. The birth certificate had to be filled out before I left the hospital. I hadn't given much thought to a name for the baby. After all, I never planned ahead, I lived for the moment. Now the moment was here and I had to make a choice. There was no one I wanted to name him after. I thought about it for several days, but I couldn't come up with a suitable name.

"You're going to be getting out in a couple of days and this birth certificate must be completed." The woman sat with pen poised above paper, ready to write. I tried to think, I've always liked the bartender at Oscar's Lounge, Pete the bartender, I turned to the woman, "I want to name him Peter, Peter Sandy."

"That's a nice Biblical name. What about the middle name?"

"No middle name, just Peter Sandy."

"Okay, and what about the father?"

"Can't you just leave that blank? I don't want to put a father on there. This is my baby and no one else's."

"In cases of illegitimate births, yes, we can leave the father out." And now my baby had a name- - he was Peter- - I liked it.

That evening Jim came to visit without Delores. "Shirley," he stammered and looked all around the room, not meeting my eyes, "I'm afraid you're gonna have to find somewhere to go when you get out of the hospital. Delores doesn't want you there, and now you're going to keep the baby. Well, she just doesn't think she can handle it. You know Delores has a nervous condition." Jim didn't want to be bothered either, but he put all the blame on Delores. "After all, she's my wife, and she's going to have my baby. I have to respect her feelings."

Jim left, and I cried all night. When I told Sandra what happened, Sandra begged Bob to let me come and live with them again. "NO," Bob said, "You know I can't stand her, and we've only got a tiny one bedroom apartment."

"P-L-E-A-S-E Sandra pleaded, Ashe'll stay out of your way. She doesn't have anywhere to go when she gets out of the hospital."

"Alright, but I don't want any trouble out of that Niger lover."

I had no baby clothes to take Peter home in. The nurses at the hospital gathered up some clothes and blankets and sent Peter and I home to Sandra and Bob.

The money for the hospital bill was taken out of my escrow account and extra money was given to me to buy some clothes for Peter.

Bob didn't want me in his house, and he didn't hide it. His favorite topic of conversation was my "nigger baby". But I only listened to this for so long, then I would explode and an argument would start. Bob would taunt me, trying to make me angry, and I fell for it every time.

A few days after getting out of the hospital, Jim and Delores came to visit. I had received some mail from the hospital, mistakenly addressed to Mrs. Sandy, and Delores had opened it. "Well, of course I opened it, I thought it was for me," Delores said, "I'm the only Mrs. Sandy."

"I'm sure it's a mistake," I told her, "I didn't tell them I was Mrs. Sandy."

"You have no right to use that name, it's my name!" Delores yelled.

"I can call myself anything I want. I was born with the name Sandy, MY FATHER GAVE IT TO ME, I have Sandy blood, my baby has Sandy blood, and you don't have a drop of it!" I yelled back at her.

Jim cut in, he didn't like people to raise their voices, and he always spoke in a calm sensible manner, he never lost control. "Shirley, your baby is illegitimate, in the eyes of the law he doesn't exist. He's a bastard."

"That's ridiculous! What do you mean he doesn't exist? He's right here, he exists."

I felt that everyone was against me, certainly everyone in my family was. I had done the unthinkable...I had gotten pregnant by a black man, I had done the unforgivable...I had kept the baby. I was an outsider, a traitor to my race. But black people didn't like me any better. They didn't want their sons messin' with a white girl.

When Peter was 10 days old, he started to cry in the night. I did everything to try and stop the crying. I changed his diaper, I tried to feed him and I tried to hold him. Frustrated, I hollered at my baby, "What's the matter with you? Stop crying!" Bob came down the stairs, "I'm sick of you, get out of my house and take your nigger baby with you!"

"I'll be gone first thing in the morning!" I yelled at him.

"No, I want you out NOW. I don't want no niggers in MY house!"

I took Peter's diaper pail, put clean diapers and bottles in the bucket. It was after midnight. I knew Sandra would stop Bob, she wouldn't let him put me out in the middle of the night! Sandra stood on the steps, watching, saying nothing, not meeting my gaze. My brother and my sister, the only two people I thought loved me even a little, both of them had turned their backs on me because of Peter.

It was the first week in February, and February can get very cold in Kansas City. I started to walk, I didn't know where I was going- - I had nowhere to go. I had on moccasins that were getting soaked form the light snow that began to fall.

Willie's family will help me, I thought. I'll go to his mother's house and show her Willie's son, her grandson. Certainly she'll fall in love with such a beautiful baby. I entertained this thought in my head as I walked. I knew where Willie's mother lived, but I'd never met her before. I imagined meeting her for the first time, both of us loving Peter. I thought about this so hard, that by the time I got to her house, I was convinced she'd welcome me home.

Willie's mother wasn't a bit happy to see me. This white girl sure had a lot of nerve knocking on her door in the middle of the night, wanting in. "So you the white girl Willie was foolin' with. I heard about you. How do you know it's Willie's baby? He hasn't claimed that baby, and it don't look nuthin like him. Since you're here, and it's the middle of the night, you can stay, but you gotta be gone by tomorrow, you gonna hafta find somewhere else to stay."

The next morning, Willie's younger sister said to me, "Why don't you go to Family Services and apply for ADC (aid for dependent children) surely you qualify for Welfare."

Willie's family gave me a ride to Family Services and left me there, glad to be rid of me. I went in the office with my bucket of diapers and bottles, with Peter tucked under my arm. I was given some papers to fill out and told to wait for my interview. People kept sneaking peeks at Peter and I, some openly stared. It was unusual to see a white girl with a black baby, and most people frowned at me. I ignored them and played happily with Peter.

"Shirley Sandy" the receptionist called, and pointed to an office. A big, fat white woman was sitting behind the desk, shaking her head.

"I'm afraid we're gonna have to turn down your application for ADC."

I COULDN'T BELIEVE IT! "Why?" I finally managed to say. I was so shocked, I could barely make a sound with my voice.

"According to your application you have no permanent address. You MUST have a permanent address in order to receive ADC."

"That's silly! My family put me out because of my baby, I have nowhere to live. I don't know where I'm going when I leave your office. I don't have a job, I don't have any money. I really need help. I thought that was what you did here. If only I can get on my feet. Can't you help me for a little while?"

The woman scowled at me, "There's no reason to get excited with ME, I'm just following the guidelines set down by the State of Kansas. In order to receive ADC in this state, you have to have an address to send the check to. You can come back and reapply when you're settled somewhere."

"COME BACK? I won't need Welfare if I have a permanent address! I need it now! I can't feed my baby!" I started to cry, but the woman wasn't moved, she wanted me out of her office. She looked at Peter with disapproval written all over her face, "There's nothing I can do, you don't meet the requirements set down by the State of Kansas, and if you continue to carry on like this, I'll call the guard."

I got up to leave, "We don't need your money! We'll get along just fine without you!" And I left.

I had no one I could call, and no money to call them with. I had my friend Joyce from Beloit, but I couldn't stay there. Joyce lived with her mother, and her mother hated white people. I was tired from carrying the bucket and the baby, I didn't know where I was headed, so I sat down at the bus stop to rest and think.

A car pulled up along side the curb and stopped. A man leaned across the seat smiling and rolled the window down. "Need a lift somewhere, little lady?"

"No, I'm not going anywhere, I have nowhere to go." I began to cry. "My baby needs a can of formula and I could use something to eat myself."

The man opened the door, "Hop in, let's get some food."

He fed me, he bought Peter two cans of formula, he got a motel room for the night, and of course, he fucked me. I didn't mind, Peter was full, he was warm and sleeping soundly on the bed. I was full and getting drowsy myself. After being in the cold for a long period of time, then coming inside and warming up makes one very sleepy.

The man fucked me and left around 8 that evening. He left $5 on the table, and I had the motel room to myself until the next day. Un''''til now, I hadn't any money or access to a phone, but before I left the room, I called everyone I knew, which wasn't but a few calls.

When I called Joyce, she said to come over to her house and hang out while her mama was at work. Joyce's mama, Jolene, didn't like white people and didn't want one in her house. She'd already told Joyce not to have that "ofay" in her house. Jolene worked all day and drank all night, so she wasn't home much. I would hang out there in the daytime, but I had to be gone when Jolene got home.

Jolene lived in the projects on 2nd Street. It was a lively place, people hangin' out on their porches, guys cruisin' by and stopping to talk. The black girls didn't like me and criticized Joyce, "You betta listen to yo' mama, Joyce, and leave that white girl alone. White people ain't nothin but trouble." This from a girl who had never been around any whites in her life.

Joyce didn't listen, she'd known me longer than any of those girls. We'd grown up together at GIS, she was my friend. "I know she ain't no sistuh, but she's okay. Shirley and that baby ain't got nobody. Don't you care about people at all?"

"Not no white girl, I don't. White people don't care about me, kept our people in slavery for 300 years, that's what I care about!"

Joyce and I spent our days trying to find a place for Peter and I to stay at night. Sometimes I didn't find a place to go, no one wanted to be bothered with me, I was a disgrace to whites and blacks alike. When it was almost time for Jolene to come home, I'd tell Joyce, "Don't worry, I'll be okay. I'll see ya later. I'd go out into the night, when it was good and dark, I'd look for unlocked cars in the neighborhoods, when I found one, I'd climb inside, tuck Peter under me to keep him warm and go to sleep. I was always gone before the Sun came up. I took Peter everywhere with me, there was no place I could leave him while I went to look for work, and I couldn't apply for a job with a baby in my arms! I didn't even have a phone number or an address I could put on an application.

Sometimes Joyce would leave, usually to see her boyfriend, and I would watch her daughter, but Joyce always returned before Jolene got home.

I started hanging out with Linda, a white girl from GIS who only went out with black guys. I didn't have a preference, I liked all the guys, no matter what color they were. But it mattered to the guys, it mattered to the white guys that I had a black baby. They would fuck me, but I was never considered a serious girlfriend, and the black guys didn't want to take me home to their families either. I was someone to fuck and that was it.

Linda's mother, who was divorced, worked at night, so it worked out, Joyce's house in the daytime, and Linda's at night. Linda was into heroin, and she hung out with a black motorcycle gang, the Zodiacs.

One of the members of the gang, Nate, had a good job and a new house. He smoked a little pot, but he wasn't into heavy drugs. He liked hanging out with the gang, he liked the excitement, he liked being accepted as one of them. The other gang members were BAD! They'd break your leg for $50 and break both for $75. Nate liked being associated with the gang, even though he never got involved in the rough stuff. He was a bachelor and let them hang out at his house drinking and doing drugs. He let Peter and I stay at his house. Of course I had to fuck him, but I was beginning to realize this was the only way I could make it! Men wouldn't do anything for me unless I fucked them, they would help me, but I had to take off my pants to get that help.

I tried marijuana for the first time while staying at Nate's. I didn't care for it, it made me dizzy and changed my view of everything, it was scary.

One day Nate and his friends were in his basement rec room, drinking and getting high. I was upstairs, bathing Peter when Nate entered the kitchen. "I'm gonna go to the liquor store and get some beer, while I'm gone I want you to take care of my friends downstairs."

"What do you mean, take care of your friends?" I knew exactly what he meant. He was drunk, he laughed, "Well, you see, I made little bet with the fellas, and I lost, so now you gotta take care of my bet for me."

"You bet me? I'm not your property!" I was angry. He was too drunk to stand up on his own, and he put his hand on the kitchen counter for support. "Yeah, told em if I lost, you'd fuck em all. After all, I gave you and your baby a place to stay. I feed you. Why can't you do this little favor for me? Huh?"

Men had always treated me cheaply, they didn't care how I felt, there was no love or romance, just sex, sex, and more sex. It was bad enough to put up with that drunken Nate, pawing all over me, just so I could eat. I really wasn't attracted to him, but it was a place to stay. We were using each other for different reasons. If he thought I was going to fuck all his friends, well, I wasn't going to do it!

"I fuck you, isn't that enough?" I said, "Do I have to fuck all your friends, too? Do you want them fucking the same woman you're fucking?"

Nate laughed and almost fell down. He didn't care if the whole United States Army fucked me! "Sweetheart, pussy is something every body can have a piece of, and it still stays whole, they ain't gonna hurt that pussy. Now go down there like I ask you, and take care of my friends."

"There's no way I'm gonna go down there, so just FORGET it!" I thought I had a choice.

"Okay," Nate said, "Just remember I asked you first," and he stumbled down the stairs. When he came back up, he had three other guys with him. "I asked you nice, and you wouldn't come, we ain't ask'n no more."

The men grabbed me, dragged me down the stairs, ripped my clothes off, tied my arms and fucked me. When they had all had a turn, which took a while, because they were drunk, Nate came over to untie my hands, "Now, that wasn't so bad, was it? Admit it, it was fun, wasn't it?"

They acted like it was a game, laughing and joking, now that the game was over and they had won, they wanted to be friendly. Only a few moments ago they had been rough and forceful, now they wanted to laugh and joke with me. I hated all of them.

The next day, Nate had a bad hangover and called in sick at work. He apologized over and over, "Hey, I'm sorry, I was drunk, it won't happen again. Anyway, they didn't hurt you. You're okay. Don't be sore at me."

"How could you let them to that?" I asked him, "I thought you liked me. You don't have any respect for me or my feelings."

"Oh baby, I respect you." Nate laughed.

*****

I was looking for a way to leave Nate's house, I couldn't stand to be in the same room with him. I knew he'd do it again, he'd do anything to keep his "biker buddies" happy.

The next afternoon Joyce called me at Nate's house. "Hey girl, what's goin' on? Doin' anything tonight?"

"No I don't have any plans, but I'd sure like to get out of here."

"Why don't you come over here? My mama gotta new honey, she ain't comin' home tonight."

"You sure? If your mama catches me there, she'll have a fit."

"Believe me," Joyce said, "Ashe ain't comin' home tonight."

I got Peter ready and headed for Jolene's house. Joyce was all dressed up, and ready to go out. "What's up?" I asked her.

"I'm going to see my man. He's waitin' on me right now! I know you'll watch my little girl. OK? I won't be gone too long," and out the door she went. I put the children to bed and watched TV, around midnight there was a knock on the door. Oh boy, who could that be? I waited a few seconds and they knocked again. It could be Jolene, she coulda lost her key, or maybe she's too drunk to find it! When I heard the knock a third time, I whispered through the door, "Who is it?"

"Hey Joyce," a man's voice came through the door, "Is that you? It's me Tokay." I knew Tokay, he was a friend of Joyce's man. I opened the door.

"Hey, Shirley, what're you doin' here? Stun or Joyce around?" He was grinning, being very friendly.

"No, Joyce said she was supposed to meet Stun, but they haven't come back here."

"Huh! I was supposed to meet em here. Why don't I just wait here a little while? Don't you want some company?"

"Jolene's gonna get awful mad if she comes home and we're here in her house."

"Don't worry, I can take care of Jolene. I'll just wait a little while."

He was smiling, so friendly, and he was a friend of Stun's, I thought it would be okay to let him wait there for a while. Tokay and I were talking when Peter began to cry. It was time for his feeding. "He probably wants to be fed. Let me check on him and I'll be right back."

I warmed up a bottle and headed for the stairs, "I'm gonna feed Peter, it shouldn't take too long." I had just gotten settled to feed Peter when Tokay hollered up the stairs, "I'm goin' now, tell Stun I waited for him."

"Okay" I shouted back.

I finished feeding my baby, rocked him back to sleep and went downstairs...Jolene's television was gone! I can't believe it! Tokay took Jolene's TV. What should I do? Maybe I should leave! No! I can't leave Joyce's little girl here alone, and then they'll think I stole the TV if I'm not here. I'll stay and tell em what happened.

Joyce came home first, her make-up was a mess, her hair disheveled and she'd been drinking. "What! You sat here and let that niggah take my mama's TV?"

"I didn't let him take it, you make it sound like I gave it to him. I was upstairs feeding the baby when he left, I guess he took the TV then."

"Why didn't you feed the baby down here? Why'd you leave that niggah down here by himself? In fact, why'd you let him in?"

"He's Stun's friend, I didn't think he'd steal your mama's TV. What're you gonna tell your mama!"

"I'm not gonna tell her anything, you gonna tell her yourself."

"Your mama's gonna be mad at you for lettin' me stay here."

"Not near as mad as she's gonna be when she finds out her TV's gone. You gonna hafta explain that one. I wasn't here."

Jolene came home around 8 a.m. with her boyfriend. "What in the fuck are you doin' in my house?" she greeted me.

"Mama, she got somethin' to tell you, about what happened last night."

Jolene turned to Joyce, "Haven't I told you not to bring this piece of white trash in my house? I don't wanna hear nothin' she's gotta say."

"Mama, somebody stole your TV last night."

"What! STOLE MY TV!" she turned from Joyce and looked at the empty TV table, then she looked at me, "I suppose YOU had something to do with it! You BETTER get my TV!"

I told Jolene what had happened, "I didn't take your TV, and I don't know where it's at. HONEST, Jolene."

"HONEST JOLENE, my ass, you gonna tell somebody the truth about where my TV's at! You think I believe that wild ass story!" and she called the police.

When the police arrive, Jolene insisted they take me to jail. She wanted to press charges for burglary. The police took Peter and I into custody. Peter was taken by the juvenile authorities and I was finger printed, photographed and put into jail.

The detectives came to question me about Jolene's television and one of the detectives was Boston Daniels. "I remember you," he said, "You're the girl from that murder in Rosedale a couple of years ago. Well, looks like you got yourself in another mess. What happened to the TV?"

I told him everything that happened and waited for him to respond. "H-m-m-m-m, you trying to tell me, he just picked up the TV and walked out the door. That right? Picked up that heavy TV all by his self and walked out? You didn't hear nothin'?"

"I was upstairs, feeding Peter. I don't know how he got the TV out, it was gone when I came downstairs."

He wasn't sure if he believed me or not. I was held in jail for 72 hours for investigation, held without bond, although that wouldn't have mattered, I couldn't have made a five dollar bond. When they couldn't find any evidence to charge me, they set me free.

I asked the officer at the booking desk where my son could be found. I wanted to get him right away.

"You'll have to talk to juvenile, that's not our department."

From the jail to the juvenile office was only a short walk. And I went straight there. I found the woman in charge of the case and asked for my baby.

"Your baby is fine, he's better off where he is, and I'm afraid I can't tell you where that is."

"What do you mean you can't tell me where he is? Where's Peter? You have no right to take him from me!"

"I'm not going to tell you where he is, look at you, you can't take care of a baby. You don't even have a place to take him, a home, you're unfit."

"Where's my baby?" I screamed in the woman's face.

"You better leave, you're wasting your time here. Leave or you're going right back to jail."

I left the juvenile office and went back to Nate's house. It was the only place I could go. I was frantic, I couldn't stop crying. Where's my baby? They've taken my baby!

I didn't know what to do or where to start, so I called the detective, Boston Daniels, "Please help me!" I was crying, "They've taken my baby and they won't tell me where he is. I'm not a bad mother." I pleaded, "I would never hurt Peter. How can they take a baby away from its mother? I know I'm in a mess right now, but I just need a little time. Can't you help me?" I sobbed into the phone.

Boston Daniels felt compassion for me, he knew everyone was against me because I socialized with blacks. He'd heard the remarks that were made around the office because my baby was black. "It's really not my department, I don't know what I can do. Let me check around and I'll call you back. Got a number where you can be reached?"

I gave him Nate's number, I didn't have to wait very long, he called back 10 minutes later, "I called the social worker handling your case," he sounded very disgusted and angry.

"What did she say? Did she tell you where Peter was?" I was almost breathless with anticipation.

"I could get into trouble for what I'm about to do, but I don't think you're being treated fairly. It's not right what they're trying to do, they're doing it for all the wrong reasons. I'm going to tell you where Peter is, and I want you to leave Kansas, go to Missouri, go anywhere, just get out of here. She's determined to put your baby in a foster home, and believe me, she'll do it, too! Peter is in a childcare center in Rosedale, she wouldn't tell you where he is because she has no legal right to hold him. Go out there, identify yourself as his mother, and they'll have to release him to you. Once you get him, get out of Kansas, she's after you and she wants to teach you a lesson, although I don't think she's motivated by what's good for Peter."

This was the great favor Boston Daniels did for me, a favor I'd always remember, all my life. Whenever I read something about him in the newspaper, or his name came up in conversation, I had nothing but praise for him.

I didn't have any money, so I began looking through Nate's clothes and in his dresser drawers. I found a twenty dollar bill and lots of silver change, I put the money in my purse and headed for Rosedale.

At the child care center they were all smiles, telling me what a good baby Peter was, and handed the baby into my arms. I took Peter and caught the bus, headed for Missouri. Peter was six weeks old.

*****

I didn't know a living soul in Kansas City, Missouri. All my family, and all the people I knew lived in Kansas. The people in KCK were like small-town, church going folks. Not much went on in Kansas. On the other hand, Kansas City, Missouri, just a few blocks away, had more of a big city atmosphere. The people who lived in Missouri thought they were slicker than the people from Kansas. They called the people from Kansas backwards and "country hicks" even though they only lived a few blocks away. When crossing State Line Road, a person could feel the difference in the two cities right away.

When the bus got to 27th and Troost I got off. Troost, I'd heard off Troost before, this seemed like a good place to start. "Well Peter," I whispered in his ear, holding him close, "We're in Missouri now, you're safe."

Twenty-seventh and Troost was a busy corner in the heart of the city. People were standing around talking, shopping or waiting at the bus stop. There was a small café and a pool hall, and across the street was a night club called "The Fandango". Some people sat in chairs on the sidewalk watching the activity, nodding at the passing pedestrians. There was a small grocery store, liquor store, hamburger stand and a hotel, "ROOMS $5-entrance around the corner" the sign said.

The old brick hotel was five stories high, upstairs over the businesses on the street. Old men, young men, sober men and drunk men were sitting around talking or playing cards in the shabby lobby.

I went up to the desk and asked for a room for the night.

"That'll be $8," the clerk said, looking Peter and I over.

"But the sign says, Rooms $5?"

"It costs more with a baby, that makes two people in the room, five bucks for one person and eight bucks for two. And if that baby cries all night, I'll put you out."

"Oh, he hardly ever cries!" I told the clerk.

"I hope you're right, for your own sake." and he pushed the registration card at me.

My room was on the third floor, a double bed with a dirty bed spread, an old dresser, a chair sitting lop-sided because one leg was broken and a sink, the toilet was down the hall. I laid on the bed and the mattress sunk down in the middle, curling around me, there were no pillows. I held Peter in my arms and rocked him until we both went to sleep.

The sun shining in my eyes woke me up. The morning light brought out every dirty spot in the room. "This is a dump!" I said to Peter, who was smiling up at me and gurgling. "I'm goin' to that grocery store and get you some formula, then I'm gonna go in that diner and have a BIG breakfast! What ya say, Peter? Then we'll figure out what we're gonna do in Missouri. Sure can't be any worse than Kansas!"

I bought the formula and while I waited for my breakfast, I fed Peter. A tall, skinny black woman in a mini-dress, puffy wig (like Diana Ross) and tons of make-up, sat down at my table. "I don't believe it! Shirley Sandy! What're you doin' here?" I just looked at the woman, totally puzzled. I had no idea who she was. But, she must have known me. She called out my name! "Hey girl! It's me! Marlene from GIS, don't you remember me?"

It was Marlene! "I didn't know who you were with that hair, and I never seen you wear make-up before!" I remembered Marlene very well. Marlene was one of the girls seriously involved in Girl Business. Marlene always played a masculine role; hair short, combed straight back, never any make-up. She walked and talked in a mannish way. I had never seen her like this before.

"This is just a wig," Marlene said, "I wear this make-up when I'm workin', but when I get home, I take this shit off! What're you doing here?" She was smiling, showing all her teeth, "It's sure nice to see one of the girls from GIS."

I grinned back, "It sure is!" We drank coffee and talked for a long time. We exchanged information about the different girls we'd known in Beloit. I told Marlene everything that happened to me since I'd been released from Beloit.

"And now," I finished, "If I go back to Kansas, they're gonna take Peter away from me, I spent the night in the hotel around the corner, but I don't have much money left. I'm gonna hafta figure out something."

"Why don't you come home with me?" Marlene said, "Ever hustled before?"

"Hustled? What do you mean hustle?"

"You know, sell pussy."

"No, but I'd do anything to make some money so Peter and I can get a place. Is it hard?"

Marlene laughed. "It's a piece of cake, girl! We'll take a cab, and I'll introduce you to my man."

We got out of the cab and went up to a house in a quiet neighborhood, a giantess greeted us at the door, she must have been 6'3", dressed in men's clothes, but obviously a woman. "This is my man," Marlene said, "This Big Dee."

"Who's the white girl?" Dee asked.

Marlene and I told Big Dee my story, laughing and interrupting each other. "She need a place to stay." Marlene said, "She ain't never ho'd before but she's willing to try."

"Well," Dee looked me over, "I don't let no girls stay here unless they my woman. If I'm gonna take care of you, and protect you, you gonna hafta be with me. You gonna hafta give me all your money."

I looked at Dee, feeling uncomfortable. Be her woman? I had never been with a woman and I had no desire to, but I didn't want to hurt her feelings, I needed a place to stay. "I don't mind being your woman, but do we have to do anything, you know, sex? I don't mind giving you my money for helping me, but Peter and I need to get a place. I'll need money for that. Can't you let me stay until I get on my feet? I'll give you half my money. Can't this just be a temporary deal? No sex?"

"You'll give me all the money and I'll put your half up for you, when you get enough for a place, I'll give it to you." If I had been wiser in the ways of the world, I would have seen the hate blazing from Dee's eyes. Dee laughed to herself and thought, "How you ever gonna get on your feet when I got all the money!"

Dee knew an old black woman everyone called Grandma, who took in babysitting jobs in her home, and Dee arranged for Peter to stay there.

Big Dee had three black girls working for her, and she was involved with a group of men who pulled armed robberies. She was a pimp, a stick-up artist and a heroin addict. She needed money, and she needed it everyday. Her women worked Troost, walking the streets. "You know," Dee told me, "A fresh, young white girl like you would be ruined workin' on Troost. You'd start actin' like those black ho's, and that would cut your money down. I know a bellhop who works downtown, that's where the money's at, the money's downtown, but only the white girls can get it, they don't want no black ho's. I'm gonna see if I can find that bellhop, he usually at the pool hall, maybe they got room for a new girl. We'll go down there. Come on girls, let's find Shirley something to wear."

First they put me in the bathtub. They put a lacy garter belt around my waist and a skin-tight, turtleneck mini-dress, it was so short you could see my ass when I bent over. Next they made up my face, there were false eyelashes on the top and the bottom glued to my lids, eyeshadow, mascara and thick, frosted lipstick. "You'll hafta get a wig, your hair's too soft." Marlene told me, "I tried to back comb it and put hair spray on it, but it keeps falling down. She's ready, Dee!" Marlene called into the other room.

No one had ever made such a fuss over my appearance before. I had never dressed like this, I kept looking at myself in the mirror. Wow! I thought, I really look good. With all this make-up and this sexy dress, why, I look like a movie star!

Jean had always told me I was plain, and I had always dressed and groomed myself accordingly. "Oh no, you can't wear that" Jean would tell me, "That doesn't look good on a girl with your coloring. Your lips are too thin, your eyes aren't wide enough, and clothes don't hang flattering on your body!" Jean was always putting me down.

Boys had always treated me badly and I thought it was because I wasn't pretty enough. Mr. Shumate had told me I was pretty, but I couldn't trust that, he'd never say anything to hurt my feelings. But now, as I looked at myself in the mirror, I knew he told the truth.

Dee came in the room and laughed, "You look different, amazing what a little make-up can do!"

I got Peter ready to go to the babysitter, this was the first time I'd ever left him anywhere. We took Peter to Grandma's house first. She was 59 years old but appeared much older, she was skinny, she had no teeth and her gray hair was pulled back with a rubber band, kinking around her face. She had a warm friendly smile and a sparkle in her eyes.

"Oh is this the little boy you told me about?" she held out her arms to take Peter, "He's the prettiest baby I've ever seen! Look, look, Vern, at this pretty baby. Ain't he cute?" she held Peter out for her husband to see.

"He's cute alright." he spoke abruptly and returned to the paper he was reading.

Grandma and Vern lived in a little two-bedroom house with an attic that served as a third bedroom. He was a retired soldier and she took in babysitting for extra money, which they could always use. Three of her own grandchildren lived with them. Grandma had a daughter when she was a teen-ager, she never had any more children. Her daughter's father was an Indian man, and she had struggled with the prejudice associated with having a mixed child. When people had turned their backs on her, she raised her child alone. She immediately felt empathy for Peter and I, she knew what we were up against. She had married Vern late in life, he had no children but treated her nine grandchildren as his own. They were good people just trying to make ends meet.

There were several children playing in the living room. I felt good about Peter being here, you could feel love in this house. We said goodbye and headed for the pool hall.

The pool hall was the same one I'd seen when I got off the bus in Missouri yesterday, the one next to the diner where I'd seen Marlene. This was where the hustler, or "players" as they like to call themselves, hung out, there were new Lincolns and Cadillacs parked everywhere.

It was a dirty pool hall, dust everywhere that hadn't been cleaned for years, there were two pool tables but no one was playing pool. In the back of the pool hall sat a man by a door and Dee called out to him, "Is Buddy back there?" He eyed Dee warily. He didn't want no trouble. It was his job to make sure there was no trouble. Everybody knew that dyke would stick a gun in your face, he had to be careful. She's got all her girls with her, he thought, she's probably not lookin' to start no shit.

"Yeah, he's here" the man said, "I'll go get him."

The man opened the door he'd been sitting by and cigarette smoke poured out the door. There was a crowd of men standing around a table, each holding a fistful of cash, other men stood behind, watching the action on the table.

"What're they doin back there?" I asked.

"They gamblin', shootin' craps. Must be thousands of dollars back there!" Dee licked her lips hungrily.

Buddy came out of the smokey room. He wasn't very tall, but he was very muscular, around 30 years old, chocolate colored skin, his hair was combed straight back in a "process". He wore Sansabelt slacks and a bright silk shirt, unbuttoned down his chest to expose a glittering gold medallion that hung around his neck. He held a wad of money in his hand, and on his finger he wore the biggest diamond ring I'd ever seen. When he opened his mouth to speak, I could see that all his teeth were trimmed in gold.

"I hope this is important," he said to Dee, slapping his wad of money against his thigh. He grinned at all the girls, Buddy had girls working for him, too, and he welcomed all new prospects.

"Hey girls, how's tricks?" his gold rimmed teeth caught the light sparkled.

"Buddy, I got a new girl here. She's never ho'd before. Come here, Shirley, meet sweet Buddy." I walked up and stood next to Dee. I could tell I looked good by the way Buddy eyed me. "I don't want to put her on the street with those slick-ass black ho's. I figure a nice white girl should be downtown, think you can get her into that hotel where you work?"

Buddy looked me up and down. "We can always use a new young face. How old is she?"

They didn't talk to me or ask me anything, I was a product and business was arranged between the men. Although Dee was a woman, she was given the respect of a man by the other players. She could whip most of them in a fight, she was dangerous and they knew it. It was easier, and safer to give her the respect she wanted.

"She's 18." Dee said.

"She don't look 18." Buddy frowned, "If they catch a minor at the hotel, I'll lose my job."

"Hey man! I wouldn't steer you wrong! She's NEW, man. New girl makes all the money, you know that. She was in that girl's home with Marlene, she's 18." Dee turned to me and spoke as if I hadn't heard any of their conversation. "Will you tell this fool how old you are."

"I'm 18," I said, "I turned 18 two months ago."

"You don't look 18, I don't know Dee. Better to be safe than sorry."

"Don't say I didn't ask you first, Buddy. You're not the only bellhop in town!" Dee turned to leave, "Come on, girls."

"Wait!" Buddy grinned, flashing all his golden teeth, "Okay, Dee,

I'll do it this one time, but you better not be lyin'. I'm not working until later, but I'll call and tell them to expect you."

"Calm down, Buddy, everything's gonna be fine. We gonna make us some money now!"

Buddy made the phone call. Dee left her three girls in front of the pool hall, they were already at work, Troost Avenue was their stroll. Dee and I got into the car and headed downtown.

Dee pulled up in front of a sign, A BROADWAY HOTEL-day-week-month. It was old, run-down, but clean. There was a small lobby with an old sofa and a chair. The front desk was a small counter, behind the counter was the pigeon-hole message boxes and an old telephone switchboard, the old cord kind.

A black man of indeterminate age leaded on the counter, reading the day's paper. Most of his teeth were gone, but those that were left on the top and the bottom, fit together like a zipper when he closed his mouth. When he talked he would wring his hands together and always laugh. His name was G.P., but everyone just called him Jeep.

"Hey, hey" he began to wring his hands together as if washing them, laughing all the while. "Buddy said you's comin'. Well, Dee, I'll take care of everything from here. You gotta go, you know Fred don't want no pimps here." Especially you, Jeep thought.

"Yeah, I know" Dee turned to me, "You do what he tells ya, I'll call you later." and Dee left.

Jeep turned to me, "I better get you out of this lobby, come on, I'll put you in a room." He went up the stairs and I followed. The room was old but clean. I was to learn that cleanliness was top priority in a whorehouse, tricks didn't like dirty whorehouses. There was no place to sit but on the bed and a phone hung from the wall.

"Buddy says you a new girl. Ever turned a trick?" Jeep asked me, while wringing his hands together and chuckling.

"No" I waited for him to go on.

"Well, there's nothing to it, you just sit here until I call you on that phone and send you to a room."

"Whata I do when I get to the room?" Jeep laughed harder and rubbed his hands faster, "Why, you give em a date, depends on what they want to do. Straight date is $15, half and half is $20 and a full French is $25. We split the money 60/40- - you get 60%, I get 40. Tips are yours. You don't have to split your tips. And ALWAYS get your money up front, okay? Don't even take your shoes off ""'til you get paid. Never give them price. Okay? Let them say what they wanna spend first, don't give them NO prices, he might think it cost a hundred bucks and you've said $20."

"How do I say it to them?" I asked.

"When they ask you how much, say it like this," and Jeep raised his voice to sound like a woman, "What do you wanna spend, honey? Okay? When they tell you how much, always try to get a little more. Okay? Don't go under those prices I gave you. Okay? Wash the tricks dick before you do anything. Okay? Tricks don't like it if you don't wash em up first, makes em feel the girl ain't clean. If you wash em real slow, it cuts down on your work in bed. Okay?"

I nodded my head at every okay. "What do you mean by straight date, half and half, and what's a French?" Jeep's hands must of been going a hundred miles an hour as he laughed, "Oh boy! You really are green, you don't know nuthin'! Straight date is just that, a straight fuck and nothing more. Half and half is half French and finish em off fuckin'."

"What do you mean, French?"

"A French is when you suck the man's dick. Half and half, you suck it until its ready and finish em fuckin', full French, you let the trick cum in your mouth."

"YUCK!" I frowned, "I've never had a man's thing in my mouth before!"

"If you don't suck dick, you might as well go home right now. You ain't gonna make any money in this business if you don't suck dick and act like you like it. If they wanna do anything else, anything unusual, call me on the phone, and I'll tell ya what to charge. That about all I can think of right now. What do you wanna be called?"

"You can just call me Shirley, that's my name."

"No, no, nobody uses their real name in this business. Only use your real name if you get busted. All the girls use "street names," that's just the way it is."

I thought about this for a moment, I'd never liked my name. A new name? To go along with my new look? I liked the idea. I had read the "Carpetbaggers" and admired the character of Rena Marlow.

"I'd like to be called Rena." I told Jeep.

"What you say? Rita?" Jeep didn't hear too good.

"No, not Rita, Rena, like in the "Carpetbaggers."

"The carpet who? What name is it again?"

"R-E-E-E-N-A-A-A" I said real slow.

"Rita?" he couldn't seem to understand what I was saying, and I didn't see why it mattered.

"Right," I said, "That's it, just call me Rita."

PART II

THE LIFE

Downtown Kansas City, Missouri in 1967 was charged with activity. The malls hadn't been built yet, all shopping was done in the city; on the Country Club Plaza, if you could afford it, or downtown where you could find several 5 cent &10 cent stores like Woolworth's, department stores like Macy's and exclusive shops like Harzfeld's. With all the shopping, city hall and office buildings, downtown was a beehive of activity in the daytime.

Kansas City, Missouri prided itself on being a convention town. Most conventions were related to the farming and livestock industries. All the major hotels and the Municipal Auditorium, where they held the conventions, were located in the downtown area.

When the stores were closing, the clubs were just getting ready for the evening business. There were restaurants, bars, live music and dancing and the Playboy Club on the top floor of the Continental Hotel. Downtown was the pulse of KC in 1967.

In the middle of all this 24 hour a day activity were a number of run-down hotels which didn't try to draw attention to themselves. If you didn't know where they were you might miss them. These old hotels were whorehouses. There were several as you walked down 12th Street; The Cordova, The Broadway, The Alton, The Howard, The Hill, The Rasbach and The Senator. These were the whorehouses on 12th Street. They catered to the out-of-towners, conventioneers and businessmen. The police knew about the whorehouses, but as long as they ran a clean place, no disease, no stealing from tricks, no rough stuff and no pimps hanging around (the police hated pimps), the vice squad usually left them alone. If the police busted the hotel by getting an undercover officer past the bellboy, it was only a $100 bond and a $25 fine. A girl that worked the streets and didn't stay in the hotels got busted all the time. The vice squad didn't want hookers all over downtown, it didn't look good for the city.

It seems like there were a lot of whorehouses in one area, but all the hotels kept several girls and they all stayed busy.

The bellhops or desk clerks ran these little houses of pleasure. All of these man were black and most of them were married, family men in their 50's or 60's. They came to work, made their 40% and went home and didn't bother the girls. Pimps, players and hustlers were kept out of these places- - it caused too much confusion. The tricks didn't like it and neither did the police.

If a girl had a pimp, they didn't want the pimps dropping the girl off at a hotel, so most of the ladies-of-the-night arrived in taxicabs. There are always exceptions to every rule, and the hotels were no different. There were a few bellhops that had girls and, of course, they gave their girls all the tricks, but these were the exception, not the rule. They could only work their women so long because tricks want new faces. A new girl makes all the money.

On the other side of downtown, on 9th Street, there were more whorehouse hotels; The Gladstone, The Frederick, The Blackstone and The Densmore. The tricks on 9th Street were mostly local. There were several bars on 9th Street, and the crowd was a little rougher than 12th Street. Usually girls who worked 12th Street stayed on 12th and girls who worked 9th Street stayed on 9th.

The bellhops didn't want the girls to sit in a room together. They didn't want the girls to know who was getting all the tricks. If a girl sat in her room alone, she was more likely to get most of the tricks. A girl would keep her own room, which she paid for, while working at the hotel. The bellhop would either call her on the phone or come and get her and send her to a room where a man would be waiting. When the date was done and the girl returned to her room, she would call the bellhop and he'd come get his money. Some bellhops waited until the end of the evening to cut the money, but not very many, most wanted their money right away.

The bellhops received 40% for providing a safe place for the girl to work; safe from the police and safe from the tricks. The bellhop was supposed to watch out for and protect the girl if the date turned nasty. If the bellhop thought the date was taking too long, he would start calling on the phone or knocking on the door. If the trick had paid for an hour the girl was supposed to call the bellhop and let him know in advance.

When the hour was up he'd call on the phone to let her know.

Most of the time this arrangement worked out for the girls as well as the bellhops, but there's always that exception. Once in awhile, when a bellhop wasn't paying any attention, a girl might get a little roughed up. It didn't happen very often and no one ever got killed in the hotels. After an unusually ugly episode, the bellhop would be more vigilant while the girl was turning a trick.

The girls weren't allowed to leave their rooms while working, except to turn a trick. They certainly couldn't sit in the lobby, that was forbidden. If they wanted food, drinks or cigarettes, the bellhop brought it to them. Some girls brought little TV's to watch, some read books, some sat in rooms together and gossiped; they occupied themselves the best they could. They were all hoping they'd be busy all night turning tricks.

The majority of the business went on at night, but there was a lot of business in the daytime too. Certain girls worked with certain bellhops; when that bellhop went home, so did the girl, unless she lived at the hotel.

A new girl makes all the money in prostitution, and everyone knows this. All the bellhops want to work with a new girl, all the pimps want to catch a new girl, and all the tricks want to fuck a new girl. Most tricks like someone different. If they wanted the same woman, they'd stay home with their wives. Some tricks would want a particular girl, some men liked a seasoned whore, but this was the exception. The rule was, a new girl makes all the money until another new girl comes along.

If the bellhop had a trick that didn't want any of the girls available at that hotel, the bellhop would call the other hotels looking for someone different. They would try the hotels closest to them first but, if necessary, they'd call as far away as 9th Street if the trick would wait that long. Most of them were in a big hurry. When a girl went from one hotel to another she always took a taxicab, even if it was only a block. This way a girl got top know all the bellhops and widen her circle of contacts. It was a business, it was run like a business, the only one there for enjoyment was the trick, everyone else was working. Some girls checked into the hotels and lived there, but other girls had a home somewhere else and only came to work during certain hours. The bellhops liked to have a girl live in the hotel, that meant he had someone available most of the time. Nothing made a bellhop madder than to have a trick and be unable to find a girl!

All the girls had a "man". They would say, "my man" this and "my man" that, but they weren't their men, they were their pimps. Some of these pimps were cold and cruel masters, controlling stables of women, men who loved no one but themselves. There were others (the exceptions), who would have only one woman, swearing devotion to her, but no matter what style of "man" they were, they were all pimps, allowing other men to fuck their women, living the high life off a woman's vagina. They were liars and manipulators, the dumber the girl, the better. They wanted young girls they could brainwash into their way of life. Almost every girl came from a dysfunctional home. Rare was the girl who was educated, from a nice family and loving parents. Most hookers didn't care if they ever saw their families again and this made it much easier for the pimp to have complete control. Some of the pimps would hang out at the bus station looking for young runaways, fresh meat for the market.

The bellhops were family men, they thought the whores were stupid for giving their money away to some guy, but they never talked openly against it or interfered. They just wanted their 40% and what she did with her 60% was none of his affair. The women were viewed as sex machines, all conversation directed to them was of a sexual nature, no one ever asked them an intelligent question, or even cared what they thought. Bellhop just wanted his 40%, pimp wanted her 60% and the trick just wanted some good head.

These girls believed that they NEEDED these pimps. "You have to have a man to protect you," they would say. Protect them from what? The pimp was nowhere around while she was working, he was having a good time with some other woman, usually a woman that DIDN'T whore, waiting for her to bring home the money. If a girl had trouble with a trick it was the bellhop who came to her rescue, not her pimp. If she got busted, it was her money that was put up for bond. These guys weren't needed and they served no function other than to suck up and throw away all the money a girl made. It didn't make any sense, but that's the way it was, and all the girls had a "man". They called it being in "The Life".

The woman or the "ho", as she was referred to, was nothing and everything was focused on the pimp, his satisfaction and enjoyment always came first, she was there to serve him. He made all the decisions and handled all the money and a girl never questioned what was done with the money. If your man dressed well and drove a big car, it was a source of pride to a girl, a status symbol, made her look like a money maker. The girls were mostly young, the pimps said it was all downhill for a woman when she turned 25. What they really meant was, it was al downhill for them by the time a hooker was 25. An old whore, one who'd been around a little while, knew she was throwing her money away with a pimp, they all wise up eventually. But by the time they get wise, their peak earning years are over and they've thrown away all their money.

Not only did the pimps want young girls, the tricks wanted them young too. Unless a girl had built up a clientele of tricks through some speciality like sadism/masochism, opened a whorehouse of her own became a madam, she was no longer in demand by the time she was 30. The young whores would laugh at the older whores, they laughed because they were still out there, they hadn't done anything with their lives, not once stopping to think that they were doing the same thing. Instead of learning from these women, they made fun of them.

All the girls dressed exceptionally well. A smart pimp always reinvested in his woman, he made sure she looked good, the better she looked, the more money she made. Boosters, people who shoplifted, would bring a car trunk full of women's clothes, good clothes, expensive clothes, and the pimp might buy all the clothes if he got them cheap enough.

The people in "The Life" didn't follow the same rules as the rest of society, they had their own code of ethics, rules made up by and for the man, the woman had no say.

*****

The phone on the wall began to ring, I threw down the magazine I'd been reading and ran to answer it. "Yes?" I said, nervous yet anxious.

"Hey Rita," Jeeps voice crackled through the wire. It took me a few minutes to realize he was talking to me. That's right, I'm Rita now, I thought.

"I think I got one for ya, go down to room 301. He's a regular spends $25 for a half and half. Call me when you get back to your room."

"Okay" I said to him and he hung up. I was scared, I stepped into the hall looking for 301 and when I found it, I knocked lightly on the door.

"Come in" a man called out. I opened the door and he was lying on the bed, around 40 years old, slightly heavy, naked, rubbing his penis. I felt uncomfortable watching him fondle his family jewels.

"Jeep tells me you're a new girl and I'm your first date! I like to break in new girls, don't get that chance very often. What's your name?" I thought I'd try my new name from the "Carpetbaggers" on him, "Rena."

"Rita? He says, R-E-E-E-O Rita. That your real name?"

"No, but they say I can't use my real name."

"None of the girls do, they pick the funniest names, Peaches, Precious, Angel, even got a Too Sweet."

"What do you wanna do?" I asked him.

"Always do the same thing, $25 for a half and half, I laid the money over there on the table." Sure enough, there it was, a twenty and a five, I picked up the money and put the bills in my purse.

"Come on, take your clothes off!" The trick was eager. I slipped off my dress and when he saw the lacy garter belt, he began to stroke himself faster.

"I'll give you $15 to leave that garter belt and hose on."

"That sounds good, I'm supposed to wash you now."

The trick got up from the bed and hung his stiff penis over the sink. "O-O-O-H, A-A-A-H" he moaned, "I can't believe I did that! Oh boy! Well here's the $15 I promised you," he pulled his wallet from his pants.

I felt bad for the trick, I had $40 for about 2 minutes of my time. I didn't want to cheat the guy! "If you wanna go again, that's okay with me. I wanna make sure you get your money's worth."

The man was putting his clothes on, "I wish I could go again, I coulda went all night 20 years ago, but I'm afraid one times enough for me now."

I took to whoring like a duck takes to water. I loved it! I'd been the object of men's desires for years now, I'd gotten used to that, but for them to put the money on the table- - in advance, I liked that. I felt this was the most honest approach to sex, all of my experiences with sex had been sordid affairs. Getting paid $40 for a few minutes was more like it! Now I had more than a wet vagina to show for my humiliation. Only it didn't seem so humiliating now. Laying the money on the table gave me value and a strange sense of power, it wasn't such a humbling affair now.

When I returned to my room I called Jeep and he came right up to get his money, "Well, how'd it go?" he asked, chuckling and wringing his hands.

"He gave me $40" I proudly announced, "he gave me an extra $15 to leave my garter belt on!"

"Hey, hey, way to go, girl!" Jeep laughed.

"When I washed him off, he cum in the sink, I told him I'd let him go again, but he said no."

"No! No!" Jeep laughed harder, "Once they cum, that's it! Dates over! Unless they wanna pay for an hour, once they cum, dates over, no matter where they cum, in the sink, on the floor, or in his pants, don't matter! If he wants to cum again, he's gotta spend more money. Don't ever tell a trick that again. Okay?"

"Okay" I told Jeep, that was fine with me, I like someone setting these rules, made the game seem more fair. "How much do I owe you, Jeep? What's 40% of $40?"

"$16, that's what you owe me, easy way to remember is $2 out of every $5." He reached for the $20 bill, gave me four ones, putting the twenty in his shirt pocket.

"Better get downstairs, might be another one waiting!"

I held the $24 in my hand and gazed at it, a couple more of these every day, and Peter and I can get a place soon. I'll only do this until I get on my feet, I thought, until I can find a place and get a job. I'll only do this for a short time.

All the dates weren't as easy as the first one, but NONE of them were difficult. There were rules and regulations in the hotel that had to be followed, by the girls as well as the tricks. All the tricks knew if they didn't get their business done quickly, they'd have to spend more money. If they were too drunk to get off, that was their problem.

I didn't mind the half and half so much, but the first time I gave a full French, I gagged and vomited on the floor. This made the date angry, and he complained to Jeep.

Jeep entered my room with a good-looking redhead right behind him. "Hey, Rita, this is Ginger. Thought she might be able to give you a few pointers. Ginger's a real pro, listen and you might learn somethin'."

Ginger sat down on the bed. She was a small round woman, very pretty with dimples and a full voluptuous figure. She was from Texas and talked with a twang. Jeep left the room and closed the door.

"Jeep told me you threw up on that trick! God knows, I've wanted to throw up on them sometimes!"

"I didn't throw up on the man, I did it on the floor. I was so embarrassed, but when he cum in my mouth, he grabbed my head, and shoved it down my throat, it made me sick," I told Ginger.

"Lots of girls feel that way. Look, when you're giving a French, put his dick under your tongue, behind your bottom teeth. That way he can't cram it down your throat, and most of em will. Stickin' a finger down your throat will make you throw up, and so will a hard dick. Lick the head and the sides, they like that, might tip you, and when it's all wet, wrap your hand around his joint, down by his nuts, and jack him off a little while you're suckin', gets em off faster. When you keep your hand on it, that stops them from pushing your head down on it and chokin' ya. Catch the semen under your tongue, behind your bottom teeth. You can't taste it too much, and some guys have nasty tastin' cum, if you hold your breath once they start to cum, you won't taste it at all!" Ginger laughed, "Hell, I'd rather give them a blow job than fuck em, pays more, it's cleaner and I think it's easier. Tricks like to get sucked off, lot of them don't get that at home. If a girl can give a good blow job, and act like she's enjoyin' it, she'll make money."

"Acts like she enjoys it? How's that done?"

"Just moan, don't over-do it, just a little, touch his body, don't be shy, they liked to be touched all over, everywhere. M-m-m-m-m daddy!" Ginger started to laugh again, "Just like that, they love it, gets em excited, makes em cum faster. The faster they cum, the faster you're out of there."

"A couple of guys wanted to lick me down there," I pointed to my vagina, "what should I do about that?"

"Same rules, let em do it, but it costs more money. Everything extra they want to do, costs more. Act like you like it, pretend to get off, it's not hard, but it takes a little practice. If you wanna make a little extra money, tell em to give you an extra $10 or so and you'll give em a hot water French or a toothpaste French."

Ginger was very comical, I was laughing at her gestures and facial expressions, "Ginger, what IS a hot water French?"

"Hot water French? It's easy! Makes em feel like they're getting something exotic. Run water in the sink until it's as hot as you can stand it, put some hot water in your mouth, about half a glass, and give em a French. They love it! Toothpaste French, just get some mint flavored toothpaste and put it on the head of their dick." Ginger was enjoying her role as a teacher, she had been a whore for 5 years, and tried to be a good one, she took her business seriously, and making lots of money was her objective. Ginger was always looking for ways to make a little extra money if she could.

"Do girls take off when they're having a period?" I asked her.

"Heavens, no!" Ginger shouted, "A good ho works all the time, makes that money while she's young. You can buy a sanitary sponge at the drugstore on the corner, comes in a blue box. The sponge is inside a drawstring pouch. Wet the sponge a little to make it soft, and when they call you for a date, put it in just before you go, it should soak up the blood long enough for you to turn a trick, and they usually can't feel it in there. Of course, if your bleeding so heavy the sponge can't hold it, just talk em into a full French."

"How do you know if you've given them enough time, there's no clocks in the room?"

"You can get a watch, but they don't like you lookin' at a watch while they're fuckin' ya. Here's what I do, after I've washed em and they're ready to get in bed, I light a cigarette and lay it burning in the ashtray. Takes a cigarette about 12 minutes to burn out on it's own. When the cigarettes burned out, I figure they've had enough time, cum or give me some more money."

I was pleased, I felt Ginger had been very helpful in teaching me some tricks of the trade.

*****

I spent most of my time at the hotel. No one ever called me Shirley anymore. Jeep was the only one I'd told my name, and he didn't remember it. The name Rita stuck and I accepted it. I would rather have been called Rena, but Rita would do.

Every day I would take a taxicab to Dee's house and hand over all the money I'd made. I never had less than $100, and usually it was more. Dee would give me cab fare back downtown and a little pocket money, the rest she was "putting up" for my apartment. Sunday was my day off. I'd pick up Peter on Sunday morning and spend until Monday afternoon with him, then I returned to the hotel.

I didn't like the idea of giving Dee all my money, Dee made me feel uncomfortable. Dee was controlling and often angry. The bellhops teased me about being with a dyke. "Dee is not my man," I would say, feeling ashamed that they thought I was a lesbian. "We have a business arrangement, and that's all!"

"Yeah! Right!" the bellhops would laugh, wanting to know how big Dee's dick was.

I didn't want to be considered a lesbian. The sooner I get away from Dee, the better, I thought as I turned a trick.

I'd been working at the hotel for about 2 weeks when I decided it was time to get my money from Dee and move on. By my calculations, I had enough money to get a place and get by until I found a job. I called Dee and told her to get my money ready, I was coming to get it. "Yeah, sure, I'll have your money ready." Dee told me. I took a taxi and had him wait while I went inside. Dee was waiting for me, and there was another woman named Angel in the room. "Hi, Dee," I greeted her, "You know I appreciate everything you've done for me, but I feel it's time to move on. If you wanna give me the money you been holding, I'll be going, I've got a cab waitin' on me outside."

Dee punched me and I fell to the floor. "Hey!" I yelled, "What're you doin'? What's the matter? What have I done?"

Dee put her foot on my throat, pinning me to the floor. "Angel, go outside and get rid of that cab," then Dee looked down at me squirming under her foot, "I appreciate everything you've done for me," Dee mimicked me, "I feel it's time for me to move on." Dee took her foot off my throat and kicked me in the ribs. "You fuckin' bitch! I'm gonna give you what I owe you! A good ass kickin'! That's what I owe you! You silly white bitch!" Dee was kicking at me furiously, in the head, in the stomach, in the ass, "You think you can come in here and change all the rules for yourself?"

"Oh, Dee, can't this just be business?"

"Ha! You bet it's business, and you ain't goin' nowhere! How much money you got now?"

Dee reached down and pulled me off the floor by my hair, "Give me all your money, you won't need any, you ain't goin' nowhere."

I was afraid, and it showed as I dug into my purse. My hands were shaking as I held the bills out to Dee. "Dee, I don't understand?" I pleaded, "I thought we had an arrangement? Why are you mad? What have I done?"

Dee punched me and I fell to my knees, the money went flying from my hands, floating slowly to the floor. I wondered what would happen next...how'd I get into this...how do I get out of this?

Dee stood over me with her knee poised under my chin. "You need to be taught a lesson! You ain't boss around here! You make no decisions! This ain't no hotel!" Dee pushed her knee into my face, pushing me back, "You can't check in and check out whenever you get ready!" Dee punched the side of my head a couple of times, then Angel broke in, Hey, Dee, that's enough, she don't know any better, she's a new girl, she don't understand the life."

"Yeah" Dee kicked me while she spoke. "I'm gonna teach this new girl a lesson. She'll understand the Life when I'm through with her, she'll understand REAL good."

Dee was right, I did learn a lesson, and I understood what the "Life" was all about. There were no helping hands in this business, everybody wanted a whore's money. If they had to hold her against her will and beat her, they would. I learned many lessons that morning, I understood why the girls had "a man", to protect them from pimps like Dee. This is not the life for me, I thought as I lay on Dee's floor, I'm getting out of here!

Big Dee was going out for awhile and told Angel to keep an eye on me. Angel turned to me, shaking her head, "Girl, I couldn't believe it, when I heard you tell Dee to give you the money she owes! You was askin' for it! If you wanna leave a pimp, you gotta sneak off, you don't tell em you're going!" Angel was rolling with laughter, "And you sure don't ask for any money! HA! HA! I wouldn't of believed it, if I hadn't seen it with my own eyes! Wait'll I tell the other girls!"

"How can you live like this?" I asked, "Why do you put up with it?"

"Ain't so bad, Dee's a bad one, but not all the pimps are like Dee, some of em are okay." Angel looked me right in the eyes, "But you can't be out here without a man! Pick your own poison!"

"I can't live this way, the sooner I'm out of here, the happier I'll be."

"Go on," Angel laughed, "I ain't gonna stop you, Dee's not my man, we're just friends. She ain't gonna beat my ass, I got a man, she wouldn't dare, she'd just tell my ol' man, and he don't care."

"I'm not gonna sit around here and wait for Dee to come back and beat my ass some more, I'm leavin'!"

"Bye" Angel called as I walked out the door.

Dee had taken all my money, so I walked. The first thing I have to do, I thought, is get Peter, then I'll figure out something, maybe I'll call Joyce, but Joyce wouldn't be happy to hear from me after the incident with Jolene's TV. I've got to get away from this! I've been running from Buck and Jean for years, I don't wanna end up in a similar situation. I don't want to be someone's whipping post.

I walked to Grandma's house, taking the side streets in case Dee drove by. Grandma and Versaille were sitting on the front porch, Grandma called out, "Dee just came and got Peter, you just missed her." As I climbed the porch steps, Grandma could see the bruises on my body, "Girl, what happened to you?"

I started crying and told Grandma everything Dee had done. "What am I gonna do now? I'm scared to go to her house, and I can't leave Peter there!"

"You poor thing!" Grandma put her arms around me and held me close, "This is no life for you! Poor thing!"

I went into the house and dialed Dee's phone number, Big Dee answered, "I'm at Grandma's, she says you have Peter, I'm comin' to get him."

"Come on, bitch!" Dee growled into the receiver, "I'm waitin' on ya!" and hung up the phone.

"Oh boy!" I turned to Grandma, "She's gonna kill me! The only way I'm gonna get Peter out of there with no one getting hurt, is to call the police. That's what I'll do, I'll call the police."

Grandma gave me bus fare downtown. I entered the police station and told the officer at the counter my baby had been kidnaped. They sent me upstairs to talk with the detectives, I told them the whole story.

"We know Big Dee. She's a bad one, she's dangerous. Can't seem to get her on anything, she always slips through our fingers. With your help we could put her behind bars for a while, where she belongs!"

"I can't do that!" I replied, "I don't want her after me!"

"We'll take care of you," the detective promised, "You don't have anything to worry about. We'll give you police protection, get you a place, make sure you got money to eat."

He called the other detectives and they gathered around his desk. "That dyke, Big Dee, is holding her baby, she wants us to get him out of there," he turned and faced me, "She wants us to help her, but she won't help us."

All the detectives began to work on me, "If you want us to get that baby, we will. We'll go right in and take him out, but you're gonna hafta sign a statement, first."

"Yeah" another detective intervened, "The Grand Jury meets next week, and I want you to testify about Big Dee's activities. Maybe we can bring State charges against her. With your testimony it's a cinch. You don't have to worry about anything, we'll put you some place safe where she won't fine you. It's best to put her away where she can't get to ya. Dee will be after you."

I trusted the detectives, "I want away from this life, can you help me until I get a job? That is, if I do what you want?"

"Sure, we will." he picked up a piece of paper and began putting it in the typewriter, You just tell me everything that happened from the time you met Dee." he started typing and I started talking.

When I finished talking he handed me the paper and a pen, and I signed it. The detectives were all laughing, congratulating each other. "We got that dyke this time! With this girl's testimony, they're sure to bring State charges!"

The detectives arranged for two cars of back-up officers, two detectives put me in an unmarked car, and we headed for Dee's house to get Peter. I was scared, seems like I'd spent most of my adolescence frightened of someone. I just want to get Peter and be free of all this.

The four uniformed officers approached the door, "Police" they knocked with their nightsticks, "Open UP!"

Dee opened the door and looked straight at me, she curled her lip but didn't say anything. "Are you Delores Ware?" the Officer asked. "Yes" she said without taking her eyes from me. "I have a warrant for your arrest." he turned to me, "Is this the woman you know as Big Dee?" I just nodded my head, I couldn't tear my eyes away from Dee's. I couldn't speak. I was terrified. I could feel Dee's evil and it was almost choking me. "Okay," a detective said, "You're under arrest for kidnapping, pandering and promoting prostitution."

The police pushed their way into the house and I went with them, I headed straight for the bedroom where I knew Peter would be. Peter looked up and grinned at me. I was so happy to see him, relief flooded through my body. They hadn't changed his diaper, and they probably didn't feed him, but he was okay! Thank Heaven! I scooped him up into my arms and returned to the living room where the arrest was being made.

"You gonna believe what some white trash girl tells ya? She didn't have nowhere to go, and I give her a place to stay and feed her and this is the thanks I get?"

"Sure, Dee," the detective said, "You give her a place out of the goodness of your heart! Don't waste your breath on me, tell it to the Judge!" he turned to the officer who had handcuffed Dee, "Get her out of here!"

The detectives took Peter and I to an old hotel over some shops on Grand Avenue. Everyday they brought me food and cigarettes, and talked with me for a while. "When am I going to get my own place?" I asked them.

"Can't do it right now. Dee's out on bond and she's lookin' for you. She wants to find you before the Grand Jury meets. It's best to keep you hid out until you testify."

A few days before I was to testify, I was moved to a convalescent home. I was to stay in the home and not go anywhere until after I testified before the Grand Jury, then after Dee was put away, they'd help me get on my feet.

The day arrived and I was scared, "Don't worry," the officer reassured me, "There's no one in there but you and the Grand Jury. This isn't a trial, you won't see Dee, the members of the Jury will decide if there's enough evidence to bring State charges. Just tell em what happened."

The Jury sat together in a box, all eyes were on me, I was led to a hard chair, I sat down with Peter in my lap. The Jury members looked at me, then they looked at Peter, my dark-skinned baby, with disapproval written all over their faces.

Not all of them disapproved, some were just surprised, but all of them reacted in some way. I saw this and I became angry. I was angry at the Jury for looking at my son that way and I showed this in my testimony, in the way I answered their questions, in the arrogant toss of my head.

Dee was exonerated of all charges. They said the witness lacked credibility. One of the detectives came to the convalescent home and told me the verdict.

"Oh great!" I told him, "Now she's out lookin' for me! I thought they were gonna put her away!"

"The Jury didn't believe your testimony. Sorry kid, we tried."

The next day an older woman from the front office of the home told me I'd have to leave. "Why?" I wanted to know, "The officers said they'd take care of everything!"

"They haven't, the arrangement was for a few days, no more. You'll have to go."

I called the Police Department and got one of the detectives on the phone. "Hey kid, we don't have money in the office fund to keep taking care of you!"

"You told me not to worry, you said you'd handle everything, as long as I testified. Now Big Dee's out there lookin' for me."

"If Dee bothers you, just call, okay, but we can't do anything else for you."

I was learning an awful lot of lessons. Nobody liked a "snitch", not even the police. They had used me, and when things didn't turn out the way they wanted, they dumped me, washed their hands of me. I had to leave the convalescent home, and I had a crazy dyke trying to catch up with me. Maybe I should go back to one of those hotels downtown, I thought. I won't go back to the Broadway, too risky, but maybe one of the others. There was an awful nice bellhop at the Howard Hotel, Jim was his name, I'll call him.

"Jim? This is Shirley, oh...I mean Rita, you remember me?"

"Sure, sure baby, I remember you, I called lookin' for you, but Jeep said you was gone."

I told Jim the whole story about Dee, I knew the police had used me, tricked me, and now I needed money and was afraid to be seen. "There's been a few stories floatin' that you signed a statement against Dee. Listen, don't ever tell anyone else you did that, nobody likes a "snitch". You can come down here and work, get a room and stay in it. Nobody's gonna come into the hotel and bother you, least of all, Big Dee. You'll have to lay low for awhile, if anyone ask you about it, deny it, say it musta been some other girl, cause it wasn't you, and never believe anything the police says again. I can understand why you did it, that dyke shouldn't have taken your baby. Dee ain't nuthin' but trouble, musta scared you to death. Yeah, Rita you can come on down here."

Next, I called Grandma who was more than happy to watch Peter. "Never," Grandma said, "Can anyone but you take Peter out of my house!"

I headed for the Howard Hotel, with all the lessons I'd learned lately, I felt I was ready for this new life.

*****

I stayed in the hotel all the time, reading books, turning tricks and laying low. I'd catch a cab to the department stores, spending money like water, buying fine clothes and cosmetics, buying things for Peter, buying things I'd never had before. I'd spend all my money, I knew as soon as I got back to the hotel I'd make some more. I was still living in the moment, never planning for the future.

I spent a few days a week with Peter at Grandma's house. I was always giving Grandma extra money, paying bills for her, or bringing groceries for her family. I felt Peter was loved there, he was safe. Grandma told me not to worry about Peter, and I didn't.

I stayed downtown reading books, shopping and turning tricks. I justified my actions. After all, I have to work, don't I? Peter is safe, he's well taken care of and Grandma loves him. I can't be there all the time, I have to make money! I pay Grandma well, I'm not shoving my responsibilities onto someone else, she wants to watch Peter.

Dorothy was one of Grandma's grandchildren, and she lived with her. Dorothy was 2 years younger than me. She was kicked out of school for various knife fights she'd had with white girls. She went to Black Panther meetings and was very militant. I really liked Dorothy, I thought

Dorothy was smart, pretty and very confident, everything I wanted to be.

Grandma and I became close. Dorothy told me I was part of her family, her "white" sister, and always made me feel welcome. "You need to do something with your life," Grandma often told me, "You need to think about that boy. This street life's no good, it's not for you."

I did want a different life, but the work was so easy and the money was good. Grandma talked and talked until she convinced me to give it a try. "Dorothy's going to the Jewish Vocational School to get her GED, they're goin' to train her and get her a good job. You can do that, too. You spend half the day in school and half the day working. They pay you for the work you do, you could stay here until you got a good job. We can squeeze you in somewhere."

I applied at the Jewish Vocational School, was accepted, and moved all my belongings into Grandma and Versaille's house. Dorothy and I were in the house watching TV when we heard a commotion on the front porch, Dorothy peeked out the window, "Grandma and Versaille are fighting," Dorothy said, "Better stay out of it, she'd be mad if we but in."

We went to bed and before the sun came up, we were off to the Jewish Vocational Center. After morning classes and a hot lunch, we went across the street to work at a small toy manufacturer. They didn't pay much, certainly not what I was used to making, but the work wasn't too hard.

That afternoon, going home on the bus, I turned to Dorothy, "I wonder what Grandma and Versaille were fighting about last night."

Dorothy turned in the seat to face me, "Oh, they were fighting about you."

"About me?" I was surprised, "Why would they fight about me?"

"Versaille don't want no white people stayin' in the house. He wanted to throw you out but Grandma wouldn't let him. She says it's her house, too. I guess they had a terrible fight and now they ain't speakin' to each other."

"What about Peter? Peter's white, too, and he lets him stay."

Dorothy laughed, "Peter's not white, you're white. You're the one he don't want there, not Peter."

I was hurt. I didn't know Versaille felt that way. But now that I thought about it, he never said anything to me. I didn't want to come in and disrupt their lives. I didn't want to cause trouble between Grandma and her husband. When we got to Grandma's, I told them I was leaving, going back to the hotel. I turned to Versaille, "I didn't know you didn't want me here, no one told me. This is your house and you have a right to say who can be here. I don't wanna stay where I'm not wanted. As long as Peter can stay, that's enough for me."

Versaille didn't say anything, but Grandma began, "You don't wanna go back to that hotel! Versaille didn't mean it, did you Versaille?" Grandma looked at him but he still said nothing.

"No" I said, "I'm going, I don't mind. I would never feel right staying here." I threw all my clothes in a taxicab and went to the Howard Hotel.

*****

I didn't want a pimp, I was waiting for love. I didn't want someone I had to share with other women, someone who never spoke words of love. I stayed away from pimps and the places they frequented. I'd heard stories, pimps would abduct a girl who didn't have a man, hold her against her will, making her turn tricks and taking all her money until she could manage to escape. After my ordeal with Dee, I knew these stories were true and I was very careful. I didn't want the pimps to catch me and I definitely tried to avoid Big Dee. I spent all my time downtown.

I was at my favorite bookstore on 12th Street, "Time To Read", it was the 5 o'clock rush hour downtown, I walked out the door of the shop, and there, in a car, right in front of me was Big Dee. I felt I'd been paralyzed for hours, but it was actually seconds. Dee started to get out of the car and I ran, I ran as fast as I could, not once looking back. When I reached the corner, I jumped in a car sitting at the light and locked the doors. "Hey, what's goin' on?" the driver yelled.

"Oh God!" I was in panic, "Just drive on, please, let's get out of here!"

There was Dee, reaching for the door handle, the light turned green, and the driver burned rubber getting out of there. "WHO WAS THAT?" the driver was shook up, it wasn't every day a young woman jumped in his car, with someone chasing her. This'll make great office gossip, something to tell his co-workers around the water cooler.

"She's a crazy woman, started chasing me, I don't even know her.

Listen, could you give me a ride, it's just a few blocks, to the Howard Hotel?"

That was a close call, I'll have to be more careful!

The bellhops liked Rita, and I was Rita now. No one I associated with downtown knew my real name and no one cared. I liked being Rita. Rita was glamorous, Rita was in demand, Rita had money and didn't have to beg for a place to stay, Rita was becoming more arrogant every day.

Shirley was still in there; unloved Shirley, insecure Shirley, plain Shirley, but Rita pushed her back, out of the way. Having two names, two different identities, made me feel like two different people and I preferred Rita to Shirley.

The bellhops like Rita because 1) she was a new girl and young, just 18. 2) she lived at the hotel and was available all the time, 3) I didn't have a pimp telling me what to do, always sticking his nose in hotel business. I didn't know anything about the business, and the bellhops trained me to be a top hotel whore.

The first thing they taught me was complete loyalty to the bellhop. Many of the girls would "burn" the bellhop (lie about how much money she made and cheat him on the cut). They got away with it for awhile, but eventually they got caught. I never burned a bellhop, I knew if they got mad at me, they'd "freeze" me out, not give me any tricks. The bellhops never confronted the girls who "burned" them, they'd just let them sit in their rooms all night, not making any money, and the bellhop would say, "Slow night, no business."

If you wanted to make a career working in the hotels, it was best not to double-cross the bellhop. Pimps were always encouraging the girl to "burn" the bellhop out of every dime she could. The bellhops knew this and preferred to work Rita. The bellhops molded and shaped me just the way they wanted.

*****

"Rita, T-Bone called," Jim's voice came through the phone, "He wants you at the Cordova, I called a cab." It was noon. I did a lot of business in the daytime, at all the hotels on 12th Street. Most of the girls worked nights, they were at home or sleeping, and by the time they came to work, I'd made my money and could relax.

I got out of the cab at the Cordova and T-Bone led me to the room where the trick waited, on the second floor. He was young, probably 20, there was something about him, something familiar, but I couldn't put my finger on it, I pushed it out of my mind and got down to business. He gave me $20 for a half & half.

When he climbed on to fuck me, he wrapped his arms around the top of my shoulders, close to my neck, when he cum, he raised his head and looked at me, then he started slapping and punching me in the face. "You bitch, I want my fuckin' money back! What a lousy fuck!"

I didn't say anything, I tried to push him off of me, but I couldn't. His arms, wrapped around my shoulders had me pinned down, I couldn't move. Better let T-Bone know what's going on, I thought. At this point, I wasn't afraid, this was the first time I'd had trouble with a trick.

I screamed, thinking the bellhop would be right there to save me, and the trick punched me in the face again, "Shut up that noise! Give me my money you stinkin' whore!" I screamed again, this time I gave it all I had, it was a blood-curdling scream. The trick reached under the pillow, pulled out a .38 and stuck it in my ear. Now I was afraid. "You scream again, bitch, I'm gonna blow your head off! I'm gettin' up and I don't want no funny stuff out of you!"

I was waiting for T-Bone to come to my rescue. The trick got up and began putting his clothes on with one hand, pointing the gun at me with the other. I sat on the side of the bed, naked, afraid to move. "Okay, open the purse slow and give me my money." I picked up my purse and pulled out a wad of bills, "Here" I said, "This is all I've got."

I handed him the money and then it dawned on me, Buck, he reminds me of Buck, the sinister gleam in his eyes, the cruel curl of his lips.

He took the money, climbed out the window and went down the fire escape. I waited a few minutes before I dared move. I was afraid he would come back. Finally I got up and called T-Bone on the phone. "That guy stuck a gun to my head and took all my money!"

"I'll be right up!" T-Bone said.

"Hey! Didn't you hear me scream?" I was angry now, now that the shock was passing, "I screamed several times!"

"Hey, Baby, calm down! I thought I heard a scream but it stopped."

"Did it ever cross your mind that it stopped cause I was dead? He put a .38 in my ear!"

"How'd he get out? He didn't come through the lobby."

"He went out the window."

T-Bone walked to the window and looked out, he seemed relieved the guy was gone.

I learned a number of lessons on this day, lessons that would prove to be valuable in the future. Lesson number one, the girl and the trick are the only ones in the room, if he wants to hurt her, no one can help, she's on her own, don't rely on the bellhop. Lesson number two, don't ever let a trick pin you down so you can't move, keep your arms around his neck, keep your arms free in case you need to protect yourself. Lesson number three, always check under the pillow for weapons. The fourth lesson, the most important one, always watch for that gleam in the eye, the sneer on the lips, the aura that surrounds a person with cruel intent. I began to look for Buck in every trick I turned, if I recognized him, I left, I wouldn't stay in the room with him. Being able to identify this look saved me a lot of trouble over the years.

*****

The bellhops were changing shifts at the Alton Hotel and they were discussing the day's events as they usually do. "T-Bone had a trick today, robbed the girl, beat her up and pulled a gun on her! Said it was a young guy. I don't like young tricks, too much trouble!"

"No kiddin'" the other bellhop said, "That's too bad. Who was the girl?"

"Rita"

"Rita? You mean Tommy's woman? Over on 9th? What was she doin' at the Cordova?" Another girl used the name Rita, but she worked at the Gladstone on 9th Street, she never worked on 12th.

"No man, not that girl. I'm talkin' bout that new girl, stays at the Howard, 12th Street Rita."

After that conversation the name stuck. When people talked about me, or about the other Rita, they always said 12th Street or 9th Street Rita to distinguish which girl was being discussed. I liked the sound of it, "12th Street Rita."

I was always reading something, a book, a magazine or the daily paper. Sometimes the other girls would tease me, "You need to put that book down and have some fun!" they'd laugh, I'd laugh too, and keep on reading. Every time I'd get to a juicy part in a book, the phone would ring and a trick was waiting. I'd turn the trick as quickly as possible, anxious to get back to my novel.

I had been at the hotel six months when a headline in the newspaper caught my eye. "BANK ROBBERS CAPTURED." Big Dee along with 3 men, held up a bank in Wichita, they were in jail, unable to make bond and headed for prison. Oh Boy! Was this good news or what! With Dee locked up, maybe I would be able to do something without always looking over my shoulder. Couldn't have happened to a better person, I laughed to myself.

*****

I adopted an attitude of superiority towards the other girls at the hotel. They were stupid. Giving their money to a man who obviously didn't care about them. I'D NEVER DO THAT! I preferred the company of books to the company of the other whores, always talking about their man, and anyway, the bellhops gave me more business if I sat in my room alone.

Two girls from Minneapolis, Minnesota, came to stay at the Howard. Pat was out-going and fun-loving, everyone liked Pat, she was always ready for a party. Pat and her man, Louis, had two children. Louie didn't have other women, he felt it was too much trouble. He didn't like women very well, he wasn't a homosexual, he just didn't like women. He beat Pat all the time, you could find him on 5th Street in Kansas shooting craps. When he was broke, he beat Pat until she came up with some money. Pat hid money from Louie, she fooled around with other pimps, giving them money, she gambled too, playing Tonk, and she made sure Louie found out, she didn't try to hide it. When he did find out she'd been up to some devilment, he'd beat the hell out of her. Pat would come in with a broken nose or a black eye, but she never got mad about it, she always laughed. Everybody liked Pat and everyone disliked Louie, but he never came around the hotel.

I enjoyed being around Pat, often we would go to a restaurant and have dinner together or go shopping in the afternoons. Although Pat had a man, she never let that stop her from doing anything she wanted. I didn't understand why Pat stayed with Louie. If she loved Louie so much, why did she always do things to get her ass beat? One evening during dinner I asked her, "Pat, why do you stay with Louie?"

"I love Louie, Rita. He's the father of my children, I'd never be with anyone else!"

"If you love him so much, why do you fool around with other guys?"

"Oh, I'm just havin' a little fun, he know how I am, and he accepts the way I am."

"I don't think he accepts anything, Pat, he kicks the livin' shit out of you! How can you stand that, known' you're gonna go home and be his punching bag?" Pat looked at me like I was retarded, "If Louie didn't beat me when I did something wrong, I'd think he didn't love me! He only does it because he cares about me."

I didn't agree with this way of thinking. I believed you didn't hit someone you loved. I'd had enough violence at Buck and Jean's to last a lifetime, and not once did I feel they beat me because they loved me. I didn't understand Pat's way of thinking, but I liked being around her anyway.

The other girl from Minnesota was Chris. She had a daughter by her man, Calvin. They came to Kansas City because Chris didn't want her family to know she was a whore. Calvin wanted to be a player, a pimp. He didn't want to work, he was lazy and wanted someone to take care of him. "Okay!" Chris told him, "I'll be a whore, but you have to marry me, you can't have other women, and I don't want my family to find out." Calvin married Chris, she started hooking and she hated every second of it. Pat and I loved being whores, we'd laugh and joke about the tricks we turned, anxious for the next one. Chris loathed it, she never tried to disguise how she felt about it, scowling when she came to work, muttering under her breath when sent to a trick.

Everyone knew how Chris felt, the girls, the bellhops and most important, the tricks. Once a trick dated Chris, he didn't want her again, unless he got off being treated like last week's garbage. With her nose stuck in the air, and a frown on her face, she would pull back and cringe when a trick touched her. She didn't want to be a whore, and she never for one second let Calvin forget it. She was doing this for him. The bellhops tried to talk to her, "You don't have to like it, just pretend, can't you act?" They said she was only hurting herself, and hurting her money. Chris didn't care, her aura of negativity was always with her.

No one liked Chris, and I was no exception. Always angry because she had to work, I found Chris to be unpleasant company. Pat pretended to be Chris's friend, and Chris clung to her. Chris didn't have any friends, and Pat was from her hometown, where Chris wanted to be. Behind Chris's back, Pat made fun of her. Chris was a big girl, she didn't know how to wear makeup or dress with style, she looked like she'd stepped off the farm yesterday. Pat ridiculed her hair, her makeup and her sullen attitude. Pat set her sights on Calvin, Chris's husband. Pat would meet him on the sly, fucking him and giving him money once in a while. Calvin liked Pat, he liked her better than Chris, who was always unhappy, but he was smart enough to know that Pat would never act right for anyone, and she'd never leave Louie, so he hung onto Chris.

Everyone knew about the affair, except Chris, and she was becoming suspicious. When she confronted Calvin with her fears, he denied it. When she asked Pat, she lied, too. There was a lot of friction between Pat and Chris. Pat didn't care if Chris knew, but Calvin did. Chris wanted to believe it wasn't true, Pat was the only one who'd talk to her!

Chris had a trick who wouldn't date anyone but her (one of the few), sometimes she would meet him at the Bar and Grill next door to the hotel. He was a dishwasher at the Muehlebach Hotel, a dirty looking guy that no one wanted to date anyway. One night he was waiting for Chris in the restaurant, she hadn't showed up yet, but Pat was there. Pat went over to the trick and sat down at his table. She was trying to get the trick to leave with her, but he refused and waited for Chris. Pat laughed at him, "You think you love her? She hates your guts! And she's married to a nigger and got a baby by him! I bet she never told you that!" Pat walked out the door as Chris walked in.

Chris didn't return to the hotel that night, everyone was worried, it wasn't like Chris to disappear, and Calvin was frantic. Around noon the next day, Pat said she might know where Chris was.

Pat took Calvin to the dishwasher's apartment, the door wasn't locked, and when they pushed the door open, there was Chris, laying on the bed, staring at the ceiling, her nylons wrapped around her throat. She was dead. The trick drove 100 miles from Kansas City, then turned himself in at some small town police station. At the trial it was revealed that the killer had just been released from a mental institution on the east coast. He'd been there for killing someone else. This wasn't his first murder. Why'd he kill Chris? Was he just crazy, or did he do it because of the things Pat had told him? That was something Pat would have to wonder for the rest of her life.

A few weeks after they found Chris, Louie came down to the hotel and beat Pat for something she'd done, beat her until she was unconscious. He beat her in the lobby in front of a number of people. He leaped in the air and landed on her head with both feet a number of times. The bellhop stopped him, but not soon enough, Pat was out.

The bellhops evicted Pat from the Howard Hotel, and the other hotels didn't want hr either, too much trouble. No one knows if it was the beating that caused it, or Chris's death, which Pat felt guilty about, but whatever the reason, her mind started to go. She couldn't remember people and started to talk nonsense. A few months after this, Louie was shot and killed on 5th Street over a crap game. Calvin went back to Minnesota with his and Chris's daughter. There were rumors that Pat lived on the street, completely crazy, remembering nothing and no one, but these were only rumors, because no one ever heard from Pat again.

*****

I took taxicabs everywhere. At first, I would count out the exact fare on the meter, and give it to the driver. I soon learned that people are more cooperative when you tip them, (especially when you're doing something on the shady side) and they always remembered you. Never know when you might need a cab right away, and I always got one. I also tipped all the waitresses that served me. I was getting out more now that Dee was locked up, and I didn't have to always be looking over my shoulder. I still didn't frequent the hustler's hangouts, but instead, I went to the shops and restaurants downtown. Most of the people downtown knew I was a whore, but it didn't matter to them, I always minded my business and I always left a generous tip.

Occasionally I would meet a man and go out with him on a date, not a business date, but dinner and maybe a movie. I didn't hide what I did for a living. Men wanted to fuck me, of course, but that was all, they didn't get serious. If a guy did like me, he wanted me to quit whoring. I wasn't about to give up whoring for anyone. I loved being Rita, the money gave me independence, I couldn't make this much money doing anything else, I had no skills or training. I didn't want to be under someone's thumb, as a wife. As long as I paid my own way, I didn't have to put up with any abuse from others. I enjoyed everything that had to do with whoring.

A young, good-looking Italian fellow named Joe began to pursue me. He was driving a cab, but only for a little while, he told me, until he could get on his feet, whatever that meant. He was crazy about me, he wanted to be with me all the time. He knew I was a whore, but he didn't seem to care. I was swept away by Joe's enthusiasm for me. I like him and thought this might get serious. He told me he was in love! He was overwhelmed with desire for me! He told me everything I wanted to hear.

Joe's family was having a big Italian get together, I'd never met his family, but he talked about them all the time. We had spent some time together, but now he had to go to the party.

"Why don't I go with you?" I said.

"Oh, that's alright," Joe replied, "This is a family thing."

"Why don't you want to take me? Because I'm a whore?"

"Because you're a whore?" he laughed, "No that's not it! I'll call you later."

"I want to know why you won't take me, are you ashamed of me?"

Joe was putting on his tie, he stopped to look at me, "Look, I like you a lot, hey, I even love you, but I can't take you home to meet my family, not because you're a whore, because you got a nigger baby, that's why. My family would never accept that. No white man is going to take you home. You understand, don't you? I like you but it could never be serious between us. I wish it were different, but that's the way the world is. Anyway, what's wrong with the relationship we got? You don't need to meet my family."

"A nigger baby, huh?" I was furious, how could he refer to my son that way? "All I can say is don't let the door slap you in the ass!" I never talked to Joe again. Although I tricked with anyone who had the money, when it came to love, I only dated black men. Joe was right, white guys would never accept Peter, and if a man didn't love Peter, he wasn't the man for me.

*****

I had turned 19 the week before, when I went to meet a trick at a motel. Snow covered ice lay frozen on the streets. After the trick did his business, he left. I was waiting on a taxicab, and because of the weather, it was a long wait. When he honked, I ran to the door, impatient, "Did you call a cab?" The cabdriver was smiling, teeth flashing, the handsomest black man I'd ever see! He was gorgeous! He looked like a movie star, all his features were perfect! I pulled the door shut behind me, and when I turned I fell on the ice, sliding half way under the cab. The driver jumped out of the cab, he was tall and he had a great body to go with that great face. "You okay?" he asked, helping me up and brushing the snow off my body. "It's slicker than I thought," I mumbled.

I wanted the ride back to the Howard Hotel to never end. He was charming as well as handsome. He had recently returned to KC after being discharged from the Navy where he'd been a cook. He was 25 years old and his name was Perry de Dunois, but everyone called him Frenchy.

"How'd you get that name?" I asked him.

"My last name is French, I'm Cajun, guys in the Navy just got to callin' me Frenchy. I kinda like it, don't you?"

"Yes" I said, looking into his laughing eyes, "I like it a lot."

He wanted to take me out and I wanted to go. There was a spark between us, a current of energy I hadn't felt with anyone else, I couldn't wait to see him again. After dinner he took me to his room at a shabby hotel. He didn't fuck me; he slowly made love to me. I told him I'd never had an orgasm with a man, and he set out to change that. It took hours, hours of licking and kissing every inch of my body until I finally had an explosive orgasm. I WAS IN LOVE! Frenchy said he loved me too, and ten days later on Peter's 1st birthday, we were married at City Hall.

Frenchy drove cab and I sold pussy. Frenchy said he didn't mind, he knew I loved only him. Of course, he handled all the money, after all, he was the man. I was blindly, foolishly in love, and if he wanted to control all the money, it was okay with me. I felt my relationship with Frenchy was different than the other girls, Frenchy wasn't a pimp, he was a cabdriver, I told myself. He's handsome, charming and he belongs to me. He loves ONLY me, he told me so! And oh, the way he makes love to me!

Frenchy and I moved into an apartment, I only went to the hotel in the evenings. Frenchy adored Peter, and while I worked, he took Peter everywhere with him. He'd go to Grandma's, they would dress Peter up real fancy, and Frenchy would show him off at the pool hall, or ride him in the cab. He told everyone Peter was his son.

"I wish Peter really were my son!" he would say. Frenchy had been married before. He had a son and a daughter that he didn't see very often. His excuse for not seeing his children was the mother. She was always giving him trouble. "I love Peter." Frenchy would tell me. Hearing these words made me love Frenchy more. Frenchy was a real smooth operator, he said whatever he thought I wanted to hear. "There's no father on the Birth Certificate, we could put your name on it, if you want to. They can't prove you're not his father."

We went to City Hall, Frenchy signed a document, swearing he was Peter's natural father, and we changed Peter's name to Peter de Dunois. Now Peter was legally his son, and Frenchy was happy.

All the bellhops liked Frenchy, he was a fun-loving guy. I didn't like intense, violent people and neither did the bellhops. Frenchy was generous, buying the bellhops food or alcohol, never causing trouble, always good for a few laughs. The bellhops let Frenchy hang around the hotel, usually very late at night, just before dawn.

Frenchy wanted to be a player, he didn't tell me this, he knew I didn't want to hear that. He was a real ladies man, he fucked every female who would let him, and they all did. He was devilishly handsome and women couldn't resist him, he had charisma. He fucked every whore in the hotel, he didn't miss one, and he fucked em at the other hotels, too. He didn't pay for it, they threw themselves at him. The whores laughed behind my back, "She thinks he's faithful! HA! HA! She's worse off than us, at least we know what's goin' on."

I thought we were building a life together, I thought we were a family. This is the way I wanted it to be, and I refused to see the truth. Frenchy liked to gamble, and he'd always lose. The luck he had with women didn't extend to the crap table. As soon as we had a little money saved, he'd lose it all. We were always broke, and that kept me working all the time.

It was Sunday, my day off, I hadn't planned on working, I wanted to spend the day with Frenchy, when he told me we had no money.

"What do you mean, no money? We had $400 in the bank! What happened to it?"

"Well Baby," Frenchy was being his usually charming self, but this time I wasn't going for it, and he could see that from my face. "I thought I'd get the money back! It didn't work out that way, I'm sorry. I'll never take the money out of the bank to gamble, never again."

"Damn Frenchy, now I gotta go to work!"

But he did take the money out of the bank, he did it over and over, until I finally learned he wasn't going to change. We began to argue frequently about money and his gambling habits. If I wanted something, I had to get it before Frenchy got his hands on the cash. Frenchy wasn't selfish, he didn't care how much money I spent, he was going to blow it all, anyway.

I was downtown at the hotel, I'd only been there a short while when I began to feel sick. My stomach was upset and I felt feverish. I never left work, once I got there, I wasn't a sickly type of person, but strong and healthy. On this day, I was too sick to work.

"Why don't you go home, Rita." Jim told me.

"Jim" I groaned, hanging my head between my legs, "I think I will." I took a cab to our apartment, I was slipping my key into the lock, I couldn't wait to lay down, when I opened the door to our studio apartment, I saw Frenchy and another woman, naked in my bed. They both had startled looks on their faces. It didn't take a rocket scientist to figure out what they'd been doing. I was in shock! What should I do? Frenchy jumped up, pulling on his pants, he started talking, and although I heard his voice, I don't know what he said, I was paralyzed, standing wit the door wide open, my key still in the lock, staring at them. Frenchy ran over, pulled me into the apartment, took my key out of the lock and shut the door. He kept talking, but I blocked it out, I just wanted him to go away. "I don't feel like talking right now." I said this in a calm, even voice. I went into the bathroom, closed the door, and took a hot bath. Frenchy started knocking on the door. "Go Away! I don't want to talk to you!" I called through the door.

Frenchy assumed I wasn't very angry, or he was hoping I wasn't too mad, since I hadn't started cussing and fighting. He came into the bathroom and started explaining, "This girl wants to work for us, she wants to be part of our family. All that money she makes, it'll be for us, baby. We might as well get the money, instead of somebody else. You turn tricks and I don't say anything, how is this any different? You can train her, tell her what to do, you'll be my main woman. Damn, Rita, you're my wife, why should you worry about some other girl. She's gonna throw that money away, she might as well throw it this way." I didn't answer him. I was so angry, I didn't trust myself to speak, I was afraid I would lose control. I lay in the warm water, silent, not looking at him. "She's real dumb, she don't know anything. Why don't I send her in, you might like her."

I still didn't say anything. Frenchy left and the girl came in. "Frenchy told me to come in and talk to you, says you're a pro!" I wouldn't speak, and I wouldn't look at the girl, I kept staring at the bath water. The silence frightened the girl. "Why don't you say somethin'? What are you? Crazy or somethin'?" I turned and looked at the girl.

"Yeah, maybe I'm crazy. I know I feel crazy right now. Truth is, I don't know what to say. It's not your fault, and I think I'm ready to get out of this tub now. If you don't mind, I'd like to get dressed." I spoke like a robot, I was still in a daze.

I got dressed and went to the living room/bedroom. Frenchy had returned the Murphy bed to it's place in the wall, they were waiting on me, "Why don't we go over to Don's and have a steak?" Frenchy suggested.

"Yeah, I'm starvin'!" the girl said. They both looked at me, waiting for me to say something.

"Okay" I responded, still in shock, still not saying much, just going through the motions.

We arrived at the restaurant and sat in a booth, Frenchy and the girl on one side, and me on the other. The waitress took our orders and brought the drinks, I started talking to the girl. "Frenchy's a good fuck, huh?"

"Oh yeah!" the girl said.

"Hey" Frenchy laughed nervously, "Why don't we talk about somethin' else? You're gonna hafta school her on turnin' tricks."

"I wasn't talking to you, Frenchy." I looked at the girl. "How'd you like the way he puts your legs in the air and licks you? He's gotta be the best!"

The girl smiled at Frenchy and put her hand on his arm. "He's the best I've ever had. I liked it a lot!"

My temper exploded, "You bastard!" I screamed at Frenchy. I took my glass of water in one hand, and I took the chili the waitress had just sat down in front of me in my other hand, I threw them both in Frenchy's face at the same time, "How could you?" I screamed at him. I ran out of the restaurant screaming like a mad woman.

Frenchy threw some money on the table and ran after me, he held me while I struggled. He flagged down a cab and sent me home. He didn't come home right away, but when he got there, he told me he'd gotten rid of the girl. "I told her I loved you, and I didn't want to upset you. I'm sorry baby, it won't happen again. I was trying to make things easier for you, I was only thinking about you." Actually, he had taken her to a hotel to work. He kept it hid from me. I loved Frenchy, and I forgave him, I wanted to believe he loved me.

Frenchy quit driving cab, he said he couldn't get along with the dispatcher. He spent all day at the pool hall on 27th and Troost, gambling and hanging out with the other hustlers, shootin' the shit. He was always telling me about a money making deal he was involved in, but I never saw any money from these deals. Frenchy started dressing flamboyantly, like a pimp, he had his ear pierced and put a diamond stud in it, he had his hair processed and he was ready to play. I was disappointed in him, this isn't the way it was supposed to go, but I still loved him.

One evening he came home broke, with a huge bag of marijuana, "I spent our money, but I can triple the money when I sell this weed." he told me, laying the bag on the kitchen table.

"Frenchy, why do you do this stuff? If you'd just manage the money I make, and quit throwing it away, we'd have plenty. I don't even smoke marijuana!"

He started with his excuses, We began to argue, but he wasn't worried, we always argued, and I'd come around. Frenchy was so smug, and sure of himself. It fueled my anger. "I'm not going to let you treat me this way!" I yelled, "I've had it with all your deals. WE'RE THROUGH! I'M LEAVING YOU!" I ran out of the apartment, and out of the building. We lived on the third floor, by the time I'd reached the sidewalk in front, Frenchy was on the balcony.

"You ain't leavin' me, bitch!" BANG! I heard the gunshot, then my whole body went numb. I crumbled to the sidewalk.

"Help me!" I cried, "I've been shot!" I knew I was shot, but I didn't know where. I lay there wondering if I was going to die. Frenchy ran down the stairs and picked me up in his arms. "Oh baby!" He was crying real tears, "I'm sorry! I was just trying to scare you. I was trying to shoot around you, you musta walked into the bullet. You know I wouldn't hurt you for anything in the world. I can't live without you!" He carried me upstairs and laid me on the bed, "The bullet's in your left knee, I'm takin' you to the hospital now!"

He was crying and I was touched with his concern. He was really worried because he'd almost killed his moneymaker. The tears weren't for me, but for himself. If I chose to think the tears were for me, he'd let me think it. "I didn't mean to shoot you, it was an accident," he told me over and over.

Just as we were about to leave for the hospital, a loud bang sounded at the door, POLICE, WE'RE COME'N IN!" The police kicked in the door on the first try, their riot guns were drawn, "GET DOWN ON THE FLOOR!" they yelled at Frenchy, "SPREAD EAGLE, ON THE FLOOR!" Frenchy jumped on the floor and spread out, he was scared with all those rifles pointing at him.

"Officer? What's the problem?" Frenchy asked.

"Where's the gun?" the police said, "Over there." Frenchy pointed to the bookcase. The cop went to the bookcase and picked up the gun with a pencil and dropped it into a bag. "We got a call there's been a shooting here." The officer turned to me "Did he shoot you? Have you been shot?"

"She's been shot in the knee, I was taking her to the hospital, it was an accident." Frenchy said.

"You shut up! Okay Miss, did he shoot you?"

"No" I said. "It was an accident, I was leaning over the bed making it up, when the dog, (we had a French Poodle named Iceberg Slim), ran into the bookcase. The gun was sitting on the top shelf, fell to the middle shelf and went off, hitting me in the back of the leg."

All the cops started laughing, "That's the dumbest story I've ever heard! The caller said the woman was shot out front on the sidewalk. If the gun went off in here, where's the shell?"

"Up my ass!" I told them. I couldn't stand to see Frenchy laying on the floor, scared. I couldn't stand the cops smug attitude. What happened between Frenchy and I was our own business, the police had no right to interfere. I hadn't called the police and I didn't want them there. Also, there was a bag of marijuana laying on the kitchen table, that I hadn't forgot about.

The cops started moving around, and I was afraid they'd go into the kitchen.

"Do you have a search warrant?" I asked, "If not, stop looking around my house."

The officer got angry, "Okay, you wanna stay here with this guy? You don't wanna press charges?"

"There's nothing to press charges for, it was an accident, the dog ran into the bookcase..."

"Yeah, yeah" the cop interrupted me, "Let's go guys. We're keepin' the gun, we wanna check it out, you can pick it up at the station in a couple of days." The police left, and Frenchy took me to the hospital.

I checked in at the emergency room and was put into an examination room where I waited to see a doctor. The officer who'd been at my apartment entered the room.

"I came by to talk to you, I thought you might be afraid to talk in front of that guy."

"I'm not afraid to talk in front of him," I said, "He's my husband."

"Look, we know he shot you. If you're afraid of him, we'll protect you."

Yeah! Right! Just like the police protected me from Big Dee. Anyway, I don't need protection from Frenchy, he loves me and it was an accident. I trusted Frenchy more than the police.

"I told you what happened," I said to the policemen in a very unfriendly tone of voice, "The dog ran into the bookcase..."

"Okay" the cop frowned at me, "One of these days he won't miss, the bullet won't be in your leg. You're playing a dangerous game, and the only loser is gonna be you. I'm giving you one more chance before I leave to tell the truth."

"I told you the dog..." the cop walked out the door.

My knee was x-rayed from all angles, "The bullet is lodged between your knee cap," the doctor began, "There doesn't seem to be any damage to the knee. If we take out the bullet, we take the risk of damaging the knee. I think it's best to leave the bullet where it is. If it bothers you, you can always have it removed later. You weren't wearing nylons, the bullet didn't carry any foreign articles into the leg. Let's leave it and see what happens." The bullet stayed where it was, and most

of the time I forgot it was there, except when it was very cold outside.
*****

Frenchy couldn't say he was sorry enough. Of course to his other women, the women I didn't know about, he bragged, "Yeah that bitch said she was leavin' and POP, I stopped that shit!" He laughed about it, and he bragged to the guys at the pool hall. He felt like a big shot, he was a player.

Again, I forgave him, after all, he couldn't bear the thought of losing me, he lost control, but it was all for love. And to me, love was everything. I didn't realize the love was only in my mind, I listened to what he said, and excused everything he did.

Frenchy liked good food, fine clothes, big cars and flashy jewelry, he bought all these things. Frenchy and I wore all the latest fashions. We still argued all the time about money, but making up was so much fun. Frenchy didn't change and the arguing was so frustrating for me. Why was I arguing? It didn't matter to him what I thought. I was getting tired of Frenchy, I knew he'd never change, he was always going to gamble and play around with other women. I'd never caught Frenchy with another woman since the day I came home early from work, but I had no doubt he was fooling around. Occasionally I found evidence; panties in the car, lipstick on his clothes, hickies on his neck. At first, I confronted him about my findings, but he always lied, he lied and lied. I was tired of arguing, it was like bumping my head against a wall. I knew he wouldn't willingly let me go, he's already proven that. I knew I had to slip away. And where would I go? Maybe he'll change, I thought, maybe he'll get bored with all his running around and realize that I'm the one who loves him. And of course, there was Peter, and Frenchy loved Peter.

Frenchy went to Grandma's often, taking Peter everywhere with him, bragging that Peter was his son. Peter was a beautiful child, he inherited all the positive traits of both races, people made over him, cooing and carrying-on, Peter had started to walk, with his flopping curls and smiling face it was a sight to behold. Frenchy's interest in Peter meant a lot to me, I couldn't spend the time I should have with Peter, I had to work.

Frenchy's birthday was April 3, I had a small party for him at home. Late in the night he left and he didn't return until the next afternoon, I was waiting on him, ready to battle. "Where have you been?" I started the fight.

"Martin Luther King's been killed- - assassinated!" he was very excited, "The police are everywhere! They think black people are going to riot!"

"I don't care about that! I want to know where you've been."

"Hey" Frenchy turned to me, with a serious expression, "This is history in the making! I wanna be a part of it!"

He was rummaging through his drawers, looking for something, he found his gun and slipped it into his waistband. "I'll be back later. Don't go anywhere! Don't leave this apartment!"

"Frenchy, where are you going?" I pleaded, "What are you gonna do? Don't leave, please, don't leave! I'm afraid something will happen to you!" He kissed me and was gone.

We lived in a racially mixed neighborhood, two blocks from Troost. I'd run out of cigarettes and decided to walk to Troost and buy a pack. It was late afternoon, there were people milling around on the streets, but they were all black people, the white people were nowhere to be seen. When I got to the store, a crowd of black youths began to taunt me, "Hey you, white bitch! You killed Martin Luther King!" They started throwing rocks and bottles at me, I ran into the store for shelter. I bought the cigarettes, loitering around, afraid to go back into the streets.

"Hey lady" the clerk said, "We're closing early today, gettin' out of here, you'll have to leave."

I tried to call a cab, but no cabs were available, they wouldn't come to that part of town. I left the store to walk the two blocks home. The youths began to chase me, calling me names and blaming me for Martin Luther King's death.

I ran as fast as I could, when I got to my own street, there were people on the roof, people I saw everyday, people I had exchanged greetings with in the hallway. They started calling me names and throwing beer bottles at me from the roof. "There's that white bitch that lives on the third floor! Hey, why don't you go home, pecker wood!"

"I am home!" I yelled back. This only made them more hostile, they must have a thousand beer bottles up there! I ran into the building, sprinted up the stairs, entered my apartment and locked the door.

Whew! I thought, what in the hell is going on out there? I wish Frenchy would come home! I'm stuck here! I can't get a cab, and I won't be able to stop someone if they decide to try and get in here! But no one bothered me. I turned on the TV and saw that the riots had started in all the black neighborhoods. No kidding!

When Frenchy got home it was dark out, he came in and his adrenaline was pumping. "You oughta see it! Niggahs is gone crazy!"

I told him what happened when I went out for cigarettes and he got angry. "You're so hard-headed, you never listen to anything! I TOLD YOU NOT TO GO OUT! Did you need a cigarette so bad you'd risk your life?"

"You should have been here with me!" I shouted back at him, "instead you're running around, God only knows where! Why did you leave me here alone? Was it so important, you left me alone and in danger."

We started to argue, when suddenly a bullet came crashing through the window and hit the wall. Frenchy tackled me, knocking me to the ground, he laid across me so I couldn't move. "Listen, don't get up, stay on the floor, crawl to the closet and stay there, you should be safe in there." The bullets were flying into the apartment now, it sounded like a war zone. Frenchy crawled through the apartment and turned out all the lights, ducking and dodging bullets as he went.

He crawled into the closet where I had gone, "I'm gonna find out what's goin' on. I don't want you to move until I get back! I brought the phone in here with me, in case you need it. I'll be right back!" He left me there, and I was very frightened. I had no idea how long I'd been there when Frenchy came back. It could have been minutes, it could have been hours. "Damn, you ain't gonna believe it! The National Guardsmen were shooting up here! Seems someone was on the roof shooting down at them and when they shot back, they shot up our place! Shootin's over now, they caught the snipers, and you ain't gonna believe this, it was some white boys on the roof, shootin' at the Guard. Damn! Those white boys was tryin' to get us killed!"

The riots started to fizzle out the next day, and after a week everything returned to normal. The people who'd thrown bottles from the roof greeted me as if nothing had happened, and I acted the same. But it was only acting, I never forgot how they turned on me, blaming me for all their problems just because I had white skin.

*****

I was at a motel with a trick, he had just handed me the money when he peeped out the window "Oh shit! The police are out there! You gotta go!"

"Why? What's up?" I replied.

"Look, don't waste time! Just go! Now!" I left the room and passed the police, when I looked over my shoulder, I saw them knocking on the door of the room I'd just left.

I had walked a few blocks when the police pulled up next to me. "Stop right there!" he demanded, I stopped and waited, not sure what was going on.

"What were you doing at the motel?"

"I wasn't at a motel." I answered, "I just left my girlfriends house." I tried to act innocent, but it was obvious I was a whore, I dressed and acted like a whore.

"We saw you leave that room. We passed you, don't lie about it!"

"You're mistaken, that must have been someone else. I haven't been to any motel." My attitude and manner of speech told the police they were wasting their time questioning me.

"Let's see some ID."

"I don't have any ID." Whores don't carry ID!

"No ID? No driver's license? Library card? Nothing?"

"No" I put my hands on my hips.

"What's your name?"

"Rita" I paused, I didn't have a last name for Rita.

"Rita what?" I remembered a girl from reform school whose name was Rita, Rita Simms.

"Rita Simms." I told the police.

"Birthday?" This time I didn't hesitate, I gave them my sister Sandra's birthday.

"1943" the cop laughed, "That's not your birthday, you're not 25!"

He turned to the other officer, "Let's take her downtown and have her fingerprinted, check her out, I think she's lying!"

"But I haven't done anything!" I yelled at the police.

"Loitering" he said, "Loitering for the purpose of prostitution. Get in the car!"

The officers took me to the police station and we rode the elevator to the top floor where the jail was. First they fingerprinted me, then they took my picture, front side...left side...right side. I was booked under the name Rita Simms with my older sister's birth date. After being held 20 hours for investigation, I was released, and no charges were filed against me. Later, I found out that the trick was a drug dealer the police had been watching. Those policemen weren't concerned with prostitution, and if I hadn't been such a smart-aleck, I wouldn't have gone to jail. After the way I'd been treated in the Big Dee affair, I wasn't about to cooperate with them.

I was arrested again, this time the bellhop sent me to a room, the man waiting was a vice squad officer. The bellhop and I both went to jail.

This time I gave them my real name. The bellhops warned me not to lie to the police, giving false information to a police officer was a serious offense, prostitution was a minor offense.

After checking my fingerprints and discovering I'd been arrested before under a different name and birth date, they questioned me about this information. I told them exactly what happened. "My real name is Shirley Sandy. I only used Rita Simms because I was afraid!" I tried to play on their sympathy, "I never been arrested before!"

The officer took a few notes and left. I was released on bond and according to the police department, I was Rita Simms alias Shirley Sandy.

*****

Frenchy and I had been together for a year, I was 20 years old, Frenchy was 26 and Peter was 2. It was a year of love and laughter, fighting and tears. Not all the time with Frenchy was bad, there were lots of good times, too. He took me out often, to the drive-in, bowling and picnics in the park on Sunday. I wasn't old enough to get in the bars, but party houses were popular in the late 60's. The party houses were private homes in residential districts. They usually opened around 10 p.m., for a small cover charge you could drink, dance, gamble or just listen to music all night long until the sun came up.

All the hustlers would get dressed up, arriving in big cars with women hanging on their arms, lighting their cigarettes. Flashing big wads of money, showing off for the other hustlers. Occasionally the police would raid the house for selling liquor illegally, but it didn't happen very often. There were a number of party houses around town, in both Kansas and Missouri, and Frenchy knew them all. He'd take me along with him, he usually spent his time gambling and wanted me there for "good luck". I had fun with Frenchy, he was handsome, and was all mine, or so I thought.

I lived in a fairy tale world in my mind. I wanted to believe everything was the way I thought it was, not the way it REALLY was. I wanted to believe my relationship with Frenchy was different, when in reality, I was just another whore with another pimp.

*****

Dorothy was pregnant and all Grandma's family were unhappy with her about it. I knew how it felt to be pregnant with your family against you. Dorothy still lived with Grandma, but there was tension in the house about the baby that was coming. The baby's father was Jack, and Air Force pilot Dorothy had met at a USO dance. Jack didn't come around, and I knew what it was like to be pregnant by a soldier who wasn't there. I gave Dorothy money and I bought her maternity clothes and other things she needed.

Dorothy was constantly making jokes about white people. She ridiculed the way they dressed or walked and how they talked. I would laugh along with her. But I didn't dare make jokes about blacks, Dorothy wouldn't stand for it, she was very militant, active in the Black Panther Party. Dorothy was fighting for her equal rights, and I understood that, I never thought the jokes were directed at me. After all, I wasn't accepted by whites OR blacks, society disapproved of my mixed son, of course being a whore didn't help matters any, but that was more acceptable than having a black baby. I didn't realize that Dorothy hated ALL white people, including me, I thought Dorothy was my friend.

As Dorothy's due date approached, she didn't have any clothes for the baby. I decided to buy Dorothy the things she needed. When I told Frenchy my plans, Frenchy, who was a very generous person, exploded, "I don't want you buyin' nuthin' for that dyke!"

"She's not a dyke!" I shot back, "And I'm going to buy the stuff, I just wanted to let you know!"

"You'll be sorry. She's not your friend."

I bought Dorothy everything she needed for the baby, blankets and gowns and towels and wash rags and diapers and socks and everything but a baby bed. Everyone was shocked at how much money I spent, but it made me feel good to help Dorothy.

*****

Frenchy and I moved out of our apartment and rented a house. The second day in the house, our dog was killed by a car. The first week in the house, someone broke in, stole some jewelry and completely ransacked the place, they even went through the garbage, leaving it on the kitchen counter. "They musta been looking for drugs," Frenchy said, "Why else would they look in the trash?"

I didn't feel comfortable in the house. I felt that my private space had been invaded, and it could happen again. I didn't want to be there when it did. I knew the burglary had something to do with Frenchy's activities, but he never told me anything, and he lied so much, I didn't know if he was telling the truth or not. "Why would someone be looking in our house for drugs?" I asked him, "We don't use drugs."

"I don't know, baby. You know how nigguhs is." Yeah, I knew how "nigguhs" were and they weren't coming in here unless they knew there was something here to get. I knew Frenchy was lying but I'd been through this so many times before, I knew it was fu''''tile.

The second week we were in the house, I got a phone call from Frenchy, he was in jail on Federal Drug Charges. His car was confiscated by the government, the interior of the car was ripped apart, looking for drugs. The FBI put an undercover cop at the pool hall, he'd been hanging around the pool hall, buying drugs from all the players.

The charges were Federal because drugs had been transported across the state line to the West Bottoms in Kansas. The West Bottoms was an industrial area with warehouses. It's where the old stock yards used to be. There were lots of truck drivers in the West Bottoms. Wherever there's truck drivers, you'll always find whores, and where there's whores, you'll always find pimps.

The liquor laws in Kansas were different than Missouri. Hard liquor was only served in private clubs, you had to be a member to get in (anyone who asked was given a membership). In the West Bottoms on the Kansas side (State line ran through the middle of the West Bottoms) there were no private clubs, but small cafes that served breakfast or hamburgers and liquor "under the table." The whores worked the cafes and the rooms above the café were rented out by the hour for tricking.

It was rough in the West Bottoms. All the girls carried a weapon of some kind, knives, ice picks and even guns. I never went to the West Bottoms, but I had heard a lot of stories about it, Big Dee used to go there. I didn't know that Frenchy hung out there, until he was arrested.

The FBI waited until they had indictments against 20 people before they made any arrests. Early in the morning, they served all 20 warrants at the same time, and Frenchy was busted at the pool hall on 27th and Troost, he'd lost all his money in a crap game when the agents arrived. The next day he was arraigned in Federal Court on four charges; two counts of possession of narcotics (heroin) and two counts of sales of narcotics. His bond was set at $10,000, I needed $1,000 to get him out of jail through a bondsman, and I didn't have a dime.

I went downtown to the hotels and checked in, staying around the clock, but the bellhops were "freezing me out" for some reason. They don't want me to make his bond, I thought. And it was true, they didn't. Each bellhop had his own reasons for not wanting Frenchy out of jail. Frenchy had fucked every girl downtown which made some bellhops mad. Frenchy's gambling had caused other hard feelings and Frenchy was so good-looking and lucky with the ladies, there was lots of envy.

No, the bellhops didn't want Frenchy out of jail, so they didn't give me any tricks. I'd sat for 24 hours and only had 2 tricks. I called Liz.

"Liz, this is Rita. I was wondering, do you still want me to work with you?"

"Sure" Liz replied, "I'll meet you at the drug store at 12th and Wyandotte, in the back at the lunch counter. 8 o'clock."

I'd met Liz at a party house. Liz was an ugly woman, skinny...no breasts...no hips...no female curves at all. She had a long horsey looking face and she was always laughing like a donkey. Some people said she was totally insane, and she probably was. She was a top money-making whore, coveted by all the pimps. Liz worked the bars and hotels downtown, not the whorehouse hotels, but the big hotels where the out-of-towners stayed. She usually sat in the hotel bar and got a guy drunk, then she'd meet him in his room, she'd try to steal all his cash and any jewelry he had and she usually got it.

The majority of these men never called the police, they didn't want to admit they'd been with a whore, so they chalked it up to experience and told their wives they'd "lost" their wallets, although Liz never took the wallets.

The bellhops didn't want Liz around, a hooker like her was trouble, bad for business. Liz didn't care about repeat customers, if she could be with them one time, she got her money. Although credit cards were around in the late 60's, they weren't that popular. Out-of-towners carried cash or Traveler's Checks.

Liz had the gift of gab, she could talk to a trick, and have him so mesmerized by her conversation, he didn't notice when she reached over and took all the money out of his wallet. He'd sit there and watch her as if in a trance. Maybe he didn't believe he actually saw it.

Liz didn't split 60/40 with anyone, all the money she made was hers to keep. But Liz always spread the wealth around, tipping the doormen at the hotels and the bartenders where she'd catch her tricks. All the bartenders knew to give Liz a shot of Coke with water, and while the guy was getting drunk on his ass, he thought Liz was getting drunk, too, but she was sober as a Judge, she never drank alcohol when working.

The bar owners like selling a shot of Coke for the price of whiskey and didn't mind Liz working in their clubs. In fact, many owners would tell Liz when a guy flashed a wad of money. "Get him to spend some money in here," they'd tell Liz, "And get the rest for yourself." And she usually did.

Liz's man was a police officer, a detective in homicide. He never intervened in her behalf because he knew he'd be fired if they found out he had a whore. But all the players knew that Liz was with a cop, they didn't mess with Liz, they didn't want to bump heads with the law.

There were only 3 other girls working the streets downtown at that time, and they usually went to jail once a month, like clock work, usually at the end of the month, and were charged with being a vagrant prostitute. It was a $25 cash bond, which was usually the fine in court, so the court kept the money. The vice told the girls to look at it as union dues. The police had an arrest quota to fill, and at the end of the month they would pick up girls as vagrants.

"Hell," the vice would say, "You come down here, you rake in loads of money, and we only bother you once a month!" The vice squad and the girls working the streets got along well together, it was like a game. They'd bust them for vagrancy, but they also tried to get them on a proposition; soliciting an undercover officer. The bond and fine for soliciting was higher than vagrancy, but it wasn't steep, a $100 bond and a $100 fine was the usual.

Liz had asked me several times to work with her. "You can "block" while I "clip" the trick." Liz told me. Frenchy was against it. He wanted me to stay in the hotels. That way, he felt he had more control. He didn't want me out in the bars meeting people, he felt threatened.

"No," he told me, "You'll be safer in the hotel. I don't want nobody to hurt my baby. And if you work the streets, you'll go to jail."

Now Frenchy was in jail and the bellhops had put the "freeze" on me. They leave me no choice, I thought, I'm going to work with Liz and get Frenchy out of jail!

When I got to the drugstore at 8 o'clock, Liz was already there. We went to the bar at the Aladdin Hotel, Liz looked over the crowd and announced, "There's no prospects here, let's move on."

All Liz wanted me to do was "block", keep the guy occupied until Liz could "clip" (steal his money). Some guys didn't want two girls, but Liz always managed to talk them into it. "Two girls for the price of one!" she'd say.

Sometimes the trick would catch Liz trying to get into his wallet, but Liz would start talking, working her way to the door. There were some close calls, and I didn't really like stealing, but I needed the money.

It took me three days to get $1,000 I needed. I made Frenchy's bond and when I told him I'd made the money with Liz, he wasn't happy. "I don't want you workin' with Liz! Her ol' man's a cop! Anyway, we can't afford for you to go to jail now, we're gonna need all the money we can get for MY case!"

We moved out of the house and got a small apartment, because the lawyers were getting all our money. The lawyers kept continuing the case, putting it off as long as they could, demanding more money from Frenchy and giving him hope that he'd get off.

Frenchy was anxious, he didn't want to go to prison. He started fooling around with other whores and he didn't care if I found out.

"I gotta have the money, baby" he'd say to me.

We had violent arguments about Frenchy's other women. I'd slap him, he'd slap me back, then we'd start throwing things at each other, anything within reach, books, lamps, chairs. I hope he goes to prison, I would think to myself. That's the only way I'll be able to get away from him!

I got my wish, he went to prison. The Judge sentenced him to 5 years in the Federal penitentiary at Terre Haute, Indiana. He was given 5 days to get his affairs "in order", then report to the Federal Marshall. I went with Frenchy to the Marshall's office, they took him into custody until transportation to Indiana could be arranged.

I played the part of the suffering wife, separated from the man I loved, but I was secretly glad to be rid of Frenchy. I was tired of Frenchy telling me what to do. I'd been working in the hotels for 2 years, I didn't make the money I used to make, I was no longer a new girl, I was working harder for return business. Working with Liz was crazy, I didn't want to rip off every trick I turned. But there was no reason why I couldn't work the bars, eliminate the bellhops cut, and give the guy a good date for his money. Frenchy wasn't here to stop me, and the first night Frenchy was gone, I hit the streets.

*****

With Frenchy locked up in prison, the other girls couldn't wait to tell me about his exploits. The other whores didn't like me, I acted so snooty all the time, always reading books and thinking I was superior to them. They wasted no time in hurting my feelings.

Frenchy had been using drugs all along; heroin, cocaine, pot, but he had hid it from me. He told me he hadn't been dealing drugs, but he was only getting drugs for someone else, doing a favor, when he got busted. Many of the girls only fucked Frenchy to spite me. I was angry with him. How could he humiliate me like this?

I moved back into the Howard Hotel. I didn't want to stay in the apartment alone where anything could happen and no one there to help me. I knew that single women unprotected by a man were easy targets for robbers and rapist.

I felt safe in the Howard Hotel, no one could get upstairs without passing the front desk. And I was always available to turn a trick when living at the hotel. I loved turning tricks, I loved making money. The more I made, the more I spent. Sometimes I spent money before I had it, but my credit was good, I always paid my debts. I never saved a penny, I spent all the money I made, usually within hours.

I bought toys and clothes for Peter and clothes for myself. I took taxi's everywhere, always tipping generously. I ate my meals in restaurants and, again, I'd tip. I gave Grandma a lot of cash, and usually anyone who wanted $5 or $10 could count on me to give it to them.

I was always working, everywhere I went, looking for a trick, except when I was with Peter, which wasn't very often. I would visit Peter on Sunday's, pay Grandma, give her any extra money she needed. Anything Grandma wanted, all she had to do was tell me. I could always be reached at the Howard in case of emergencies. If Grandma called, I'd come, with my money, ready to take care of the problem. I thought money could solve all problems. Grandma took care of Peter and I paid her well for it. I told myself there was no reason for me to feel guilty, what else could I do? Peter's taken care of, better than I could do, and Grandma loves him.

I wasn't there when Peter took his first step or said his first word, I was downtown turning tricks. When he started to talk, Peter called Grandma "mama" and he called me "Charly". I neglected Peter, I could have spent more time with him, but I told myself Peter was happier at Grandma's. I pushed all responsibility for Peter onto Grandma, and she accepted it. Over and over Grandma told me, "You go on, girl, don't worry about Peter, I'll take care of Peter." and she did.

Dorothy had her baby, a daughter she called Alice. Dorothy moved out of Grandma's house and was staying with her mother. I didn't interfere in their family affairs, but I was aware of all the hostility directed at Dorothy and her baby.

I rented an apartment and shared it with Dorothy and her baby. I was never there, I stayed downtown working, I was only trying to help Dorothy. When I did spend the night at the apartment, something would always come up missing, usually my money but sometimes clothes.

First it was the coins I'd saved, then money out of my purse and dresses, wigs. Dorothy would always have someone to blame and I would always believe her. Dorothy was my best friend. "You're my white sister!" she'd tell me. I kept my things downtown and only brought a change of clothes when staying at the apartment because of Dorothy's thieving' friends.

*****

I would work the bars once in awhile, but I still preferred the safety of he hotels. When the bellhop got a trick who didn't want to get a room at the Howard, but instead, wanted the girl to come to his hotel, the bellhops could count on me to turn the trick and bring back their 40%. I'd go anywhere as long as it was downtown.

For a period of a couple months, the Howard kept getting calls from someone at the TownHouse Hotel in Kansas. Twice they sent a girl, but I never wanted to go, and both times the girl was robbed outside as she exited her cab. I stayed downtown, there was plenty of activity to keep me busy, and lots of police to keep it safe.

Getting in and out of the big hotels downtown was considered an art, but I thought it was easy. If the police saw a known hooker enter a big hotel, they'd arrest her for trespassing. The police also considered it blatant disrespect for the law, to walk into a hotel while they were watching. The police didn't like to be disrespected, they wanted the girl to sneak in.

Some of the hotels had an underground tunnel leading to the parking lot, some hotels had a service entrance in an alley, and some hotels, I just took my chances and walked through the lobby, hoping no one would recognize me. All the major hotels had house detectives, usually police officers moonlighting. Some house detectives would arrest a whore on the spot, others would just throw her out and some would turn their heads the other way. A smart girl, who was on her job, kept up with which shift each detective worked.

I learned all the ins and outs of the hotels and even discovered new ones. Although some girls were afraid to try and enter certain hotels, there was no hotel I wouldn't try. It was a challenge to get in and out of the hotel without being caught. And if I did get caught? All they would do was put me in jail. They weren't gettin' no cherry, I'd been there before. I wasn't afraid of getting busted like some girls, I could always make my bond.

"Rita?" I heard Jim's voice when I answered the phone. "I got a guy at the Downtowner Motel, you wanna go?"

"Sure, I'll be right down. What's his room number?" Jim told me the man's room number.

The Downtowner Motel was next door to the Howard, the tricks room was in back. I made it my business to know where the room numbers were located in a hotel, so I'd know the best way to get in and out. All I had to do was go out the back door of the Howard, cross the alley and enter the back stairs of the Downtowner. It was a piece of cake, no one would see me. I entered the motel and knocked on the door. A young guy answered, about 30, he was very polite and mild-mannered. I gave him a half and half and returned to the Howard.

About an hour later, Jim called again, "Rita, you know that guy you dated at the Downtowner, well, he's got a buddy in the room next door, he wants a date, too. Wanta take it?'

"Get that money!" I laughed into the phone.

I went back to the Downtowner, and this time I knocked at the room next door. A big, husky man answered, he was older than the other trick and very drunk. There were two empty fifth bottles of Scotch sitting on the dresser.

I got my money, washed him and lit a cigarette, putting it in the ash try, something I always did when turning a trick to keep track of time. It was one of the things Ginger had taught me when I first started hustling.

The cigarette completely burned out and the trick wasn't finished. "Hey, you're gonna hafta cum, I can't stay here all night, the bellhop will wonder what's going on."

"Just give me a little more time," he was still pumping away, "I'm almost done."

"Maybe," I said to him, "You should give me a little more money to stay."

"I don't have any more money. I gave you all the cash I had."

"Okay," I told him, "I'll give you ten more minutes, then I'm leavin'."

When the ten minutes were up, the trick still hadn't ejaculated. "Okay, I'm leavin' now, I don't think you're gonna get off, you're too drunk." I got up and started to wash myself.

"You fuckin' bitch," the trick snarled at me, still laying on the bed, "Who do you think you are? You're just a whore. You're NOTHING!"

"If I'm a whore," I said to him in my most sarcastic voice, "What does that make you? A Whoremonger, that's what!"

I didn't like the way the trick was acting, I didn't like to argue with them, I began to dress rapidly, and when I looked at him, there it was; the cruelty in the eyes, the sneer on the lips. Oh shit! Now I was really scared!

The trick got up from the bed and was screaming at me, "You're nothing but the child of Satan, you're evil, corrupting the rest of us! I'd be doing the world favor by killing you!"

The only thing I could think was how I was going to get to the door. Please God just let me make it to the door. "I don't see how you can judge me," I said, "If there weren't guys like you, there'd be no whores. You're just as evil as me."

"I can judge you," he roared at me, "and I judge you GUILTY!"

I ran for the door, he caught my arm and threw me on the bed, he climbed on top of me, pinning me down.

"You're nothing," he screamed at me, all the while I was struggling with him to get away. He held me down, screaming in my face, "If I were to kill you now, no one would look for you. You're a whore, a parasite on society, no one cares about you!"

He was drunk and that gave me a advantage but not much of one, I had turned myself around and was now kicking the wall where the other guy stayed next door. I banged on the wall, all the while struggling with the crazy man on top of me. He relaxed for only a second, but it was long enough to push him off and head for the door. I was dressed, my shoes were on the other side of the room, but I wasn't worried about my shoes. I made a dash, but he caught me by my upper arm and held me in a superhuman grip, I couldn't pull away.

"I think I WILL kill you! I'm going to smash this bottle," he held me with one hand and picked up the empty fifth bottle with the other, "Into your head! Oh, it'll be easy. Then I'll roll your body in one of those blankets. Think about it, that's your fate! I'll take your body down the back stairs, put you in the trunk and dump you in a park somewhere! No one will ever know I did it! You'll just be another dead whore! NO ONE CARES!"

I looked into his eyes and I saw the madness, I had never been more frightened in my life. I grabbed his upper arm with the arm he was holding and flipped him over my head, when he landed he was stunned, I ran to the door, unlocked it, it seemed like the lock would never turn, and ran as fast as I could. I turned once, and there he was, running after me, completely naked. I started running faster.

That was a close call. I didn't see Buck in him, not at first. I'll have to be more careful. And how did I ever flip that guy over my head? I only weight 105 pounds, I can hardly lift anything! It's amazing how

much strength you have when you're afraid!
*****

I wrote to Frenchy once a week and I always put a money order in the envelope. Frenchy wrote back almost every day. He loved me, he wrote, and all the things he'd done to hurt me, well, he was sorry. I was his wife and Peter was his son (this always touched me). He knew things hadn't been perfect, but he wanted to make it up to me. When he got out, he'd get a job and everything would be different. He'd been under the influence of drugs, he wrote, and couldn't be held responsible for the things he'd done.

He knew what I wanted to hear, and he had no problem telling me. Maybe Frenchy will change, I thought to myself, maybe being in prison has made him see how foolish he's been. I bought a bus ticket to Terre Haute, I was going to visit him.

We had a romantic visit, as romantic as it can be during a prison visit, and we renewed our love. We talked about when he would get paroled.

"I'm gonna try to get transferred to Leavenworth, sometimes they do that, send you closer to home, that way you can visit me more often."

Frenchy was transferred to Leavenworth Federal Penitentiary, and I did visit him more often. I asked Frenchy to put Dorothy on his visiting list, so I could have a travel companion when I came to Leavenworth.
*****

I was waiting for Frenchy but I liked to flirt, after all, I was a whore, I wanted men to notice me, and they did. All the pimps wanted to catch me, but I stayed downtown, out of their reach. Some of the bellhops were pimps, and they tried to "cop" me. I enjoyed leading them on, making them think there was a chance, when there wasn't. I wasn't about to be with some guy who had a stable of women! Some of the bellhops didn't like me, and wouldn't use me. More and more, I was catching my own tricks, outside of the hotel.

The vice squad became familiar with me and I started going to jail once a month for vagrancy. It was a small price to pay for the privilege of working downtown in the bars, kinda like union dues. "Be here tomorrow night at 2 a.m., in front of the Pioneer Grill," the vice would say, "Tomorrow's jail night."

The girls would always show, if she didn't, she couldn't work downtown, the vice made her life hell. If the vice had more girls than they needed for their quota, they'd let us throw dice, and the winner went free. The cops would bet among themselves on which girl would win.

During my years at the hotel, I'd talked to my sister, Sandra once in a while, but not very often. I had forgiven her for not saying anything when Bob had put Peter and I out in the winter night. "What could I do?" Sandra said, "I was pregnant. I was afraid he'd put me out, too!"

Sandra and Bob were breaking up, she'd found someone else, someone who really loved her. His name was Phil, and Sandra wanted me to meet him.

"Tell you what," I said into the phone, "I'll meet you at the Muehlebach Coffee Shop, tonight, 9 o'clock."

"Oh Shirley" Sandra gushed, "I can't wait for you to meet Phil!"

I was a few minutes late getting to the Muehlebach, I was turning a trick. Sandra and Phil were already there. Oh boy! I thought, when I looked at Phil, he's one of my regular tricks! Phil saw me, but he didn't acknowledge me, he had no idea that RITA was Sandra's sister SHIRLEY! When I sat down at the table and greeted Sandra, Phil's heart leaped into his throat. He didn't have to worry, I was cool, I acted like we were meeting for the first time, and he did the same.

"This is Phil, we got married today!" Sandra was excited, gazing at Phil, hanging on his arm.

"What? Got married!" I was shocked, "Is your divorce from Bob final?"

"Not for two more weeks," Sandra was starry-eyed, "But we couldn't wait, we're in love!" Sandra and Phil embraced each other, displaying their impatient love. I started laughing.

"Sandra! That's bigamy!"

"I know," she replied, looking into Phil's eyes, "but we wanted to be man and wife, we didn't want to wait two week."

I laughed to myself. Who would have thought that one of my tricks would end up my brother-in-law!

*****

I started taking diet pills, amphetamines, I didn't abuse them, but would take only one when I got up, to get me going. I didn't get to sleep until the wee hours of the morning, and often was up early to turn a trick for the bellhop. I started having a few drinks to bring me down at night.

Sandra had gained so much weight with her last baby, the doctor was giving her diet pills regularly. She gave me the first capsule I'd ever taken, Dexedrine, called "Christmas trees" on the street because they were green and white. They were easy to get, you had to have a doctor's prescription, but in 1969 the physicians were giving them to anyone who had the money for an office visit. The clinics of the diet doctors were packed with people, all getting diet pills. Some were keeping the pills for themselves, and others would sell the pills and make a profit.

I would be up all night and half the day, making money, spending money, never thinking about tomorrow, still living for the moment.

I liked the diet pills, I liked the way the pills made me feel. They gave me energy and confidence. When I didn't get much sleep and had thing I wanted to do, I'd take another pill. This second pill made me very intense, I'd be really paranoid about the police or a trick. The second pill made it difficult to work with a clear head. If I took a second pill I didn't work, I played cards. There was always card game going on in the back room at the Howard, and they always played for money. The game was Tonk, low hand wins.

I started playing, gambling. The first time I played, I won. After the first time, I won once in a while, but most of the time I lost. The card players were bellhops I saw everyday, and cab drivers I rode with everyday. It never occurred to me that they were cheating, stealing my money. They expected me to be honest on the 60/40 cut, and I thought they were honest when gambling with me. Marked decks, cards up the sleeve, cards under the table, mirrors, you name it, they did it to me and I didn't have a clue what was going on.

It took several years and thousands of dollars before I discovered the truth. When I found out what a sucker I'd been, I lost my taste for cards and never gambled again. But at the close of 1969 just before my 21st birthday, I was taking pills, playing cards, turning tricks and waiting for Frenchy to come home.

*****

I'd done a few bachelor parties but I didn't like doing them, they never turned out well. The girl was hired to screw the groom, spend a little time with him, give him one helluva a fuck before tying the knot. If any one else at the party wanted a date, they had to pay for it out of their own pocket. That was the deal, but it always turned into a fiasco. The party-goers were young, usually drunk and I'd be there with all those men, alone. I didn't like the odds. The men would feel me freely and laugh, they didn't respect the fact that I was a whore and wanted to get PAID for everything I did. I usually waited a whole night, not making nearly the money I was promised. I learned to steer clear of bachelor parties.

More girls were leaving the whorehouse hotels and working the streets. They were getting away from the 60/40 cut and the bellhops, who controlled how much money a girl made. Prostitutes were more visible in the downtown area, but it wasn't a problem...yet.

One whore had parties at her house frequently. Her name was Linda but everyone called her "Crooked Jaw." Her jaw had been broken and was never set. As a result, her face leaned to one side. She was petite and would have been attractive if not for her crooked face and sad, weak eyes. You knew when you looked at her, she was weak. She wouldn't do anything if you insulted her or slapped her around, she begged for abuse and she got it, too, from her pimp. He was always kickin' in her ass.

Crooked Jaw was always trying to get a party together, but these weren't bachelor parties, they were called "shows". Show is exactly that, you put on some kind of show and the tricks pay to watch only. If they want to fuck the girl, that cost more. Crooked Jaw would try to get at least 10 men together at $100 a piece (if she had only 4 or 5 guys, she's still do her show) and she'd suck and fuck her Great Dane. I'd never been to any of Crooked Jaw's parties, but everyone knew about them. "If you run across a trick wants to see a good show, give em my number," Crooked Jaw would tell all the girls, "I'll give you a little kickback (money) for every trick you send."

*****

Liz's best friend was a Mexican whore named Bea. Bea never worked the streets, only the whorehouse hotels, but mostly she worked out of town on "appointment". There was a network of whorehouses all over the United States where a girl could call and book an appointment to work. When the girl called, she had to have a reference, someone they could call to check her out. The appointment was usually for two weeks but some were as long as a month. Lots of these whorehouses were close to military bases. The girl checked in, fucked her brains out for two weeks and went home with piles of money. Bea had a book an inch thick with the phone numbers of appointment houses in almost every state, in small towns that were always looking for new faces.

Bea was an "old" whore, past her prime, she was 29 years old, and Joe was her pimp. Bea was his bottom (main) woman, but he was always playing around with the other whores, especially when Bea was out of town, which was most of the time. Joe was dealing drugs; heroin and dilaudid (synthetic morphine), and raking in the dough. He'd gotten busted for dealing drugs and was facing a prison sentence.

Monk was a heroin addict, he was a mean heroin addict. He didn't mind using violence to get what he wanted, he enjoyed it.

It was a Sunday night, Bea was home, she was leaving for North Carolina in the morning. Joe and Bea were asleep in their bed when they heard a noise and woke up. They'd heard guns cocking, and standing over them was Monk and another man.

"Okay man, I want everything you got, drugs, money, jewelry, EVERYTHING!" Monk was laughing, pointing the gun at Joe's nose.

"I don't have anything here!" Joe's eyes were big and he was scared.

"MOTHAH FUCKAH, GIVE ME THE STUFF!" Monk pushed the barrel of his gun in Joe's mouth, shoving it down his throat. "I'LL BLOW YOUR FUCKIN" HEAD OFF!"

Joe started to cry and Monk was stunned, he didn't expect this, he thought Joe was tough. This will be easy! Joe gave Monk everything he had, all the while, crying and begging for his life.

Bea was still laying in the bed, the other gunman was watching her. "Hey Monk!" The gunman called out, "I wanna fuck this Mexican bitch! I wanna try some of that hot tamale pussy!"

"Go ahead!" Monk called back, "Take your time!" The gunman fucked Bea, he used her body like a toy, doing whatever he wanted, when he was done, Monk fucked her, then they both fucked Joe.

"You know, Joe," Monk sneered at him, "You was so good, and I like the way you cry, better than a girl, I'm gonna let you live."

A month later, Joe went to prison for dealing drugs and Bea chose Monk as her man. Joe was gone for a year before he made parole. He was on his ass, no money and his woman was with the man he hated most, the man who had witnessed his humiliation, the man who caused his humiliation. That fuckin' bitch, Joe thought, of all the people she could be with, she chose him!

Bea and Liz had booked an appointment in Birmingham, Alabama, they were both down South. One evening Liz went to pick up dinner and when she got back, Bea was dead.

"I was only gone 10 minutes!" Liz said. It was ruled an accident, she'd had a heart attack. Liz brought Bea's body back to KC, to her family.

"I saw the body," Liz told me, "I found her. She didn't have a heart attack, she had bruises all over her body. Bea was murdered but nobody cares about a whore. If a whore gets killed, the police don't even look for the guy. No, no one cares about a whore, she got what she deserved."

Some people thought Monk had something to do with Bea's death, but others felt it was Joe. There was even speculation that Liz was involved, after all she was there.

*****

Every afternoon I would begin getting dressed for the night, turning myself into Rita. I always wore dresses, that's what men liked, I had great legs and showed them off at every opportunity. I wore cocktail dresses, they were called "after 5's" because that's when you wore them. I wore lots of make-up, I hid behind this mask of make-up, hiding Shirley, who no one loved, and becoming Rita, the big-time whore. I never went anywhere without my make-up being applied first. I was very skillful at putting on make-up, turning plain Shirley into desirable Rita. And my hair? That was the easiest part, I had a number of wigs in all colors and lengths, human hair wigs, professionally styled. I changed my looks all the time, sometimes a blonde, sometimes a brunette, sometimes a redhead. All the whores dressed well and were always trying to out-do each other.

The whores that worked the streets would get together in one of the coffee shops downtown, killing time, talking shop, and trading information on the whores, tricks, the pimps and new places to work. I didn't have coffee with the other girls, the only one I was friendly with was Liz otherwise I was a loner.

When a group of whores would get together in a coffee shop, sometimes they'd get loud or try catching tricks in the restaurant, disturbing the other customers, and the management would get upset. They'd only order coffee, usually didn't tip, and tie-up a table for an hour. Some of the coffee shops began to refuse service to the girls, asking them to leave and not come back. This never happened to me, I could go anywhere I wanted, I always went alone, never drawing attention to myself (although you couldn't help but notice me) and I always left a generous tip. All the serving staff knew me and wanted me to sit in their section.

One night I was sitting in the Pioneer Grill at 12th and Baltimore. I'd finished my cherry pie and was sipping on some coffee, smoking a cigarette when a girl, a whore I'd seen around but didn't know, sat down in the booth across from me.

"Slow tonight, huh?" the whore said, "My feet are killing me!" Some girls didn't go into the bars, but walked the streets downtown, their pimps didn't want them wasting money on drinks, they wanted all the money to come home to them.

The waitress came over to the table with pen and pad ready, "Ready to order?"

"No thanks," the whore said, "I'm only gonna sit here a minute, I'm talkin' to my friend." The waitress didn't say anything, rolled her eyes and walked off.

My friend? I thought as the girl talked. Hell! I don't even know her name. I don't wanna sit here with some dumb whore who's got a pimp and she doesn't even have enough class to order something...spend some money. This cramps my style!

"I'm Honey Dew," the whore said, "What's your name?"

Honey Dew! I wondered where she got that name but I was afraid to ask!

"I'm Rita." I started to gather my things off the table, cigarettes, lighter, putting them in my purse, preparing to leave, getting away from Honey Dew.

"You're Rita! My man told me about you, he said to stay away from you, you a gangsta ho'."

I laughed, "I'm a gangsta ho'? What's that?"

"Ain't got no man, out here by yourself, a GANGSTA HO'. You ain't got no right to come out here and work with no man, somethin' might happen to you. You better get yourself a man!"

"I've got a man, Frenchy."

"He's in jail. You ain't got a man that can look out for you now, tonight. My man told me to stay away from you. The girl got up to leave. "Better get yourself a man," she called out over her shoulder.

A Gangsta Ho', sounded like something out of Prohibition, sounded bad, I liked that. So, I thought, the players call me a Gangsta Ho' and they don't want me around their women. I smiled, I know I'm different than the other whore, I'm better than they are, they're all fools!

*****

I was in the alley, headed for the service entrance to the Phillips House, when coming the other way was Morgan, Detective Dave Morgan of the Vice Unit.

"Been to jail this month?" he'd been drinking, he wasn't drunk, but was getting there fast. All the detectives received free drinks or food in the establishments downtown, perks of the job. There were rumors that certain girls fucked the vice, and this was a job perk, too.

"I went last week." I told him, trying to be friendly, hoping he'd leave, I had a trick waiting.

"I could take you to jail right now." he was smiling, "But you don't hafta go to jail, we can work this out. You know what I mean?" he leered at me.

I know exactly what he meant, and I wasn't interested, I put my hands on my hips (my signature stance) and said the words I'd later regret. "If you have to use your badge to get a piece of ass," I was laughing, "You must be a lousy lay. I'd rather go to jail!" I had made lots of enemies with my smart-ass mouth, but never a cop.

"You filthy whore!" he said, "I know all about you. Get out of here!"

I knew he was going to arrest me, I stood there waiting, looking at him, "What?" I finally said.

"You fuckin' cunt! GET OUT OF HERE!"

I turned and left, forgetting about the trick. I had a bad feeling, a feeling I'd just made a mistake.

Every time Morgan saw me, he took me to jail. Sometimes his partner didn't want to be bothered with going to the station and booking someone for vagrancy, but Morgan insisted. Morgan told everyone, the bartenders, doormen, bellhops, pimps, whores, anyone who would listen that I was a "snitch", a "rat", I'd testified to the Grand Jury. Most of the bar owners were Italians with Mafia ties. They paid no attention to Morgan, they were smart enough to know that if I was a snitch, Morgan wouldn't tell everybody. But the whores and pimps passed the word like wild fire. A couple of whores confronted me one night, "The police say you're a snitch, they tell everybody to stay away from you."

I looked at them. Being a snitch was the worst thing that could happen to a person in the hustling life. "How many times you been to jail this month?" I asked one girl.

"I went last week," the girl said. I turned to the other girl.

"And you?"

"I ain't been to jail in about 5 weeks."

"I've been to jail four times THIS WEEK," I told them, "I went three times last week. I thought the police took care of their snitches. If I'm a snitch, why do I go to jail so much?"

The two whores looked at each other, "Probably just a cover-up for your snitchin'!" one of them said, and they left.

*****

I had taken Peter shopping. When I returned to Grandma's, Loren was there, Dorothy's older brother. Loren and I were the same age and we'd once had a little fling. It never turned serious but we remained friends, we enjoyed eachothers company. We talked awhile, exchanging news, when Loren stood up, "I'd like to stay and shoot the shit, but I told Chicken I'd pick her up at the Greyhound." Chicken was the family nickname for Dorothy.

"At the Greyhound?" I asked, "Where'd she go?"

"She's been up to see Frenchy." I looked at him, saying nothing, puzzled. Finally I spoke.

"Why would she visit Frenchy? Why would she go up there without me?"

"Oh boy!" Loren said, "You don't know, do you? I thought you knew by now."

"Know what?"

"It's time someone told you, it's not right everyone lyin' to you. Alice, Chicken's little girl, that's Frenchy's baby. I'm surprised you hadn't noticed by now, Alice is the spittin' image of Frenchy. You remember when Chicken first got pregnant and everybody was mad at

142

her? They was mad because it was your husband, you puttin' food on Grandma's table and Chicken's out fuckin' your husband. Then you bought her all that stuff for the baby! Grandma told her. "Don't you feel bad, now." But Chicken kept foolin' with him ""'til he went to prison. I thought you knew. Everybody else does. Chicken says they gettin' married."

"No, Loren" I answered, "I never suspected anything, never! Dorothy and Frenchy always acted like they hated each other." I stood up, "Where are you taking Dorothy?"

"I'm bringing her here, Grandma's suppose to watch Alice..."

I waited for Dorothy, not wanting to believe what Loren had told me. Loren stopped in front of the house, he didn't come in, when Dorothy got out of the car, he pulled off.

When Dorothy saw me she was all smiles, "Hey Sistuh, I didn't know you was comin' today", she called out to me, "What's goin' on?"

I saw Dorothy smiling and I knew it was all a lie, "Dorothy, I just heard the craziest story, you won't believe it. Somebody told me Alice is Frenchy's daughter." I looked at her, waiting for her to deny it, and have a good laugh over it.

"Who told you that?"

"Your brother told me. Why would he make up a story like that about his sister?"

"Probably cause it's true." Dorothy was no longer smiling, she had taken off her mask of friendship, and revealed all the hate she felt towards me.

"I thought we were friends, Dorothy, you said I was your white sister."

"I ain't got no fuckin' WHITE SISTER! You thought we was friends, HA, I can't stand the SIGHT OF YOU! Black girls ain't friends with white girls! Look around you, white women are taking our Black Brothers, makin' pimps out of em! Elijah Mohammed is right, you're devils here to torment us, blue-eyed devils!" Dorothy was screaming in my face, her eyes were blazing. "You think Frenchy loves you? He don't love you, he loves me. We're gettin' married when he gets out. He has no respect for you, you're just a whore. All the pimps got square women on the side, a woman they hide from their whores. The woman they love, the woman they give YOUR money to. These are the women they care about, not you nasty whores. He's just stringin' you along until he can get his hands on your inheritance. He talks about you like a dog behind your back."

I didn't say anything, I wasn't angry, but deeply hurt and it showed. Dorothy was pleased with the hurt she saw, and she felt triumphant that she'd caused it, she continued to talk. "You white girls. You was born with all the advantages, you can do anything, and you want to come down here and take our men! Why don't you stay in your own race? Leave our men alone!"

Finally I spoke, "If that's how you feel, why'd you take those things I bought? WHY did you pretend to like me?"

"White people been takin' from blacks for hundreds of years, I was just gettin' what you owe me!"

"How can you say that?" I shot back, "I've never done anything but be nice to you! I tried to HELP you!"

"You wasn't tryin' to help me, you was tryin' to buy me, make me your slave. You may have bought my Grandma, but I ain't for sale!"

Grandma came into the living room, "What's goin' on in here?" She looked at Dorothy, frowning. Dorothy smiled at her Grandma, pleased with herself.

"I was just givin' Shirley lessons in race relations."

"Well, come on in the kitchen, dinner's ready."

"I'm not hungry." I said to Grandma, "I think I'll call a cab." Then I turned to Dorothy, who had put her friendly mask back on for Grandma. "Oh Dorothy, I don't have blue eyes." I sat on the front porch to wait for my cab.

I was crushed, not because of Frenchy, he had betrayed me many times before, and I wasn't hurt about the baby, Alice. I was in the business of sex, I knew how weak some men were. I was hurt because Dorothy hated me and there was nothing I could do about it. I hadn't done anything to deserve her hate, but I was white and I was nice to her. Dorothy would have had more respect for me if I'd been a red-neck, who belonged to the KKK. Dorothy knew how to deal with that, she understood hate. Dorothy didn't know how to deal with my kindness and she thought I was a fool.

Why didn't I see it before? Why was I so blind? Dorothy was always ridiculing white people. I didn't see that it was me Dorothy was making fun of. But I saw it all now, I saw it very clearly.

I took the bus to Leavenworth the next day, told Frenchy it was over, I wouldn't be writing or visiting him any more. I wasn't sending any more money.

"I won't get a divorce until you get out. I know it looks better on your record to have a wife waiting for you. I'm not out to hurt you, Frenchy. I just want out, I don't want anything to do with you. It's over."

"Oh baby," Frenchy pleaded, "You don't mean that! That bitch was all over me, every time I went to get Peter. She was out to get me cause she hated you."

"If you knew she hated me so much, why'd you fool with her, Frenchy?"

"Oh baby, I don't know. I was high. I don't know what I was thinking of. I love you Shirley, I love Peter, and I want us to be a family when I get out. You ain't gonna let that bitch come between us, are you?"

These were the things I liked to hear; I LOVE ONLY YOU, I WANT ONLY YOU, but I was learning. You can make your mouth say anything, it's what you do that counts. When I said I loved you, I meant it, but I learned that not everyone was like me, many people used the word love casually, it was a word they used to get their way, like saying PLEASE. I stood up, "Good-bye Frenchy."

"Baby! WAIT!" he called after me.

*****

Dorothy was happy now that I was out of the picture, Frenchy was coming home to her. Frenchy had been writing a number of girls while in the penitentiary, telling all of them the same thing.

"I didn't mean that stuff I said," Dorothy told me, "I was just mad cause you had Frenchy."

"There's no reason for you to be mad now," I replied, "He's all yours."

And you're welcome to him! I thought to myself, you'll find out when he comes home that you don't have him either.

To all outward appearances, Dorothy and I had made up. I was friendly to Dorothy, sharing in her excitement about Frenchy coming home. Dorothy thought everything was okay, that I had forgiven her. But

I knew that it was all an act, I'd seen Dorothy without her mask, I always remembered the look in Dorothy's eyes when she'd said, "You're devils, here to torment us- - blue-eyed devils!"

Dorothy missed the money I used to give her, she pretended that she hadn't noticed I was no longer helping her. She's not for sale? We're all for sale, Dorothy!

"Don't mind Dorothy," Grandma told me, "She'd full of hate and I don't know why. She goes around with them Muslims and Panthers, they teach hate, and Dorothy listens, now she won't eat any pork. She's really a sweet girl when she wants to be."

"Grandma, I ain't mad at Dorothy. She has a right to feel any way she wants. Any way, she'll have her hands full when Frenchy gets home."

"Lord, girl, ain't that the truth!"

*****

I received my inheritance several months after my 21st birthday. I got $2,500; I bought a 1966 Mustang for $1,000, which I only had for a week before I wrecked it beyond repair. I spent $500 on this and that, and the other thousand dollars I put in a savings account for Peter. It was only there a month, I took the money out and gave it away. I had been seeing a guy, it wasn't a serious relationship, he said he'd triple my money, I knew I'd made a mistake as soon as I handed him the money. After he got my cash, he wouldn't take my calls.

The Mustang was turquoise. I didn't know anything about cars, I never had a car before, I didn't even know how to drive a car. Frenchy had taken me out a few times and tried to teach me, but I wasn't interested. It was easier to call a cab. Frenchy had a car when he went to prison, I wrecked into a city bus trying to get the car home. I parked it in front of our apartment building, it was repossessed within a week. At least I think it was repossessed, it wasn't in front of the building anymore.

I had my own car, in my own name, it made me feel good. The car wasn't new but it was only four years old, and it was clean, not a scratch on it. Of course, the transmission had a leak and the tires were bald, but I neither knew nor cared about those things. It looked good. I wouldn't know a good tire if it ran over me!

I gave the car lot a thousand dollars, cash, and went downtown and bought tags for the car. I didn't have a driver's license, but I didn't give it much thought. What could happen? Give me a ticket? Take me to jail? HA! My whole life was illegal! What's a traffic ticket?

I parked the car behind the Howard, I could see it from my room, I would glance at it as I got ready for the evening. My chest would swell with pride! MY CAR!

I went out to work, leaving the car parked. No sense asking for trouble with Morgan out there. A big national convention of Firefighters was in town, staying at the Muehlebach, and I wasn't about to miss it. This was the first day of the convention, the day they spent the most money.

I turned a few tricks early and was having a hamburger when Liz came in the drugstore.

"Firemen keepin' you busy?" I greeted Liz.

"I'm cleanin' up, Rita." Liz turned to the waitress. "I'll take one of those hamburgers and some coffee." Liz was a loner, too, and she always ordered, even if she didn't eat it and tipped generously, she was smart. Liz turned her attention back to me, "I hear the vice are going to take us all to jail tonight. Get us off the streets because of the convention. Dirty Bastards! First good convention in a couple of months and we're going to jail for vagrancy!"

I didn't ask Liz how she knew this and I didn't question its truth. Liz got the inside scoop from her man, the homicide detective.

"How shitty can you get!" I said, "You know, I bought a car today, it's sittin' behind the Howard, but I don't have a driver's license."

"You got a car?" Liz said, starting to get excited.

"Sure did! I bought a Mustang!"

Liz's eyes got bright. "I've got a driver's license. We can park at the side door of the Muehlebach. They can't take us to jail for vagrancy when we're sittin' in a car. Let's try it, see what happens."

"Wouldn't hafta spend any money in the bars either. Okay." I told her, "Let's do it!"

I couldn't wait to go sit in MY car. I stood up to leave. "Oh yeah," Liz said, "I forgot to tell you. The vice stopped me last night, they told me to stay away from you, it was Morgan." Liz knew the whole story about Morgan, I had told her all about it. "He said if I wanted to hang around you, I was going to jail, too. He wanted to warn me."

"That fuckin' Morgan! I wish he'd get off my ass! Maybe you better listen to him, Liz. No sense in asking for trouble."

Liz laughed, "Fuck Morgan!" I laughed, too.

We parked on Baltimore at the side door to the Muehlebach. There were lots of people on the street. Liz and I had collected several room numbers to call later. A good whore always spent the first part of her evening setting up dates, while the people were out, and the last part of her evening turning them.

"Oh Shit!" I said, "Here comes Morgan!" He was with another man I didn't recognize and he was staggering drunk.

He rested his arms on the roof of the car and leaned down into the window. "Where'd you get this car?" he asked.

"It's mine." I said, "I bought it today."

"Oh you did, did you? Well get out of it. You're going to jail!"

The other man stepped forward, "Hey Dave, this is our night off, we came to have a few drinks, not bust whores."

"I'm takin' this whore to jail," Morgan turned back to me, "Get out of the car, and let's go! I'm gonna have this car towed in!"

"You can't take me to jail." I told him, "We haven't done anything. You can't take us to jail for vagrancy, we're sitting in my car, LEGALLY parked and PROPERLY registered."

Morgan jerked open the car door and grabbed my arm, trying to pull me out of the car, "Take your fuckin' hands off me!" I screamed at him. Two conventioneers, firemen, heard my scream, they ran up, grabbed Morgan by both his arms and pulled him away from me.

"Leave the lady alone!" one of the men said.

"LADY! This is a prostitute, and you're interfering in an arrest!" Morgan was fumbling in his suit jacket for his badge.

"Sure," the firemen said, he knew Morgan was drunk. By the time Morgan had his badge out, I had slammed the door and Liz was pulling away from the curb. He ran after the car, pounding on the trunk.

"I want you out of town in 15 minutes," Morgan screamed after us, "I don't wanna see you in Kansas City, again!"

The next night Liz and I were riding around in my Mustang, when Morgan and his partner pulled us over. Morgan was sober, and he walked up to the car, ignoring Liz, who was driving, speaking directly to me.

"Okay, let's go! Get out of the car!"
"What's the charge?" I asked.
"Driving without a license."
I laughed, "Are you blind or what? I'm not driving this car."
"Oh yeah," he said, "That's what you say, I say you ARE driving. It's my word against yours in court. Let's go!"

Morgan gave me three traffic tickets and warned Liz, again, to stay away from me. Morgan didn't charge Liz with anything.

A few days later, I totaled out my Mustang in a rain storm. The tires were bald, the rain was pouring, and I was an inexperienced driver. I lost control of the car. Sandra was with me, but we didn't get hurt. I had a cut by my eye that required 7 stitches, tiny stitches. I only had the car one week. The wreck scared the hell out of me. I forgot about driving and took cabs everywhere. Let someone else worry about the traffic.

The court cases were piling up, and my lawyer wasn't that good. He had an alcoholic's red face and was often late for court. I'd even gotten a conviction for vagrancy! I had a lot of cases coming up, and I was looking for a new lawyer...fast!

A whore didn't go to court without a lawyer, the Judge always frowned on this, and it was best not to irritate the Judge. Some of the girls tricked with their attorneys, instead of paying them cash, but I noticed that the lawyers lost interest in the case once they got "paid." I needed a lawyer that would fight for me, and that took cash.

Liz and I were working a convention in Kansas. We met some guys downtown who invited us to come out to the motel where the convention was being held.

It was some kind of Law Enforcement convention, but they weren't out to bust anybody, they wanted to party. One of the tricks worked in the Sheriff's Department. He didn't say which Sheriff's Department, and I didn't ask, but one thing I did know, cops know lawyers.

"I'm lookin' for a lawyer. You wouldn't happen to know someone, would you?"

"It's funny you should ask," the trick said, "I heard about a new guy yesterday. He's young, real gun-ho, just got out of law school. He's lookin' for some business." He gave me the lawyer's name and the next day I looked him up. His office was downtown and I hired him to represent me. His name was Joseph.

*****

I was standing in front of the Jet Lounge when the red convertible drove by. The car went by and the man driving gave me our secret sign. I walked four blocks away from the hubbub of 12th Street, where he was waiting for me. I got in the car and he headed away from downtown. I saw him every week, sometimes twice a week, and he always took me to a nice motel in the outskirts of the city.

Sometimes, after sex, he'd take me to dinner. He always paid me well for my time. I started spending extra time with him, I liked him and I enjoyed talking to him. He was smart, educated. He was around 50 years old and he enjoyed my youth. He bought me gifts; jewelry and expensive perfumes. He said his wife paid no attention to him, he was lonely. "The only thing that's kept us together was our son, but he's in college now and we don't have anything in common."

All tricks like to tell whores how badly their wives treat them, I was used to this. "Why don't you go away with me?" he asked. "To California. Start over, have a new life. I'd be good to you, and I'd send your son to the best schools." I laughed at this, I was having too much fun being a whore, I didn't want to go anywhere! I'd told him I had a bi-racial son, but he didn't care about that, he was crazy about me.

He said he was a lawyer, a well-known lawyer, that's why he always met me away from 12th Street, in case someone might see him. After my troubles with Morgan began, I asked him, "You're a lawyer, can't you handle these cases for me?"

"No, I can't, Rita." he replied.

"Why not? I won't tell anyone I know you. Strictly business! I'll pay you!"

"I'm afraid you couldn't afford to pay me." he said.

"Oh, you're one of those big-shot, high-priced attorney's. Well, I make a lot of money!"

He laughed, "Rita, I'm a lawyer, but I'm not practicing law, at least not that way. I'm a Judge in Jefferson City, State Court of Appeals."

"Really? A Judge?" I was impressed.

"I can't represent you, but I can give you advice on your cases if you like."

After that, I always called him, "The Judge". We talked about my cases and he gave me advice on how they should be handled. I told my new lawyer, Joseph, who didn't have much courtroom experience, what the Judge would tell me. I didn't tell Joseph who was giving me pointers, but he knew it was someone with extensive knowledge of the law. He not only listened to my advice he took it. We had won all my cases so far.

I was getting tired of Morgan taking me to jail. How can I stop this guy? I decided to call Clarence Kelly's office, he was the Chief of Police in KC. I didn't get to talk to Kelley, but someone in his office. When I insisted on talking to the Chief, the man on the phone said:

"I'm his right hand man, you can talk to me."

I told him about Morgan and he listened. "My advice to you," he said, "Is to file a complaint with Internal Affairs." So that's what I did. All the cops got mad at me for that. They said I had a lot of nerve filing a complaint! They took turns taking me to jail.

My lawyer continued my cases, juggling them around until five cases ended up on the same day, with Morgan as the arresting officer. When we approached the Judge's bench, Joseph started, "Your Honor, my client has been continually harassed by Officer Morgan. As you can see, she has five different arrests here, on five different occasions. He seems to have a personal vendetta against her."

The Judge looked at the papers in front of him, then he looked up, over his reading glasses, he looked at me, then he looked at Joseph, "I'm throwing these cases out, all of them," then the Judge turned to Morgan, "Officer Morgan, it appears you've been harassing this girl. I don't want to see this woman in my courtroom again with you as the arresting officer. Next case."

Morgan was embarrassed, he wasn't used to a Judge chewing him out. Morgan looked at me and I was smiling like a cat who just stole the cream. Morgan never busted me again, but the other officers did. I went to jail frequently, there were lots of other cops to bust me, and this went on for several years. They couldn't convict me, but it cost me a lot of money for bondsmen and my lawyer. The vagrant prostitution ordinance was ruled unconstitutional, and the girls no longer went to jail once a month, the cops had to catch them doing something. Solicitation, trespassing in the hotels, these were the charges they could bring. By the time the law was changed I had been arrested 90 times on prostitution related charges. But that was a few years away, yet.

*****

I was seeing Bobby, he was a new bellhop at the Senator Hotel. He was only four years older than me. He had a huge Afro and a FuManchu mustache, and he was very good-looking. Bobby was a pimp, and he had a woman, Virginia. But I wasn't worried about her, she was an old, old whore, in her 40's, and she had only one arm. They used to call her "the one-armed bandit". Virginia was very good at disguising her handicap. She had her arm to the elbow and that's where it ended. But she couldn't hide her age, and in the whore business, youth is everything. Nope, I wasn't worried about Virginia. There was a chemistry between Bobby and I, we liked each other right away.

I was supposed to meet Bobby three blocks away from the Howard, away from 12th Street. I'd never been out with him before and I was looking forward to it. It was just getting dark when I walked out the back of the Howard, walking through the parking lot, when someone jumped out of the shadows and grabbed my arm.

"Hey baby!" It was Frenchy, "Ain't you glad to see me?"

"Jesus! Frenchy! You scared the shit out of me! What're you doin' out here? When did you get out?"

"Got out yesterday. I had to see you, baby. Been waitin' out here for an hour," he was turning on the charm.

"What for? Why aren't you with Dorothy?"

"I don't want that square bitch, she can't do nothin' for me!"

"I guess you should have thought about that before you fucked her."

"I don't wanna talk about that bitch, I wanna talk about us."

"Nothing to talk about, Frenchy. I told you it's over. Anyway," I smirked at him, "I got someone else!"

"Who?" he said, "You ain't got nobody, I been keepin tabs on you." He pulled me close, putting his arms around me, burying his chin in my neck, "Oh Shirley," he whispered, I could feel the hot puffs of air on my neck from his words, "I missed you so-o-o-o much!"

I wanted to get away from Frenchy, Bobby was waiting, he might think I'm not coming. I put my hands on Frenchy's chest and pushed him away, "Frenchy, I'm in a hurry, I gotta go!"

Frenchy didn't like being pushed away, "Get your inheritance?" he asked.

"Last month, and I spent it all!"

"It's gone?" he looked surprised.

"Yes, it's gone. That's all you cared about anyway, what you could get from me."

"I can get money anywhere, I care about you, baby," he was turning on the charm full blast now.

"Get it through your head. I DON'T WANT YOU, I DON'T LOVE YOU ANYMORE, FRENCHY!"

He slapped me, a hard open-hand slap on the side of my head. My ears were ringing! I wondered if my jaw was broke.

"FUCK YOU!" I screamed at Frenchy and ran as fast as I could. I should have run track, as much practice as I got running.

*****

I ran all the way to 14th and Broadway, where I was supposed to meet Bobby. My head was throbbing with pain. I didn't see Bobby's car, I looked around, and over in the parking lot someone was blinking their headlights on and off. There he is! I ran to the car and slid into the seat.

"I didn't think you was comin'." Bobby smiled at me. I always fell for the charmers, the guys who could talk a good line.

"I just ran into Frenchy," I told Bobby, "I think he broke my jaw."

"Open your mouth." Bobby instructed me. I opened my mouth, "Now close it. Okay, now move your chin back and forth." I did everything he asked. "Looks okay to me," he announced, "Musta hit you awful hard, I see his finger marks on your face. When did he get out?"

I told Bobby everything that happened with Frenchy. I was upset, seeing Frenchy was a surprise, an unpleasant surprise. I was hoping he'd forgot about me and go away with Dorothy, or anyone for that matter.

"Wanna get high?" Bobby asked, "Might make your head feel better."

"What ya got?"

"I got some acid, LSD. Got it from a white boy at Volker Park. He said it's real good."

"Oh, I don't know," I told him, "I've never had acid before. What's it do?"

"Makes you trip, mind trip. You'll like it, I've had it before." He took out his wallet, and pulled out two pieces of paper, he handed one to me. It was small and square, not much bigger than a child's fingernail, with a picture of a man who resembled Father Time. I held the paper between my thumb and forefinger, looking at it, "This is acid?" I asked, "I thought it was a pill or something, not paper! This is some kind of joke, a test? Right? You wanna see if I'll eat this paper."

"I wouldn't do something like that! Trust me! I'm gonna take it." He put the piece of paper in his mouth. I examined the paper in my hand.

"Who's this? The Grim Reaper?" I pointed to the picture.

"That's Mr. Natural, the acid is in the ink of the picture."

"I feel kinda silly eating' this paper, I think you're playin' a joke on me, but here goes!" I popped the paper into my mouth and swallowed.

He drove around the city while we talked. I thought Bobby had fooled me, when all of a sudden everything changed. My head stopped hurting, and the lights, the city lights, headlights of the cars, starlight, and the lights were glowing and flashing, streaming by, it was fantastic, it was beautiful.

My body felt different, too. In fact, I couldn't feel my body at all, my mind had taken over.

"Bobby, I feel it now. I guess you weren't kidding me."

"Yeah, me too. I'm gonna stop at this Holiday Inn, I don't trust myself to drive."

We were having fun, tripping on the acid, laughing about the visions we were having. We talked about our lives, when Bobby asked:

"Where's your family? They live in KC?"

"Yeah, my brother and sisters are here. I don't see them, except Sandra. I don't see her very often."

"What about your mom and dad?"

"They're dead, they died when I was 11." I had said this many times before, to many people. It was like saying the Pledge of Allegiance To The Flag, I said it without ever thinking about the meaning of the words. When I said the words this time, the acid was working on my mind, opening doors I'd kept locked, making me look at things I'd tried to avoid. I looked at Bobby, "They're dead," I said, and for the first time in my life I knew it was true. "And they're not coming back. EVER!" I started screaming, pounding my fist on the wall, becoming hysterical.

Bobby grabbed me, I fought him, he got me to the bed and put his hand over my mouth to keep me from screaming. "Go ahead and cry." he whispered in my ear." It's okay."

I cried. I cried for my dead parents and I cried for myself, while Bobby held me in his arms, rocking me, comforting me. It had taken 10 years and a hit of LSD, but I finally grieved for my parents and I KNEW they were NEVER coming back. After that, I stayed away from the psychedelic drugs. I didn't like my mind wandering off, out of my control.

*****

I got back to the Howard around noon the next day. I was exhausted, I'd been up all night crying. I stepped in the back door and there was Frenchy, standing at the counter talking to Jim. I knew he wouldn't start trouble in here, the bellhops wouldn't stand for it. I'd rather he was in here, than lurking around out back!

"Hey, baby," Frenchy said. He was all smiles and his hand was in a plaster cast.

"What happened to you?" I asked, nodding towards his cast.

Frenchy looked at me, holding my eyes, a serious expression on his face, "I had my hand where it didn't belong." WHAT AN ACTOR! This guy should have been in Hollywood, not on 12th Street in KC, but I had seen many "Oscar" worthy performances from Frenchy, and this time I wasn't buying it. He saw this in my eyes, he laughed.

"That's what I get for hitting a hard-headed woman! Are you okay? When you didn't come back last night, I got worried, I thought you might be hurt."

"My face is a little sore, but I'm okay."

"I broke my thumb in three places," he laughed and laughed, "Hey," he turned serious again, "I just wanted to tell you that I won't bother you no more, okay?"

"Okay." I replied and went upstairs to my room.

*****

A few days later Dorothy phoned me, "Can you come over?" she asked.

"When?" I said.

"Right now. I need to talk to you."

"Is it about Peter? Is Peter okay?" I got worried.

"Oh no, Peter's fine, I wanna talk to you about something important."

"Can't it wait?" The evening was just getting started and I didn't want to leave right then.

"We need to talk." Dorothy was almost pleading, unusual for her, "Right away."

"All right, Dorothy, I'll be there as soon as I can get a cab."

Dorothy was living at Grandma's. She couldn't afford her own place without my help. Dorothy was watching out the window when the cab pulled up, she went to the door, she didn't say anything, she held the door waiting for me to enter.

I walked into the living room and there was Frenchy. He was fidgety, looking at the ceiling, looking at the floor, but looking at neither Dorothy or me.

"What's so important?" I looked at Dorothy.

"Frenchy has something to say to you." Dorothy looked at Frenchy, he was staring at the floor. "Go on, tell her," Dorothy prompted him.

"I don't want you botherin' me any more. Dorothy and I are going to be together."

I turned to Dorothy, "Is this why you called me over here? To have some kind of show-down? I don't want Frenchy." I turned to Frenchy, "I haven't bothered you, it's the other way around."

"I thought it best we all get togther, and get things straight." Dorothy was smiling, she looked like the cat who ate the mouse. "Frenchy wants a divorce so we can get married and raise our daughter together. Isn't that right, Frenchy?" He nodded his head.

"Well, if that's all you wanted, you don't have to worry about me. You can have him."

"I know you want him," Dorothy turned mean, "But he don't want no white girl!"

I called a taxi and went back downtown. I hadn't been there 15 minutes when Frenchy called. "Dorothy made me do it, she said she'd call my parole officer, get me sent back to prison. I didn't know what to do! I love you, Shirley, not Dorothy, let's be together, let's be a family again."

"Frenchy, you just said those same words to Dorothy not 30 minutes ago. I don't want to be in the middle of your silly games!"

"Oh baby, I just got out, I'm on my ass, you won't be with me. What am I supposed to do? Just say we'll be together, I'll tell Dorothy..."

"Please, Frenchy," I interrupted him, "Dorothy lives at Grandma's, and so does Peter. I don't want this trouble! Any way, you don't want a white girl, remember?"

"That black bitch! I didn't say that, she did!"

I hung up on Frenchy. Now it's my turn. I dialed Dorothy's phone number. Dorothy was on Cloud 9, making plans for her and Frenchy, hoping I wasn't mad.

"Oh, I'm not mad," I told her, "Where's Frenchy?"

"He left right after you did, said he had to be back at the Y." Frenchy was staying at the YMCA.

"He just called me," I said, "He said he didn't mean all those things he'd said, said you made him do it, said he loves me and wants us to get back together."

"You're lyin'!" Dorothy spat out, "You're just mad!"

"Believe what you want. I don't want him, and I don't want to be in the middle of this mess. You want me to leave Frenchy alone? Why don't you tell him to leave me alone. He's tryin' to play us against each other. Tryin' to cause trouble! Frenchy's not going to be faithful to you, he's not gonna be faithful to anyone! I just thought you oughta know." I took satisfaction in telling Dorothy these words.

A few nights later, Jim called. "Rita, they want you over at Broadway." It was 2 a.m., the bars had closed and the hotels were busy.

"Can't you send someone else?" I asked.

"Bellhop said the guy wants Rita."

"Okay," I told him, "I'll be right down." Can't disappoint my regulars, I thought, not good for business.

I went out the back door and headed for the Broadway Hotel. A car pulled up next to me, the back door flew open, and out jumped Frenchy. He grabbed me and I began to scream. He picked me up and threw me in the back seat of the car, the car took off.

He laid on top of me in the back seat so I couldn't see where we were going. He took me to someone's house, I don't know whose house, and held me prisoner, fucking me and telling me I was his property. I was going to be with him whether I liked it or not!

I argued and fought with Frenchy. I realized the only way I was going to get away from him was to agree to be his woman, but I couldn't bring myself to do it. I refused to cry when Buck beat me, and I wasn't giving in to Frenchy. The first two nights he tied me up while he slept, but on the third night he didn't tie me, and I tip-toed away while everyone slept. Frenchy left me alone after that.

Dorothy and Frenchy never got together, Dorothy was a square, and Frenchy wanted a whore, he wanted to be a pimp, a player. Within a few weeks he had caught a couple of girls and Dorothy was forgotten.

*****

I was considered a top whore by everyone, the bellhops, the pimps, the police, the bar owners and the other whores. I was in my prime money making years, still young, only 22, with four years experience as a prostitute. I knew what I was doing, and the money rolled in. I spent it all.

I liked Bobby, he spent a lot of time with me, but he never said he loved me, and I have to have those words in my relationships. Bobby wanted to be a pimp and now he had another woman beside old Virginia. He'd caught a young girl named Bunny. He turned her out to the Life. She was beautiful and I couldn't deal with that. I was insecure about my looks, although I acted arrogant. In my heart, I was still that plain little girl.

I had a special affection for Bobby, he was the one who comforted me when I grieved for my parents. But I didn't want to be some pimp's woman. If I couldn't have love and romance, and commitment, I'd rather be alone.

I teased Bobby, giving him a little money, making him believe there was a chance. After all, if he could catch 12th Street Rita, that would be feather in his cap.

"It's a shame," the pimps would say, "Woman like that, always workin', and she ain't got no man. I'd sure like to catch her, but she don't like pimps and she don't like no ass-kickin' either!"

"That's what she needs!" another pimp put in, "Woman needs to be slapped around a little, keeps em in line. Her problem is, she ain't had the right man. I could make that bitch act right, and love it!"

"Oh yeah," the pimps would laugh, "Then why ain't you got her?"

Bobby started putting the pressure on me. He put a deposit on an apartment and wanted us to move in together. I was having too much fun to move in with anyone, especially a pimp. I didn't want to give up my freedom.

I had several men I saw besides Bobby, men he didn't know about. I liked an Italian guy with green eyes, who hung out in the bars on 12th Street, and the other was a vice cop. This cop had never busted me, and I could see the desire in his eyes when he looked at me. We began an affair, but it was hush-hush, top secret. He could get into a lot of trouble if the Police Department found out he was involved with a prostitute. Lust had a hold of him, and I enjoyed the idea of fooling with a cop.

I was supposed to meet Bobby at the apartment to sign the lease and give them the rent, but I didn't go. I couldn't bring myself to go through with it, even though I told him I would. I avoided Bobby for two days, I spent time playing cards, I spent time with the Italian and I spent time with the vice cop. Bobby would be mad that I stood him up, and I was giving him time to get over it. On the third day he found me.

"Get in the car!" he said. I got in. "Where you been" he was angry, "Why didn't you show up at the apartment?"

"I've been busy workin'." I said.

"You haven't been workin', I been looking for you for two days. Where you been?" he was on the freeway now, shouting at me, and not watching the traffic, "You tryin' to make a fool out of me? HUH?"

I didn't want to keep lying, I was tired of it, "Bobby, I'm not trying to make a fool of you, but I was with another man, two men to be exact." He pulled over to the side of the freeway and hit me.

"What! Two men!" and he hit me again.

"That's right! TWO MEN, YOU GOT TWO OTHER WOMEN, WHY CAN'T I HAVE TWO MEN!" I was screaming at him.

"You think you're smart! You think you can treat people any way you want!" Bobby pulled back onto the freeway and drove to Blue Valley Park where he beat me, screaming and kicking at me. When he was done, he said he was sorry, he didn't know what came over him. He took me downtown, I had two black eyes and a broken nose and lots of bruises. I never fooled with Bobby again.

*****

I didn't go to the hospital and I didn't know my nose was broken. After it healed, I discovered my nose slanted to one side. But the day after the beating I had so many bruises and swelled up places, I knew I couldn't work. Tricks don't like to be with beat up whores. I got into a card game at the Alton Hotel, we were playing Tonk 25 cent/50 cent a hand and I won $300. This was one of the few times I won at cards.

As soon as I got back to the Howard Hotel, my sister, Sandra telephoned. Sandra had divorced Bob, and Phil whom she'd already married had joined the Army. They had a baby boy. Phil went AWOL and nobody knew where he was. Sandra had fallen in love with an Astrologer who lived in California, and she wanted me to drive to California with her and her new baby. She said she didn't have enough money to go alone. Hell, why not? I thought, I can't work.

"Okay," I told Sandra, "I'll go. We'll split the expenses and I'll have enough money left for a plane ticket home. When do you want to leave?"

"Tomorrow," Sandra said, "Is that too soon?"

The next day Sandra picked me up at the Hotel. She was driving an Oldsmobile, about fifteen years old, and she had a U-Haul trailer hooked up to the back of the car. She also had a purse full of diet pills. We left in the late afternoon, taking I-35 to Wichita, where we got on 54 to Tucumcari, from there we took the "Mother Road", Route 66.

We drove all night, and the next day, taking diet pills to keep us going. When we got to Albuquerque, the car stopped, it wouldn't go any further. It was the middle of summer and boiling hot. A New Mexico Highway Patrolmen stopped to help us.

"I'll call a tow truck," he said, "and you can sit in my car until he gets here. It's air-conditioned."

We were sitting in the patrolman's car when I told Sandra I would pay for the car repairs and she could buy the gas for the rest of the trip.

"I don't have any money." Sandra said meekly.

"You don't have any money!" I was screaming at Sandra. I'd been up all night and day, taking pills, I was out of control. "HOW AM I SUPPOSE TO GET BACK TO KC IF I PAY FOR THE WHOLE FUCKIN' TRIP."

"I don't know," Sandra tried to reason with me, "I had to get to California and I knew you wouldn't go if I told you I had no money. I spent the money I had getting the U-Haul trailer."

"This is great! You wait until we're broke down in the desert, a thousand miles from home, to tell me you have no money!"

"You'll have to calm down," the patrolman said, but I went on and on.

"You deceived me! On purpose, to get what you want!"

"Shirley, don't be mad at me, please."

"DON'T BE MAD AT YOU! HOW AM I SUPPOSE TO GET HOME?"

"Okay," the cop said, "Get out of my car and wait for the tow truck in the heat!"

The tow truck driver looked the car over then he came over to us, standing in the heat by the side of the highway. "I think I've found your problem," he held up a small gadget.

"What is it?" Sandra asked.

"Clogged fuel filter. I took it off, it should run okay now, but I'd get another one as soon as I could. They only cost a couple bucks."

He charged us $5 and we were on our way to California. We were both relieved there wasn't anything seriously wrong with the car, we didn't have the money for car repairs. I calmed down and we drove until we crossed the California state line. When we got to Daggett, we rented a room and slept 13 hours.

*****

Los Angeles, the city of Angels, I had never seen so many cars, or so many freeways for them to travel on! Sandra drove to Redondo Beach, where the Astrologer lived. This was the only area of the city she was even slightly familiar with. We checked into a motel on Highway 101 and now we only had $20 left.

Sandra called the Astrologer, but every time she called, he was either not home or too busy to talk to her. He said he'd come by the motel in a couple of days, when she finally got a hold of him.

"Sandra, you drove 1800 miles to see a guy that doesn't have the time to come and see you!" I laughed at Sandra, square girls sure do stupid things! I would never have chased a guy down, I let the guys chase me, the pimps the tricks, I was in demand. Of course this gave me a superior attitude. I found it hard to believe that a woman as beautiful as my big sister would do something like that, when she could have any man she wanted, and get paid for it, too. I was a whore, I'd been a whore for over 4 years and I thought like a whore. I was sitting on a gold mine and I knew it!

"What are you going to do now, Sandra? I'm going back to KC as soon as I can."

"Oh, Shirley," Sandra moaned, "What am I gonna do? I don't know anybody out here. I WON'T go back home!"

"Don't worry, we won't go hungry." I wasn't worried about being broke, I knew SOMEBODY was going to give me some money. I didn't know anything about California but I knew ALL about men, and I knew there was a man somewhere in Redondo Beach that was going to give me some money.

"You stay here with the baby, and I'll see what I can do."

"Do you think you can get some help? Will you be okay?"

"Sandra, I'm a whore, and I'm a good whore, I'll be right back."

I left the room and walked to the front office. "Is there a bar around here?" I asked the desk clerk, "I'd like to have a drink."

"Sure," the clerk answered, "Right behind the motel," he looked me up and down, "But you might not like it, mostly truckers, older people, hilly billy bar. Young people go to the clubs on the beach."

"I'll have to remember that." I said to him as I walked out the door. A TRUCKER BAR! PERFECT!

It was still daylight out when I entered the bar and I had to wait for my eyes to adjust to the darkness. A woman was mourning the loss of her love on the jukebox, and it was Country & Western. A man and woman were shooting pool and two men sat at the bar. I looked the place over, I was in a strange place so I proceeded with caution. I knew some objected to whores in their establishments. A lone bartender, a woman in hr 30's was running the place.

I stepped up to the bar, ordered a beer, left a tip (you have to spend money to make money) and sat down at a table alone. A good whore knows never to sit at the bar in a strange place.

If a woman makes it obvious she is alone, the men who are interested will come to her or send her a drink. If she sits at the bar, she is inviting the bartender into her conversation. A whore NEVER wants to do that, unless she knows the bartender is COOL.

Not much here, I thought, but it only takes one. The bartender came to my table with a beer in her hand.

"Guy at the bar bought you a drink." She sat the beer down in front of me.

"Which one?" I asked.

"Tall guy, on the end." I turned to look and he was watching me. I smiled invitingly. He picked up his drink and joined me at the table.

A good hustler never jumps around in a bar, it doesn't look good, and you can also determine something about the man. If a man crooked his finger, wanting you to join him, he wants you to COME to him, best to leave those guys alone, they were usually trouble. I believe that all money is not meant for me, and sometimes I have to turn them down. I always let the man COME to me. And this guy was acting just the way I like.

I asked the man if he wanted a date and he did. We finished our beers and left together. He gave me $50 and when I told him I was stranded in California with my sister and nephew, that I was a whore from KC, he took me to the grocery store and bought food for several days.

I walked into the motel room, with the trick behind me, carrying the grocery bags. Sandra was amazed, I'd only been gone 30 minutes!

"Sandra, there's nothing to it!" I told her, "If you let a guy know you're available for a price, they'll either buy it or they won't, and most of them will if you look good."

"I could never do that! I have to like the guy, I can't be with just anybody!"

I laughed at her, "You'd rather be with a guy that won't take your calls, hungry, with no money in your pocket! You're silly! What difference does it make? At least this is more honest. All a man wants, any man, is some pussy, love comes later. All I want is some money, if he wants to give me some money for a little pussy, well then, we've both gotten what we wanted, without hurting anyone."

"I just couldn't do it with a strange guy! I couldn't get excited." Sandra replied.

"You don't have to get excited, he does! I get excited when I look at those Hamilton, Grants and Franklins in my pocket! I find that very exciting."

I went back to the bar right away, I walked up to the bar tender and handed her a ten dollar bill. We looked at each other knowingly. The bartender took the money and stuffed it into her jeans pocket. She smiled at me.

"What's your name?"
"I'm Rita."

*****

I went to the bar everyday, always giving the bartender a little "kick back" for letting me work there. I didn't wear the place out, but made enough to pay the motel everyday and have money in our pockets.

"Sandra," I began, "You're gonna have to do something, cause I'm not stayin' in California. I'm going back to KC."

"Why do you want to go back there?" Sandra asked, "When you can stay out here, in Los Angeles, palm trees, movie stars, mountains, oceans. Don't go back, Shirley, we could have so much fun out here together."

I wasn't interested in California, I didn't care about palm trees and oceans. I wanted to get back to my own life on 12th Street, where I was somebody, where everyone knew me.

"I'm going home, Sandra, I didn't want to move to California, you did."

"You could change your life. You don't wanna go back there and be a prostitute, you could start over out here."

"Stay out her and be like you? Broke on my ass? Running after guys that won't talk to me? You don't understand, I don't wanna start over. I want to be a whore, I like being a whore!"

Sandra learned that she could get assistance from the Red Cross because her husband was in the Army, even though he was AWOL. The counselor told her to find an apartment and they would pay for it. Sandra also applied for welfare, she was all settled now. I called the vice cop I'd been seeing and he paid my plane fare home. I gave Sandra all the money I had, packed the few things I'd brought and I was ready to go.

"Time we left for the airport." I told Sandra.

"Don't leave, Shirley. Don't go back! Stay here!"

I caught the flight to Kansas City. It was the first time I'd been on an airplane and I didn't like flying. I couldn't speak, I was so frightened for most of the flight. When the plane approached downtown KC, I could see the lights of the city. I'm home, I thought, I can't wait to get back to 12th Street!

After I arrived in KC safely, the plane didn't crash, I felt that flying wasn't so bad after all. At least it didn't take 3 days to get here! I had been gone a month.

*****

I would meet my vice cop lover at his apartment, usually about 4 a.m. I was finished working for the night and so was he. I never stayed all night with him, I never slept there, it was too risky. I was aware that the relationship could never go anywhere. He was a police officer and I was a known, convicted prostitute. I was playing around with him, amusing myself and waiting for true love. I knew I wouldn't find true love with a cop, unless he was willing to sacrifice his career, and this guy didn't want to do that.

He could lose his job if the Police Department knew he was meeting me, but he couldn't help himself he was in lust. And I knew how to please a man. It was my job to know what a man wants, and I was good at my job.

Early one morning, I was waiting on my cab after a session with the vice cop when someone knocked on the door. The vice cop thought it was my cab driver and opened the door. Standing in the door way was his partner, a fellow police officer, he walked in.

"I thought you might still be up," he was talking as he entered, then he saw me sitting on the sofa. First his face registered shock, then humor. "Oh! Oh!" he chuckled, "I guess you're busy."

"I'm not busy." My lover said "Whatcha need?"

The partner glanced at me, "I'll talk to you later. I didn't want anything important." He stepped out and pulled the door shut.

A week after his surprise visit, two vice cops came to the Howard Hotel. It was late, all the bars were closed and the night people were going home. "Sergeant wants to talk to you. He told us to pick you up and bring you down to the station," one of the detectives told me as I walked down the stairs.

"What about?"

"Didn't say. You're not under arrest, but if I were you, I'd see what he wants."

The officer escorted me to the vice unit and they went home. The Sergeant and I were alone.

"I hear you're seeing one of my officers." He sat with his elbows on the desk in front of him, looking at me.

"Who told you that?" I replied to his stare.

"It's my job to know what all my officers are doing. If I feel one of them is behaving foolishly, I try to help them." The Sergeant wasn't hateful, he was concerned, and it showed in his tone of voice. I didn't say anything, I waited for the Sergeant to go on. "You don't have anything to lose, but he's throwing away a career that he's worked years for. If he loses everything, he'll hate you. If you really like him, do him a favor and leave him alone."

"What if he won't leave me alone?" I said, "After all, I didn't chase him down, he ran after me."

"Don't worry about him, I'll handle him. You just do your part, if he wants to see you, tell him anything you want, tell him the truth if you want. If you do this for me, I won't forget it."

I didn't say anything else, there was no need to, he wasn't asking anything, he was telling me.

"Oh, by the way," he said, "Don't tell anyone about our little chat. I'm going to talk to him, but I don't want anyone else to know. You can go home now."

I avoided the vice officer and he avoided me. I wasn't going to jail as much, only when the other girls went. So, I thought, the Sergeant kept his word, he didn't forget.

*****

Grandma's husband, who was 70 years old, died at the VA Hospital in Leavenworth. I attended the wake, but I didn't go to the funeral. It was a family affair, and although Grandma's family always said I was one of them, part of the family, I knew it wasn't true. Grandma and I were close, but that's where it ended, I wasn't going to be taken in again, like I had been with Dorothy. Grandma's family tolerated me because I was good to Grandma, they put up with me because I always had money, but I wasn't part of the family.

*****

Players were coming to Kansas City from all over the Midwest, Chicago, Des Moines, Denver, Omaha, St. Louis, Oklahoma City, Dallas and everywhere in between. The pimps were coming to attend the Mack Ball being held in the Grand Ballroom of the Muehlebach Hotel.

The Banquet Manager at the hotel didn't know what a Mack Ball was. If he had, he wouldn't have booked the event, but everything was paid for in advance, and the Banquet Manager didn't know a Mack from a mackerel, so the Ball was booked.

A Mack is a pimp, but not just any pimp. A Mack has the gift of gab. Mack refers to conversation-he either could Mack or he couldn't. A Mack didn't have just one or two women, but large stables of girls.

"Cop and Blow" was the name of the game according to the pimps. They tried to cop as many girls as they could, they didn't expect to hold them, hence "Cop and Blow." A good Mack had a conversation so smooth he could catch any girl for awhile. And these Mack's were going to have a Ball at the Muehlebach Hotel, the most prestigious hotel in Kansas City.

I didn't attend the Ball, but I knew about it, all the hustlers knew, it was all they could talk about. I stood in the drugstore across the street and watched as the players arrived. Chauffeur driven limousines pull up to the entrance of the hotel, and before the doorman could open the car door, women jumped out of the limo, opening the door for their man, beautiful women. But the women paled next to the pimp, who wore lavish tailor made clothes, custom made jewelry with their initials or their full name in diamonds, fur coats draped over their shoulders and hats cocked jauntily over their eyes. The women ran ahead of the pimps, opening doors, lighting his cigarettes, he was their King! Car after car pulled up, each trying to outdo the others, making a grand entrance. It was better than the Academy Awards, and just as glamorous. It was obvious that these people were pimps and whores, they weren't trying to hide it, they were flaunting it, and some of the guest at the hotel wanted to know what was going on.

He doorman contacted the night manager, "I don't know what to do," the manager shouted, "Everything's been paid for in advance, the Ballroom's ready, the food's prepared and the banquet servers are here."

"But, sir," The doorman said, "The guest are complaining."

"It's too late now. I can't tell these people to leave, then we would have a mess. We'll just have to make the best of it! They don't seem to be bothering anyone, but they're so gaudy!"

The players didn't bother anyone, they had a first-class Mack Ball in a first-class hotel, there was no trouble of any kind. Pimps were widening their network, meeting pimps from other cities, AND meeting whores, which was their main objective. A pimp is always on the look out for new whores and what better way to meet them, than at a Mack Ball.

The day after the Ball, no one could talk of anything else. How hip everyone was, what clothes they wore, how lavish the decorations were, and how delicious the food was.

"Hey, Rita," one of the girls said, "You shoulda been there."

"Who would I go with?" I answered, "Any way, I work downtown, I don't want to be seen going to a Mack Ball."

"You'da liked this! They voted among themselves and chose the best Mack! You'll never guess who won! Frenchy! Your ex ol' man!"

"Why should I care if Frenchy wins?" I felt bitter towards Frenchy. For all his talk of love, he was just another pimp, he had deceived me and made a fool out of me for everyone to see.

"Hey girl, you should be proud. You turned Frenchy out to the Life. You was his first woman."

Frenchy had become an important pimp. Traveling around the country with a stable of no less than 8 girls and as many as 15. "Cop and Blow" was the name of the game, and Frenchy was the best. With his movie star looks and his pleasant manner with the ladies, he turned out lots of new girls. They never stayed very long, but there were always new ones out there. The other pimps liked to hang around Frenchy, so when the girls left, they might catch one.

Frenchy liked being a pimp, he was always looking for new girls to fuck. If Frenchy hadn't been a pimp, he would have been a trick. Frenchy once said he wanted to fuck every woman in the world, no exclusions. He didn't care how old they were or what they looked like, he wanted to give them all a try. It was his destiny to be a pimp, with his horny nature he was suited for the job. Yep, Frenchy was definitely the Best Mack.

*****

Things were changing, the Vagrant Prostitution Ordinance was no longer in effect. This saved me a substantial amount of money. The only way they could bust me now, was if I solicited a cop, and I could smell a cop a mile away.

A police officer had a certain manner, he was trained in the Police Academy to always be in control of a situation. It wasn't anything they did or said, it was just a feeling I'd get. I always had my senses turned on high when meeting a man for the first time. I knew my safety depended on it.

I didn't date aggressive, demanding men, I liked my tricks to say please. In any relationship, whether it lasts for years or only 15 minutes, there's always one in control and I felt uncomfortable when it wasn't me.

I trusted my instincts, and I never went against my 6th sense. A few times I misjudged and missed out on some good money, but most of the time I was right. In this game, I was only allowed one mistake, and it could be my last. When I met an aggressive trick, I'd take his room number, just to get rid of him, but I'd never call or show up. He was forgotten as soon as I walked away.

Whenever I was approached by an undercover vice cop, my 6th sense would tell me that this guy was not interested in fucking, he was up to something else. What the something else was, I didn't know or care. I wasn't going to find out. I always had my guard up. I knew they wanted to bust me, but it wouldn't be an easy bust, the vice would have to work for it.

With the Vagrant Prostitution Ordinance no longer in effect, more girls began working the streets. Before, a trick had to look around for a whore, now they were on every corner. The owners of the businesses downtown, 86'd the girls, refused them service. The whores had bothered their customers and didn't spend any money, they jumped from table to table, drawing attention to themselves. There was a city ordinance that a convicted prostitute could NOT be in an establishment that served liquor by the drink, and they began to enforce it. The bar owner's made an exception in my case, they let me work in the bars and were always turning me onto tricks. They knew I'd give the guy a date and not try to steal his money.

I was changing, too. I no longer felt that I was unlovable, that something was wrong with me, that I was bad. My experience as a prostitute had taught me that Buck was the sick one, not me. I never understood before why Buck only beat me and not my brother and sisters. But I saw it clearly now. The way I responded to the beatings turned Buck on. He got a perverted pleasure from inflicting pain, being in power. Although only I got the beatings, Buck and Jean enjoyed giving emotional pain to all of us. They'd put us down and watch with glee as disappointment spread across our young faces, we were called stupid and worthless. I'd grown up, I knew what had happened wasn't my fault, there was nothing I could have done to change it.

This knowledge set me free, I felt better about myself, about who I was. I wore less make-up, took off the wigs, I was more comfortable with myself. Hell, I'm not worthless, I thought, I'm one of the best known whores in Kansas City, and proud of it! I was no longer angry, I was leaving the past where it belonged, in the past.

I was ready for love, waiting for love, looking for love everywhere, I knew it was coming. I listened to all the songs on the radio and I felt the love songs were written for me, I knew all the lyrics by heart. I read about love in novels, laughing and crying with the heroine, but this was the only experience I'd had with love. No man had ever loved me, I knew that. It was always about sex or money, but my day was coming and I was anxiously waiting.

I came down off my high-horse and became friendlier with the other girls. I still worked alone, but I would sometimes stop to talk shop with a girl. What I found out was that the other girls didn't like me; I didn't have a man, I dressed in the latest fashions and I could go into the bars and restaurants. The other whores were jealous of me.

*****

Joe, the same Joe who had the whore Bea, Joe who'd been robbed by Monk, he had several girls now. Two of his women, Toni and Kelly, worked together sometimes. Toni was bi-sexual and she and Kelly were fooling around together. Many pimps had bi-sexual women in their stables. A bi-sexual whore could help her pimp cop women, help hold women, and make more money putting on shows.

Although Toni and Kelly had a sexual relationship, there was still a lot of competition between the two for Joe's attention. One night Toni made a pass at me, and I turned her down in no uncertain terms. Toni got angry, she began to taunt me, calling me names whenever she saw me; slut, bitch, wanting to fight, but I ignored her.

Since Toni didn't like me, Kelly did. Kelly would call, wanting to go to a movie together or just meet for drinks. Kelly wasn't like the other girls, she thought about the future. She was going to school and getting an education so she could take care of her five children. Kelly was older, in her late twenties. She had started whoring after she and her husband divorced a few years earlier. Toni was young, younger than me, and she made more money than Kelly. Toni had no children, her body was flawless, Kelly had five children and her body was stretched out of shape. Toni was beautiful with coal black hair and vivid blue eyes with a porcelain complexion. Kelly was a little over weight with mousy brown hair and a forgettable face, but Kelly loved Joe and Toni was in the way.

Joe worked as a bellhop at the Densmore Hotel on 9th Street, so he knew all the girls.

"I'd sure like to catch that Rita." he'd tell everyone, "She knows how to make money, she's smart and she sticks to herself."

I'd never met Joe before, I'd seen him and he'd seen me, but I didn't work the hotels very much anymore, and I never worked on 9th Street.

One day Jim called while I was still asleep. "Rita, Densmore called, they want you to come over. Whatcha want me to tell em?"

"Can't you send someone else?"

"Don't want nobody else, he asked for you only."

"It couldn't be a regular," I said, "I've only been to the Densmore a couple of times and that was a long time ago."

"Well, he only wants you. What should I say?"

"Okay, call me a cab."

When I arrived at the Densmore, the bellhop took me upstairs in the elevator and showed me the room. When I walked in, I saw Joe sitting on the bed, I knew who he was, but this was the first time we'd ever spoken.

"The bellhop said there was a trick in here, he musta give me the wrong room number." I turned to leave.

"There is a trick in here," Joe smiled, "I'm the trick." I opened the door to leave, "Wait!" Joe called, "I've got your money right here! I see somethin' I want, I don't mind payin' for it." He laid a hundred dollar bill on the table.

I came back into the room and closed the door. I eyed Joe suspiciously. "What's the catch?" I asked.

"Ain't no catch, I heard you had the best head in town. Here, take the money and put it in your pocketbook."

I took the money and turned the trick. After we were done, Joe laid back and lit a marijuana cigarette, a joint. "You don't hafta give the bellhop no cut," he told me, "I told him I was givin' you $15, 60% of $25. You tell him the same. I want you to keep all that money for yourself." Joe didn't want the guys he worked with to know he'd spent $100 on a whore.

"You're Toni's ol' man, aren't you?" Joe nodded, "I don't know what's the matter with her. She hit on me and I turned her down, ever since then, she's been screaming names at me, trying to pick a fight while I'm trying to work." Joe laughed.

"I sent Toni after you."

"What? Why? I don't like girls."

Everyone says you're a lesbian, that's why you ain't got a man, you like women. I told Toni to go after you, I wanted to meet you, but you turned her down. She's mad cause she knows I want you, not cause you turned her down, I guess she's jealous. I didn't know she was trying to cause trouble. I'll talk to her."

"Everyone thinks I'm a lesbian!" I was laughing, I couldn't believe it!

"That's what they say," Joe told me, "I'm glad it's not true."

*****

Joe called me over to the Densmore about every 10 days, always tricking, trying to talk shit to me, wanting me to choose him for my man. I liked Joe, I enjoyed talking to him, he was smart, and he was a pretty good fuck, but there was something about him that made me feel leery of him. A coldness in the eyes, a current of violence just below the surface, ready to erupt at any time. He was always extremely polite, but I felt he was very dangerous. I never teased Joe, made false promises or in any way tried to lead him on. Joe was no one to play with and I felt this in every bone of my body. I heard he slapped his women around and I believed it. I was afraid of him and yet I kept seeing him, he excited me. His desire turned me on.

I wondered why he kept tricking with me. He had lots of girls who wanted him, gave him money, but he kept spending their money to be with me. He didn't even try to catch me anymore.

"I can't be with a pimp," I told him, "I don't want to share my man with other women."

"I know how you are. You don't like pimps and you don't like violence." Joe looked at me and my spine tingled with fear, his eyes were so cold, "I wouldn't like it if you was with some other dude. I want you to be with me, but if I can't have you, I don't want no one else to have you, either."

I kept seeing Joe, but of course, I didn't tell Kelly. After all, it was business, Joe was spending money, it wasn't personal. Toni left me alone, but I could see the fury in her eyes. I wondered how much Toni knew.

Kelly and Toni fought all the time about which one was Joe's main woman. Joe had kept a copy of Bea's appointment book and he kept Kelly out of town most of the time, and kept Toni at home with him. This pissed Kelly off, and often she would call asking me to cover for her on an out-of-town appointment. She wanted to stay home and keep her eyes on Joe and Toni, but if she didn't show up for the appointment, they wouldn't let her come back.

The first time Kelly asked me, I was skeptical. I'd never worked out of town, except when I went to California with Sandra, and that was different.

"It's the same as working in a hotel here," Kelly was trying to convince me, "This place is in Danville, Virginia, it's only for a week."

"Have you been there before, Kelly?"

"No," she reluctantly admitted, "But I've heard about it, supposed to be good money. Please Rita, do this for me, PLEASE! I can't leave town this week!"

I took a flight to Atlanta, and there I caught a small plane that stopped at every small airport along the way. I took a taxi to the hotel in Danville, checked in, introduced myself to the bellhop and went to my room. I had arrived in the afternoon, and all night I sat and waited for a trick but nothing happened.

"Slow" the bellhop said when I asked.

I was sitting there waiting for all that big money the girls talked about making out of town.

The next afternoon the bellhop came to my room. "Thought you might like to meet some of the other girls."

"I'd rather have a trick." I told him, and followed him down the hall.

There were three girls in the room and one of the girls was from Kansas City. I didn't know the girl, but she said she'd heard of Rita before. I talked with them awhile then went back to my room. All that night I sat, not making a dime. Finally I called the bellhop and asked him to come up to my room.

"What's going on?" I asked the bellhop when he arrived, "I've been here two nights and I haven't turned a trick. If you don't have any business, why do you have so many whores here? I think you're freezin' me out!"

"Okay," the bellhop replied, "I'll tell ya, nobody on the circuit knew ya. We didn't know the other girl that was supposed to come, but at least some of the other places knew HER, NOBODY knew you. When the other bellhop took you to see the girls, the whore from KC said you was a snitch. So we decided not to use you, to be safe."

"JESUS CHRIST!" I shouted, "Why didn't you tell me? Why'd you let me sit here for two days, thinking business was going to bust wide open at any moment." I stood up and immediately started packing my few belongings. "How long were you guys gonna let me sit here? Huh?"

The bellhop didn't reply to any of my questions, he was glad I was leaving.

"You don't have to worry about me!" I told the bellhop, "I'm going back to KC."

I left the hotel and waited at the airport for the next flight to Atlanta, and made connections for Kansas City. I was furious, not only had I made no money, but I was out the money for round trip airfare to Danville. That damn Kelly. You wait until I talk to her!

Kelly was full of news when I got back. Her and Toni had gotten into a hair pulling, eye gouging, clothes ripping fight in front of the Pioneer Grill, in the heart of downtown! "Rita, I'm sorry about what happened in Virginia. I told you I'd never been there. I guess I'm never gonna go now, if that's the way they act. I can't believe they froze you out after you traveled a 1,000 miles. Look, I got a number in North Dakota, I've been there, you'll clean up. I'll give it to you." Girls guarded their out-of-town numbers, often they sold them, they didn't give them away.

"No thanks," I told Kelly, "I'm perfectly happy right here."

The next time Kelly called wanting me to cover for her, I told her to find someone else.

*****

A new girl started working downtown, she never spoke to any of the girls, she'd never worked the hotels, no one knew who she was. She called herself Karen and said she was from Kentucky. Karen grew up dirty poor in the Kentucky hills. When she was a young girl, a good looking white boy named Tony, found her in those hills and took her to Louisville. He turned her out to the Life, and she'd been with him ever since. Karen claimed she was 25 years old, but everyone suspected she was much older. Tony was an Italian wanna-be who dyed his hair black, and thought he was tough.

Tony told Karen not to work with the other girls, don't have anything to do with them, if she did, he'd beat her ass. He wanted complete control over her.

Tony and Karen had to leave Louisville. I thought they were on the run from the law, but I wasn't sure. Karen's mother and step-father lived in KC, so Karen and Tony ended up in KC.

Tony and Karen had a daughter 9 years old, and when Karen worked, Tony stayed at home with their daughter. Tony and Karen always lived way out in the suburbs, on the outskirts of the city. They moved around a lot, but they always stayed in the suburbs.

They had one car and Karen drove it to work every night. She knew Tony was home babysitting, with no transportation and she could do what she wanted, he didn't know anyone in KC, he never would find out.

"I got two tricks at the Hilton," these were the first words Karen said to me, "They want me to bring another girl. Wanta go?"

"Sure" I told her.

Karen and I started hanging out together. Karen was a party animal, she wanted to have fun. She'd been tied down by Tony all her life and she was ready to break loose! She'd come to work early, make enough money to satisfy her man, and have hours left to party.

Karen and I became inseparable at work. When you saw one, the other was close behind. We'd make our money early, then go to all the disco's in town, drinking, dancing and flirting the night away. Of course, all the hustlers said we were lesbians. We neither denied it or admitted it, we didn't think the question deserved an answer. We didn't care what other people thought, let them wonder! We were partners, best friends, we swore our loyalty to each other. Neither one of us had ever had a close girlfriend before, and we cherished our relationship.

But although we were closer than any sisters could ever be, I'd never been to Karen's home, I didn't know where Karen lived! I didn't have her phone number, and could never call her or get in touch with her when she wasn't working.

"If anything ever happened to you," I told Karen, "I'd never know, Tony wouldn't tell me, how could he, he doesn't know I exist. Hell! I don't even know your real name. You know mine. What's the big deal? Why can't you tell me?"

Karen got serious, she was very secretive about everything concerning her life with Tony. "Gee, Rita, if it means that much, I'll tell you my real name, but don't tell nobody."

"Who am I gonna tell? I don't talk to any one but you."

"My name's Linda."

"Linda what?" I asked.

"Linda Gardner"

"Linda?" I laughed, "You don't look like a Linda."

"Well", Karen was laughing too, "You don't look like a Shirley either."

"You're right," I said, "We look like Karen and Rita, two Kansas City ho's."

I had a feeling Karen was lying to me. I didn't believe her real name was Linda Gardner, but I didn't care, I was sure Karen had her reasons for being so secretive.

*****

One evening Karen didn't show up for work, it was unusual, but it had happened before, and there was no way I could call her. I went on to work alone. The police stopped me, a patrolman, "I'm suppose to give you this number to call," he told me.

"Who's number is it?" I asked.

"Police Department in Kansas, Johnson County. They wanna talk to you."

I took the number. It was best to settle all problems with the police, you couldn't be on the streets working when the police were looking for you.

I wondered what they wanted, I never went to Kansas! I thought about brushing it off, forgetting it. Hell! They're in Kansas, what do I care what they want! But I learned the hard way to respect the law, and those who represented it, so I found a phone booth and called. I dialed the number and asked for the officer on the card. When I told him who I was, he began asking me questions about Karen.

"I don't know anyone named Karen." I told him.

"Everyone knows you're friends, it's no secret. But it's not her I'm concerned with, what about her man?"

"I don't know anything about him, I've never met him."

I didn't talk to the officer long, I told him nothing, I didn't know anything to tell, but I don't think he believed me. The next night Karen showed up for work.

"What are you up to, Karen?" I greeted her.

"I was sick last night."

"That's not what I'm talking about." I told Karen what had occurred the previous evening.

"Why are the police in Johnson County asking questions about you or, I should say, your ol' man? How do they know we work together? Are they watching you?"

Karen was visibly shaken, "I gotta go home, Rita, I'll see you in a couple of days, I'm moving! I live in Johnson County!"

When Karen returned to work, she'd moved out of Kansas into Missouri.

"What ARE you up to?" I asked her over and over, "What are you afraid of? Why did you move so quick?"

"I don't know what they wanted," Karen replied, I felt she was lying, "But I wasn't staying in Kansas to find out."

We never talked about it again. In the Life, everyone respected each others privacy.

*****

I was seeing another cab driver, he'd take me to the movies or dinner. He was an older man, just how old, he wouldn't say, but I figured he was in his 40's, late 40's, and to me that was ancient. He was a black man from Arkansas, and he had the soft spoken, Southern manner. He tricked with me a couple of times when I first met him, but now we were seeing each other, and it was getting serious, his name was BJ.

"BJ wants to get together." I told Karen, "He's not a pimp, he wants to open a business. I really like him."

"No , Rita," Karen was upset, this was not good news to her, "Don't be with him. You're better off like you are. You have no idea how I envy you. I wish all the time I wasn't with Tony, but I'm afraid he'd kill me if I left him. If you get with BJ, he won't let you party anymore. Everything will change."

"Karen, you've got your man, you have a whole life I can't be a part of. I want a man, too. No one's ever loved me before, but I believe BJ does."

BJ told me he loved me and, of course he was good to Peter. At first I didn't love him, but I was lonely and I thought he loved me.

Joe was upset with me, "Why him?" he asked.

"Because he loves me!"

"HUMPH!" Joe looked at me, I knew he was holding his anger back, trying to control his emotions. "You've made the wrong choice. I'm the best man for you, you just don't know it yet."

"But you have other women, and you know how I feel about that!" I always used this as an excuse for not being with Joe, but the real reason was he scared the hell out of me.

"Those other girls are silly. I need a woman like you by my side, you're a star, BJ don't know what to do with you, I don't know why you gotta be with some fuckin' square! Ho's don't belong with squares, you'll see." He was starting to lose control and I wanted to calm him down, and I knew only one way to do it.

"Joe, please don't be mad," I spoke softly. Laying on the bed, I patted the place next to me, "Come here, Joe, don't be mad at me." I spread my legs and began to massage myself. I watched his eyes and saw his anger replaced by desire. He laid down next to me and took me in his arms.

*****

It's often said that whores are hardened against sex. It's a common belief among "squares", the most frequently asked question is; a whore has been exposed to so much sex, she no longer enjoys it. Some even say that whores hate men, nothing could be further from the truth.

There were girls like Chris from Minnesota, who hated what she was doing, but she was dead. Girls with this kind of attitude never lasted very long in the life. Lots of girls tried hustling for a short while, for the fast money, but they soon drifted away to other parts of society. It takes a certain personality for a girl to become a career whore.

Sex is a very powerful thing, it crosses all racial, religious and social boundaries. "A hard dick has no conscience," the whores would laugh among themselves. All the regular whores, the career whores were on a power trip. They bragged among themselves on how good they were in bed. Each girl thought she was the best. All of these women were lusty creatures. None of the girls were above having a liaison for free with a good-looking man. Nothing excites a man more, than to know the woman is enjoying herself.

Many tricks didn't care about the woman's pleasure, they were only concerned with their own. These guys were the "quickies", the $25 and $30 dates. But there were other tricks who did care. They were satisfied only when the woman was, they spent more time, and they spent more money. These tricks would ask for the same girl again and again.

Some of these men knew just how to turn a woman on and others wanted to learn. I liked these kind of tricks and they liked me. I had a long list of regulars.

I had learned that love and sex do not go hand in hand. You can love someone you've never fucked, and you can fuck someone you've never loved. Sex, with pleasure being the only objective can be very refreshing. If I could enjoy myself and get paid for it, WHY NOT? Many men, successful, good-looking men went to hookers because they didn't expect an engagement ring for a romp in the hay. After sex, each person would go their own way, with no commitment, no hang-ups attached to the relationship.

I didn't do shows and I never did sadism/masochism, but I gave pleasure and received pleasure. This made me very popular, I was a "hot number".

"I don't need those weird-o tricks." I'd say, "I've got plenty of regular guys who want me." My head was swelled a mile wide.

Karen had a trick at the Holiday Inn, he wanted Karen to whip him, a business man from down South.

"Why don't you go with me, Rita? After I'm done, we'll go party."

"I don't think so, you know I don't like those kind of tricks."

"Come on, Rita, you don't have to do anything, you don't have to take your clothes off, just wait until I get done."

"Maybe he don't want two girls."

"Fuck him," Karen replied, "let's go!"

"Okay, Karen, but I'm not taking my clothes off with some sicko who wants his ass beat!"

He was a stout man of about 50, with a very pleasant manner, probably a salesman. Karen got her money, but she didn't get undressed, the trick wanted no sexual contact with her, he wanted to be whipped with wet towels.

Karen went in the bathroom and soaked all the towels in hot water. She twisted all the water out of the towels and left them twisted. The trick, laying on the bed naked, turned on his stomach. Karen raised the towel over her head and SMACK, hit the trick across his back, he moaned, she laughed and hit him again.

"Hey!" the trick called, "You just gonna sit over there? Why don't you join in?"

The situation didn't look that dangerous, "You'll have to pay me," I said to him. He gave me the money and Karen handed me a towel. I raised the towel to strike, but I couldn't bring myself to do it, it wasn't in my nature. When I brought the towel down, it brushed gently on his back.

"Come on! You can do better than that!" I tried again, and again I couldn't bring myself to make the towel SNAP, when I hit his skin. Karen was working away, small red welts began to rise on his back. I think Karen's enjoying herself!

All of a sudden the trick reached out and grabbed my skirt in his fist, pulling me closer to the bed. "You don't seem to like swinging the towel. Maybe you'd rather be here, gettin' some of this!"

"OH MY GOD!" I yelled, I pulled my skirt out of his hand, picked up my purse and ran out the door. "I'll meet you at the car." I called to Karen over my shoulder as I went to the door. Karen came out the door behind me, doubled up with laughter.

"Rita, you shoulda seen your face when that trick grabbed your skirt!"

Tears were rolling down Karen's cheeks, she could hardly get her breath from laughing so hard. I didn't think it was funny, the guy had scared me, and I got angry with Karen.

"You wouldn't be laughing so hard if that trick had snatched you and beat your ass!"

"Rita, he wasn't gonna do anything." She was still laughing, but not as hard, she knew I was angry.

"You don't know that! A trick like that can turn on you at any time! MAYBE YOU'D LIKE SOME OF THIS!" I mocked the trick. "He likes getting his ass beat, and he probably thinks we like it, too!"

"There was two of us there," Karen tried to reason with me, "I don't know what you're so scared of! Girl, you turn down a lot of money!"

My anger was fading, Karen was right, I did turn down a lot of money. A top whore doesn't turn money down, and this bothered me, caused I wanted to be a top whore, but I just couldn't turn some tricks no matter how bad I felt about it.

I make plenty of money, I thought to myself. Not all money is meant for me. I turned to Karen.

"Don't ever ask me to do that again. Someday you're gonna make a mistake, and it'll be your last mistake, you won't get a second chance."

"Rita, you're a chicken shit!" Karen said this in a friendly way, trying to lighten the mood.

"Maybe I am, but I think you were having fun, slapping those towels on his ass!"

"I was!" Karen laughed and I laughed with her.

*****

BJ and I rented an apartment and moved in together. It was a new building, some of the apartment units weren't completed when we signed the lease. It was a two bedroom apartment, we bought a bedroom set and a dinette table and chairs. The rest of the apartment was empty, no furniture, but we planned on buying all those things later. It had been several years since I had a stove and refrigerator, I'd lived in the hotels and always ate in restaurants. Now I could go to the grocery store. A new adventure! But I didn't know how to cook, and I wasn't interested in learning, so the refrigerator stayed empty and the stove collected dust, I still ate in restaurants.

I continued to work as a prostitute, I would never consider being with someone who wanted me to quit, that was out of the question. I wasn't looking for a way out of the Life, I wanted someone to accept it.

I was ready to settle down and be with a man, and I thought BJ was the perfect man for me. I had tricked with older men, but never been involved with one emotionally before. Of course, he loved me, I never doubted it for a minute. Why shouldn't he? I was young, I was good-looking and I made lots of money. When it came to love, money wasn't an issue with me. I let him handle all the money, he had big plans, and I couldn't save a dime. We were a couple, anything he did would be for OUR future together..

One thing he insisted upon, I MUST divorce Frenchy immediately, Frenchy and I were still legally married. BJ said he didn't want his woman being married to another man. How romantic I thought.

I contacted Frenchy and told him what I wanted and he said NO.

"What do you mean, no? We haven't been together in years."

"What are you gonna do? Marry somebody else?"

"Maybe," I replied and grinned.

"I'll get custody of Peter!" he shot back.

I started laughin, "Frenchy, Peter's not your son. That paper you signed, swearing your Peter's father, you forged it, you lied. If you don't give me a divorce, if you make any attempt to take Peter, I'll go downtown and tell them you forged a government document!" I didn't know if he'd broken any laws or not, but it sounded good, and it made Frenchy think twice, so he gave me a divorce.

BJ wasn't a pimp, he didn't have other women to attend to, he wasn't on the prowl looking for new women, he spent his time with me. "That old' man'll suck up your youth!" people warned me, but I was happy, and I was falling in love, BIG TIME! They're jealous, I thought, they're jealous because I have a man who wants ONLY me.

Karen hated BJ and talked against him from the beginning. I no longer wanted to party but Karen did.

"It's no fun by myself." Karen would whine, "Come on, Rita, I can't have any fun if you're not there."

"I'd rather work. BJ's got big plans, we're gonna open a business," I didn't go, I'd lost my taste for the party life. I didn't get mad at Karen for talking against BJ, I knew Karen wanted to party and she wanted me to go with her. Karen had lost her running partner, and I understood how she felt.

"Karen, nothing can come between our friendship, you know that. But I'm in love and I don't want to go out and party all night! I want to make as much money as I can while I'm still young enough to make it! I've been hustling almost 5 years, I'm ready to do something, secure my future."

I wasn't living for the moment so much anymore, but started looking to the future. Before, I worked and spent my money as soon as I made it. Before, I worked when I pleased and partied when I wanted. But now I had something to work for, I had a goal, life took on a new meaning, I was in love. Different people tried to warn me, but I stopped them, wouldn't let them finish, didn't want to listen. People don't like it when they see someone who is happy, I thought, they want everyone to be miserable like them.

Every evening I'd go to work and come home around 3 a.m. I worked all night, I was dedicated, I was making more money than I ever made before.

"WE'RE going into business TOGETHER! What kind of future do you have with your pimp? I'll tell ya, NONE! He's not gonna share with you!" I'd brag to the other girls.

BJ had promised to marry me when my divorce was final, but he didn't. I was waiting for him to bring the subject up again, but he didn't. When I asked about marriage, he laughed, made some excuse to put it off for awhile, I didn't mention it again and neither did he. I pushed the subject to the back of my mind, I wouldn't think about it, might spoil the image I had of a perfect relationship.

BJ, Peter and I wet out often as a family. BJ was good with Peter who was 4 1/2 years old, he was going to school next year! Peter still lived at Grandma's, but was spending a good deal of his time with BJ and I.

BJ and I spent most of our time together at home, alone. He'd take me to the drive-in movies once in a while, but he said it made him nervous to be seen with a white girl in public, he'd grown up in the South.

"BJ, this is 1971! They're not gonna lynch you cause you go to dinner on the Plaza with a white woman."

"We'll see," he said, "Myself, I'm happy here at home with you."

I accepted this, even felt sorry for him because of his brutal childhood in the South. I loved him and respected his feelings. If it makes him feel uncomfortable to go out, we'll just stay home!

He also wouldn't tell me how old he was. He acted like his age was topsecret information. He said the age on his driver's license was incorrect, but he wouldn't tell me the real number.

It didn't take long for me to discover that he couldn't read or write. He never picked up a book, magazine or newspaper. When he had something that needed to be read, such as mail, he said his eyesight was poor and would hand the material to me. He always had to be home to watch the news on TV.

"I'm not ready to go home," I'd say, "Why don't you get a newspaper?" but he never did.

When I saw him slowly, painstakingly sign his name on some paper that required his signature, I knew he was illiterate. I asked him about it, I even offered to teach him to read.

"I can read!" he was embarrassed, "I don't read real good, but I can read." I picked up a magazine I'd been reading earlier, I opened it and pushed it towards BJ.

"What does this say?"

"What's this? A test! I don't have to prove to you I can read."

He never admitted that he couldn't read. He stopped asking me to read things for him and he never signed any papers in front of me. But he still rushed home to watch the news on television. He doesn't trust me, I thought, he won't tell me anything. I pushed this thought back into the farthest reaches of my mind. I refused to think abut it.

*****

BJ grew up in Arkansas. His family were sharecroppers, who eventually bought a small piece of land. But they were always poor, there was never enough. BJ didn't go to school, he and his brother and sister were needed to help pick cotton and work the farm. Going to school was a luxury his family couldn't afford. He was a country boy who came to the city as soon as he was old enough to live on his own, he wanted to escape the drudgery of farm life. His brother fled to California and his sister lived in KC, running a popular café that sold liquor "under the table" after the bars closed on Sunday.

BJ was having a mid-life crisis, he was 49 years old, (I didn't know that and I wouldn't have cared) and he felt this was his last chance to do something...be successful. Having no education had always held him back from getting the good jobs, then here I come, giving him more money than he'd ever had in his life. This was his chance and he wasn't going to blow it!

BJ was insecure about his lack of education. When I went to bed, I always had a book with me, at first BJ admired this, then he began to resent it.

One morning I found the book I'd been reading, propped on the pillow where BJ's head should have been. The pages had been ripped out, and scattered all over the floor. I asked him why he did that.

"You love those books more than me!" I didn't laugh, although it was ridiculous. "You lay in bed for hours, not talking to me, reading a damn book! I get tired of it!"

I let him blow off steam, I understood it was his own frustration at not being able to read the books himself. I felt compassion for him and loved him even more, but I didn't give up my books, he eventually got used to it.

BJ had no sense of fashion, he'd wear green pants, with blue socks and a purple shirt. Not only were his clothes uncoordinated, they were cheap. I decided he needed a make-over, so I took him to Woolf Bros. and picked out new clothes for him, having them altered for a perfect fit. BJ was proud of his clothes, but he was starting to resent me.

I wasn't aware he felt that way, I thought I was helping him, I loved him, I didn't mean any harm. After all, if you're seen with 12th Street Rita, you don't want your ensemble to come from Sears!

It was the Spring of 1971, I was 23 years old and making a small fortune. BJ was saving money, hiding it away in the apartment, he said he didn't trust banks. I knew there were thousands of dollars in the apartment, but I never bothered to look for it, I let BJ handle the money.

We settled into a regular routine, I worked 6 nights a week, taking off on Saturday. The other whores took Sunday off, so I worked on Sunday, and it was usually my best night of the week. Afternoons and Saturday's were spent with Peter. BJ was still driving a taxi, but he talked about quitting and I encouraged him. He wanted to spend his time trying to open a business, he wanted a nightclub.

"Won't be long!" He'd say. Although BJ was very secretive, one night he couldn't hold it any longer, he was excited.

"You know how much money we got?"

"No," I said, I joined in his excitement, "How much? Tell me!"

"Guess."

"I can't guess! Tell me!"

"We got almost $10,000," he went to the closet and pulled out an old black overcoat, one he no longer wore, he held it out to me. "Here, take a look!" I took the coat and looked in the pockets...nothing, then I began to pat the coat..there at the bottom...something was in the lining. I tried to find my way into the lining when BJ said, "look in the pocket, there's a little tear."

I pulled the money out of the coat, it was rolled up, a lot of little bundles, held together with a rubber band, each bundle amounting to $100. He was happy, for the first time he was going to do something, be somebody, own a business. And I was happy for him, for US.

*****

BJ never answered the telephone, I had numerous regular tricks who called to set a date for the evening. It was always nice to have a couple of dates set up in advance, something you could count on. Tricks don't like to call a girl when a man answers the phone. Makes them nervous and they won't call back, they don't want any trouble. It's just not good for business to let some guy answer your phone.

Most of the tricks knew the whores had pimps, but they didn't want to be confronted with it. If a trick found out a girl had a black man, it meant death for that girls business, she'd have to find somewhere else to work.

All BJ's friends knew to ring once, hang up and call again. That was the signal that the call was for him. BJ had lots of friends, mostly people from Arkansas, people like himself, country people, people he felt comfortable with. He was always going to visit his friends and family but he never took me along.

"You don't wanna meet my aunt! She's old! She'd bore you." BJ would say to me.

"I WANT to meet your aunt. What's the matter? Are you ashamed of me?"

"Oh no! I'm not ashamed of you! How can you say that?" But he never took me along and I didn't push it. I was trying so hard to make this the ideal relationship, exactly what I'd dreamed of. And this, too, I refused to think about.

BJ was making plans to open his nightclub, looking for a location. I was working to make BJ's dream come true, to make OUR dream come true. After all, BJ's dream was my dream, or so I thought.

*****

"The Godfather" was going to be playing in Kansas City, downtown at the elegant Empire Theater. I had read the book and couldn't wait to see the movie. The opening was tonight, but I was working, BJ and I planned to go this weekend.

I'd gone to a motel with a trick and, when he took me downtown, he drove right by the Empire Theater. He stopped for a traffic light, I gazed out the window at the parking lot, I couldn't believe it! There was BJ's car, parked in the theater lot!

"Let me out on the corner." I told the trick. I went to the parking lot and circled the car in question, it was BJ's car alright!

BJ's around here somewhere, I thought, but where? There was nothing open except the theater. I stood in front of the theater, leaning against a post under the canopy, waiting until the movie was over. People started pouring out, the theater was sold out, half the crowd had passed when I saw BJ coming out of the theater with a woman, a black woman, an older woman his own age.

I started to cry immediately, I stepped forward and blocked their path. They had been laughing, enjoying each other's company, unaware of anyone around them. When they saw me, they were shocked, speechless.

"Who's this bitch?" I screamed at BJ, pointing at the woman, I didn't wait for his answer. I turned and walked away, left them standing with their mouth hanging open. Maybe I was afraid to hear what he'd say.

I ran down the street, tears streaming down my face, I didn't know where I was going, running blindly. Finally, I stopped and stood on the street sobbing. How could he? I thought, he was supposed to take me! Who was she? I knew I was in no condition to work, I hailed a cab and went home. He's probably at home waiting on me, I thought, worried about me, but he wasn't there.

I sat at the dinette table and waited on him. It was the only place to sit, the apartment was empty except for one bedroom and the dinette table. We hadn't bothered to create a home environment, there was time for that later, everything was going towards BJ's dream.

I sat at the table and cried, no longer sobbing, but quietly, tears flowing from an inexhaustible source. A broken heart, I thought, is real, I can feel it, it's pain, real physical pain, vibrating in every fiber of my being! I wish it would stop hurting! My heart is actually going to break in two!

BJ showed up around 1 a.m., hours after I'd seen him at the movie theater. He immediately ran to me.

"Where've you been?" I asked through my tears.

"I've been looking for you! Oh, look at you! You've cried until your eyes are almost swollen shut! What're you cryin' like that for?"

"I can't believe you ask me that! I find you at the movies, a movie I wanted to see, with another woman, and you ask me why I'm crying." I started to cry harder.

"That woman ain't nothin' to me! That's my cousin's wife. He asked me to take her." BJ had a Kleenex and was catching the tears as they fell, patting my face lovingly.

"I don't believe you! Why didn't you tell me you were going?"

"I didn't know until tonight. My cousin got called to work at the last minute and he asked me to take his wife. If you hadn't run off like you did, we'd have told you, and saved you all these tears for when you need em, cause you don't need em now. We're still going to the movie this weekend, aren't we?"

"No" I answered, "I don't want to see it now. It wouldn't be the same. You've already seen it! Oh BJ, I thought you'd been with another woman!"

"Why would I do that? I've got you."

I accepted his story, I didn't try to analyze it, I pushed it to the back of my mind (my mind was starting to get crowded like an attic, crowded with things I didn't want to think about). Anyway, I thought, that woman was old, and I'm young, he wouldn't want her.

*****

BJ leased a club on Troost Avenue. I had been there many times with Sandra when I was pregnant. It had a long bar with a bandstand, dance floor and enough room for 20 tables. The place sat empty for a year and needed a little fixing up. BJ hired carpenters and painters, bought tables, chairs and bar stools, picked out glassware. He was waiting on his license to operate, you can't order your liquor stock until you're approved by the Liquor Control Department.

His application for a license to serve liquor by the drink was denied. He was crushed, all his dreams went up in smoke! The Liquor Control

Department didn't give him the courtesy of a written denial, they told him over the phone. All replies to Liquor applications, denial or approval, were supposed to be in writing, they treated him like a chump.

"I told you not to use the black lawyer," I said.

BJ clenched his teeth, he didn't want to hear I told you so from some smart-ass kid. Kansas City is a segregated city, each ethnic group with it's own community, with some racial mixing in midtown. In 1972 the powerful people were white, blacks were just beginning to get in the door. I knew all this from my many court appearances, I wasn't being racist, just practical.

"If you're trying to make a statement, use any attorney you want, but if you really want that license, you gotta learn to play by THEIR rules. I always hire a Jewish lawyer," I told BJ, "They'll never sell you down the river to the prosecutor. They're the best, pay em the money and they'll work for YOU. A Jew understands the meaning of loyalty to his client."

How could I be so smart in handling all my business affairs and so dumb in my emotional affairs? BJ hated taking my advice, he always did things his way, ignoring me. This time he had no choice, all his dreams were at stake.

The attorney I recommended got immediate results, Liquor Control treated BJ with a little more respect now. The Liquor Control Department said BJ had no records to show how he'd acquired the money to open the club. Of course, the Police Department knew that BJ and I were a couple, he was my pimp, they made it their business to know who each girl was giving her money to. This was probably the real reason he was denied, but a lack of tax records was the excuse.

BJ's sister, who owned the café, said she loaned him the money. The Liquor Control Department reluctantly gave their approval. They knew if it was denied again, the lawyer would take it to a higher court.

"It'll be easier for us to watch him real close and bust him. He'll fuck up!" The cops laughed among themselves.

The club was ready to open, he hired a band and was having a big Grand Opening, he called the club "My Place". He wanted me to come to the Grand Opening.

"BJ, they didn't want to give you a license, they were forced to. Believe me, the police don't like to be forced to do anything. They're just waiting to catch me in there, that's what they want. I'm a known, convicted prostitute, I think I should stay out of the club. It's in OUR own best interest." BJ agreed with me.

I wanted to be there, but I wouldn't do anything to hurt BJ's dream, and that was fine with him.

*****

The club made money from the minute it opened the doors. BJ was in heaven, floating on a cloud, and my head swelled even bigger. We OWNED a business. It didn't matter that I never stepped foot in the place, it didn't matter that my name was on none of the papers for the place, I'd made the money, I made it all possible and everyone knew it. Without me it would never have happened, it was OUR nightclub.

I was still working hard, although the club made money, BJ always needed more. I didn't pay attention to money, I never paid any bills, I just went out and earned it. I never knew how much money we had. Actually, I never had any money, it was BJ's.

Karen and I worked together every night. We took diet pills and drank beer, smoked pot, while we worked. Working was not something I wanted to avoid, it was a big party. We didn't go to the dance clubs anymore (Karen and I both loved dancing) since I was so dedicated to BJ's cause.

One Friday night, Karen and I had made a lot of money early in the evening.

"Bobby D's is open for another hour," Karen said, "Why don't we have a drink? We haven't done anything in ages. You're gettin' to be a pain in the ass, Rita!"

"BJ wouldn't like it."

"Fuck BJ! He won't know."

"Okay, but just one drink." I replied.

Karen did a U-turn in the street and headed for Bobby D's.

"That's all we'll have time for by the time we get there!"

Bobby D's was in Waldo on 75th Street. You had to drive through the Plaza to get there. We had a drink, danced to a few songs and it was 1:30, time to close. We talked and flirted with some guys in the parking lot, then we got in the car and headed downtown.

We were on the Plaza when suddenly I had to use the bathroom, I had to pee urgently.

"Can't it wait?" Karen said, "We'll be downtown in 10 minutes."

I was holding my crotch and squirming around in the seat, "I gotta go, Karen! NOW! Karen pulled over and parked at a 24 hour café in the Plaza. The café was crowded, it was a popular place to have breakfast after the bars closed. It was Friday night, and people were waiting on a table. Karen and I went to the women's restroom, took care of our business, and were leaving the restaurant. Standing by the front door was BJ and he was holding hands with a woman, the same woman I'd seen at the movie theater. I walked up to them, looked him in the eye, then glanced at his hand, the one holding the woman's hand.

"Oh," the woman said, "You the one that called me a BITCH!" She turned to BJ, "I told you if I saw her again, I was gonna kick her ass!" The woman lunged for me, but BJ held her back, and I walked out the door in a daze.

"RITA, don't let her talk to you like that !" Karen said, "That's YOUR man!" I didn't say anything, I headed for the car and got in. Karen got behind the wheel and started to pull off, all the while talking, "You are CHICKEN SHIT! I'd go back and kick her ass! What's the matter with you, Rita? You scared of her? I'll go with you."

We had only gone a block when I shouted, "Take me back! I'll show that bitch!"

BJ and the woman were sitting in his car, arguing, I approached from the passenger's side, they didn't see me, when I opened the door, they both turned and looked, and I kicked the woman in her face, shouting, "STAY AWAY FROM MY MAN!"

The woman came flying out of the car, we were both on the ground, I was on top, when the woman screamed in my face, "He's been my man for years!" The woman reached up and sank her teeth into my right eyebrow, and wouldn't turn loose, finally she did. Karen ran to help and BJ held her back. The police were there within minutes and the fight was broken up. No one wanted to press charges. BJ turned and left with the woman. Karen was staring at me, a look of horror on her face.

"What is it, Karen? What's the matter?"

"Your head," Karen said, digging in her purse for a mirror, "You've got a hole in your head! That woman bit you!" She handed the mirror to me. Until then, I felt fine, but when I looked in the mirror I got weak, dizzy. There was a bloody hole where part of my eyebrow should have been.

"Oh God!" I sank to the sidewalk, "Where's BJ? I need to go to the hospital!"

"He's gone, Rita." Karen told me, "He left with that woman. I'll take you to the hospital.

Karen dropped me off at the hospital emergency room, she couldn't stay cause she had to get home. I waited for hours while the doctors decided what to do. The nurses gave me numerous shots.

"A human bite is the worst bite you can get. Humans have more infection causing bacteria in their mouths than any other animal." The nurse informed me as she stuck me with needles.

At first the doctors wanted to do a skin graft, then another doctor said no, it's best to stitch it together. So they pulled the hole together, 6 stitches in all.

"You'll have headaches for a few weeks," the doctor said, "Until the skin stretch, but it won't leave a bad scar, not like a skin graft. The skin has enough elasticity, that it should be okay in a few weeks. I'll give you a prescription for pain."

By the time I got home it was daylight, and BJ wasn't there. He came in just before noon.

"Oh, look what that bitch did to you!" was his greeting to me.

"Where've you been?" I asked, "Why did you leave me there, bleeding?"

"The police told us to leave. You know they don't want no niggahs on the Plaza!"

"You were with the same woman I saw at the movie theater. Why? Who is she?"

"I told you before, she's my cousin's wife, she'd been at the club, and I was taking her home, we stopped to have breakfast first."

"But you were HOLDING HANDS!" I began to cry, "Why are you doing this to us?"

"What!" He acted surprised, "We weren't holding hands! You're wrong about that! I wouldn't hold that bitch's hand! She's a trouble maker. I told my cousin to keep his wife out of my place."

"BJ, she said you've been her man for 7 years. What about that?"

"She's lyin'. I ain't her man, she's got a husband. She said all that stuff to hurt you, she don't like white people. I wouldn't have no woman like that. All she does is cause trouble everywhere she goes. I could tell you all kinds of stories about her."

This is what I wanted to believe, I wasn't ready to let go of my illusion, even though all the evidence was there for me to see again, I accepted his excuses.

"What's her name?" I asked, BJ hesitated a moment, "Pauline" he said, "Bitch's name is Pauline."

*****

Her name was Tina and BJ loved her, but he couldn't have her, she was married to someone else. Her husband was an over the road truck driver (Not BJ's cousin). When Tina's husband was out of town she was with BJ. Tina had been married since she was a teenager and she had grown children. She wasn't about to leave her husband, but she liked stringing BJ along.

BJ wanted Tina, he showered her with presents and cash. He tried to make her understand about me. Tina knew I was the one who provided all the cash for the presents BJ bought. She liked the presents, but she didn't like the hold I had on BJ. BJ was Tina's toy, and Tina didn't want anyone else playing with her toys.

"Damn!" BJ told Tina, "I don't know why you had to bite a hole in her head. I thought sure she'd be gone, clothes and all, when I got home!"

"I suppose she was patiently waiting on you, full of forgiveness!" Tina spoke sarcastically and BJ laughed.

"Yeah, she forgave me. Believed everything I told her. Might not be so lucky next time."

"Why don't you let that bitch go? You got your club. I'm tired of sharing you!"

"I'm tired of sharing, too, Tina, but you got your husband. When you leave him, I'll let Rita go."

When BJ and Tina first began their affair, he always wanted her to leave her husband and be with him. Now, he didn't mind her husband so much. He'd gotten used to the money I brought him and he didn't want to give it up. He no longer encouraged Tina to leave her husband and Tina noticed this.

Before, when BJ chased Tina, he had no money to spend on her, but now he was a successful nightclub owner, and it was all because of me, without me the whole thing would crumble. BJ started calling the shots with Tina, instead of the other way around.

Tina was at the club every night, helping BJ manage the place. They were a couple and everyone knew it except me. He didn't try very hard to hide it from me, I took everything he said as gospel truth. He was confident he could handle me, but Tina was another matter. Tina had started acting foolishly, being jealous, not caring if her husband found out about the affair. But now BJ cared.

It was Saturday night, I was at home, not working, still healing from the bite wound, when BJ came home early from the club.

"Shouldn't you be at the bar?" I asked.

"The bartender's gonna do it." He said, (Tina was closing that night) "I come home early to give you a Christmas present."

"Christmas is months away!" I laughed.

"So, I'm early, close your eyes." He stood there, holding a full length red fox coat. It was beautiful!

"Oh, BJ, I don't know what to say!"

"Say thank you. Here, try it on."

I jumped up, slipped on the coat and caressed the fur. I loved beautiful clothes and I'd always wanted a fur coat. It was the perfect gift.

"It musta cost a fortune!" I said to him, admiring the coat.

"It wasn't cheap, but you deserve it."

BJ didn't tell Tina he bought me a fur coat, but he felt bad about my eyebrow, he felt guilty. He was beginning to like me a little bit, he'd sure miss me if I left.

*****

When I returned to work, I told Karen about the fur coat.

"If some bitch bit a hole in my head, Tony'd hafta give me more than a fur coat!"

"You don't understand, Karen, that woman was BJ's cousin's wife."

"I don't understand? You're the one that doesn't understand, Rita. She bit a hole in your head, she spit your eyebrow out on 47th Street, HE left you bleeding on the sidewalk, HE LEFT with ANOTHER WOMAN! I saw it with my own eyes! Say what you want about pimps, but Tony would never do that to me. He knows which side his bread is buttered on!"

"He didn't want to leave, the police told him to go. Anyway, let's not talk about it, we'll only argue."

My head healed, there was only a very fine scar, and I filled my eyebrow in with a dark pencil. Not too bad! I thought, kinda like Al Capone, adds character. When I told people the scar was the result of a human bite, WOW! It was a great conversation piece.

"There's a new club where the hustler's are hanging' out." Karen informed me one night, "They got go-go girls, and I hear they'll let you catch tricks in there. It's on 9th Street, and it's called JJ's. You know the guy that owns it. Why don't we go over there and check it out?"

Joe owned JJ's, and Karen knew all about my previous relationship with him, because I told Karen EVERYTHING! I hadn't seen Joe, except from afar, I hadn't talked to him since I'd told him I was going to be with BJ, and that had been almost two years ago.

When Karen mentioned the place, I realized I missed Joe. I missed the sexual desire he had for me. Although my occupation was sex, I didn't have much of a sexual relationship with BJ. Sometimes we went for weeks without having sex. He always had an excuse, or he'd be sleeping when I got home. He made me feel dirty, said I'd been with other men, and that turned him off. I didn't even tell Karen about my sex life with BJ, she'd tell me what a fool I was. Of course, he doesn't want me with other men, I thought, he loves me!

But when Karen mentioned Joe, I felt a longing to be with someone who truly desired me. I thought of the times I'd spent with Joe, times I'd never had with BJ. "Sure" I told Karen, "Let's go check the place out."

When we entered the bar, we passed a stage where a girl was stripping, taking her clothes off to the beat of the music, grinding her hips and shaking her tits. She didn't dance very well, but she didn't have to, the men didn't care, they were stuffing money into her G-string, and the place was full.

We sat down at a table and ordered a drink. I looked around the bar, and Joe was standing in the back, I smiled at him, and he frowned at me, then he stopped the waitress.

The waitress returned to the table without our drinks. "I'm sorry, I can't serve you." She announced.

"What?" Karen said, "I thought you was friends with this guy, Rita?"

"Not you," the waitress said, she turned to me, "Just you, the Boss told me not to serve you."

"Fuck him!" I said and I got up to leave, shooting Joe a dirty look.

"Yeah, fuck him!" Karen echoed, and we walked out the door.

We were parked behind the bar, and when we got to the car, Joe was standing at the back door, waiting. I ignored him and got into the car, he grabbed the car door before I could shut it.

"What're you doin' here?" he said, sarcasm dripping from his words. "Why ain't you at "My Place? Huh?"

"We were going to have a drink" I was trying to pull the door closed, but he wouldn't let go, Karen sat there, all ears, taking it in. "But we're not wanted, or I should say, I'M not wanted here."

I looked at him, I had been anxious to see him again, and this was the way he treated me! "So, if you'll kindly let go of the door, we'll leave."

Joe started laughing and he smiled at me, "Okay, okay, so I got a little pissed off when I saw you come in." He leaned down, pushing my hair away, whispering in my ear so Karen couldn't hear, "I've missed you." He stood back, looking at me, "Come on," he said, "I'll buy you both a drink."

We went back in the bar and Joe sent us a drink, but he didn't come to the table, he stood in the back of the bar, staring at me with a mixture of anger and lust in his eyes.

"Boy!" Karen said as soon as we were in the parking lot, "That guy Joe couldn't take his eyes off you! What'd you do to him? You oughta be with him, Rita and not that creep BJ." Karen wanted me with anyone but BJ and she encouraged every flirtation.

"He's a pimp, Karen, that's all, he's just after my money."

"And I suppose BJ isn't?" Karen said dryly.

"I don't know why you're so against BJ, you don't understand him, he's okay."

"I understand HIM perfectly," Karen said, "It's YOU I don't understand."

*****

"I don't want you around Karen. I want you to stay away from her." BJ told me one night.

"Why? Because she doesn't like you? She's not your friend, she's mine."

"She's a trouble-maker. If it hadn't been for her, you wouldn't have come back to the restaurant that night and got that hole in your head. It's her fault."

"It's not Karen's fault! You make it sound like she bit me!"

"Might as well been her!" BJ shouted, he was getting angry, but I was getting angry, too. "Just do like I tell ya, stay away from that bitch. I don't want you workin' with her no more!"

"BJ, I do everything you want, but I'm not giving up my friend. I don't see you givin' up your friends for me! I just can't do it, so forget it."

"Why? You two fuckin' or somethin'? I'm suppose to be your man! You'd rather have her?"

"Why do I have to make a choice? Why can't I have my man and my friend, why do I have to give one up?" I was shouting at him, something he wasn't used to, he thought all he'd have to do is tell me to stay away from Karen and I would, he didn't expect me to argue about it.

"You gonna stay away from that bitch!" He picked up the telephone receiver, and held it above his head, threatening to hit me with it. "You heard what I said!"

"Go ahead!" I was really screaming now, "GO ON AND HIT ME, but I'm not giving my friend up for anyone!" I was right in front of him, daring him to hit me, but he didn't, he put the receiver down, I'd called his bluff.

"You'll be sorry, she ain't your friend, she'll just cause you more trouble. I'm only telling you this because I care about you."

"Look, don't pick my friends and I won't pick yours." I turned and left him standing there.

*****

I was getting obscene phone calls several times a day, for weeks, then the calls would stop for a month or longer, then start again. The caller disguised their voice, and I wasn't sure if the caller was male or female, but the caller ALWAYS mentioned BJ, he was a fag...a homo...he had a disease...get away from him!

At first I was angered by these calls, I argued with the caller, defending BJ, exchanging profanities. But after a while, I got tired of the calls, and hung up when I recognized the voice.

Whata you expect?' BJ said, "Every trick in KC's got this number."

"But BJ, they always talk about you, ALWAYS! It's somebody YOU know. They want me to leave you." I told BJ everything the caller said, he was furious.

"Probably somebody from the club." he said, "Somebody I fired. You know how people are. I'll find out who it is."

BJ confronted Tina about the calls, "What're you trying' to do?" he shouted at her, "Fuck everything up?"

"I didn't make those calls," Tina replied, "I wouldn't do that to us, I know you need the money right now."

And he did need the money, because things weren't going so well at the club. BJ and Tina made up a code of conduct for their club, monetary fines for profanity, and men had to remove their hat while in the club! This was the 70's and all the fellows wore hats, and they didn't want to take them off, the hat was part of the outfit! As far as profanity was concerned, it was expected in a bar, these people wanted to drink and party, not pray. Business slowed down, people found another club where they could dance, drink, cuss and wear their hats.

Not only were the customers avoiding "My Place," but BJ had trouble hiring a bartender. He was always accusing his help of stealing; stealing money and giving away drinks. He watched his help like a hawk, the word had got around that he was hard to work for, and most people didn't want to work for him.

BJ was emotionally stressed out. Between the bar and Tina always threatening to tell me everything, he felt he needed a vacation, so he sent Peter and I to California for two weeks, to visit my sister, Sandra, who now lived at the foot of the Hollywood Hills on Ivar.

I'll get Rita out of here for a couple of weeks, that'll give me time to get things straight with Tina, he thought. Although Tina denied making the calls, she WAS the caller, and BJ suspected her. Two weeks, he thought, should be enough time to settle her down, make her see reason, and stop trying to destroy everything!

"I want you to have a vacation." BJ told me, "You and Peter can visit your sister in California."

"You're coming, too, aren't you?" I replied.

"I can't, I gotta stay here and run the club. But you deserve a vacation. Take Peter to Disneyland, have some fun."

At first, I said no, but I thought about it. I haven't seen Sandra in two years, it might be fun to fly to California with Peter. It's only for two weeks, everything will be fine ""'til I get back...

***

Sandra rented a huge house on Ivar, "Clara Bow used to live here!" Sandra gushed.

"Who's that?" I asked.

"Who's that? Why she was a movie star!"

Sandra rented out rooms to a various assortment of people; "Nik, the photographer from Paris, who was a lesbian; Judy, the militant writer who worked as a social worker, and hated it; Sarah, from London, who thought people were always stalking her; Douglas and his girlfriend, aspiring actor and actress; Paul the psychic; and in the back was a rock band, four more people! It was a very artsy-craftsy crowd, totally different from the people I was accustomed to in my hustling life.

Judy and I instantly disliked each other, but she worked most of the day, and was tired at night. She was a radical feminist, and she disapproved of my profession. Judy tried to tell me that I was an object for men, they were debasing me, I needed to stand up to them, take pride in myself and stop letting them use me in such a sordid manner. But I laughed at Judy, made fun of Judy.

"They can debase me all they want, as long as they pay me, What's the difference? All a man wants to do is fuck, and at least I'm getting paid for it! You see all those women on welfare, at your job, if they'd get up off their asses and sell it instead of sitting on it, they wouldn't need welfare! You're just a man hater, nothing they do is right, as far as you're concerned. I'm glad they like to fuck, if they didn't, I'd be out of a job, and a good paying job at that!" Spoken like a true whore! Judy was angered by my words. Judy was the only one in the house holding down a regular job, everyone else was trying to do the Hollywood thing, get discovered, make it big.

I met a handsome, single man at Sandra's named Lou. Judy hated Lou (she hated all men), so I liked him out of spite. He was a successful copy-machine salesman, with a home in the San Fernando Valley. He came by everyday, showing me all the highlights of Southern California. He was fascinated with me because I was a hooker and proud of it. His main topic of conversation was always about sex.

I was impressed with Lou, too. He owned a long, one-story stucco house, with a swimming pool, and a couple of horses. Lou and his wife had recently divorced, and he got the house.

I had sex with him, but he was a disappointment. He wasn't concerned with my satisfaction, only his own, he was a selfish lover. But I found him extremely interesting out of bed. Lou had been to college, he was educated, and he was interested in Astrology. He knew how to draw up a chart, this was before the days of computer charts, and he passed this interest on to me.

I left Sandra's house in Hollywood and took Peter to stay at Lou's in the Valley, swimming and riding horses everyday, and talking about Astrology all night. Instead of staying in California two weeks, I was gone a month. BJ had been calling Sandra frantically looking for me, wanting to know what I was doing, wanting to know when I was coming home.

Besides being a lousy love, Lou had another fault, he didn't like children, and I would never be with someone who didn't like Peter. After a month, I went back to Sandra's, called BJ and told him I was ready to come home.

"Where've you been?" he yelled, "I've been trying to find you for two weeks! I should just leave your ass in California!"

"I've been staying with a girlfriend of Sandra's, in the Valley."

"Sandra said she didn't know where you were!"

"I don't know why she'd say that! The woman has kids and swimming pool where Peter could play." I wove the truth around my lie, feeling very guilty. I'd never done anything like this since I'd been with BJ. The guilt was awful. Why did I do this to BJ, I thought, after he'd sent me on a vacation?

BJ was relieved I was coming home. He'd gotten worried when he couldn't find me in California. He didn't like the idea that I might not come back. After I returned, I found a piece of paper on the dinette table, scribbled all over was the name TINA, it looked as if someone had been sitting at he table, doodling.

"Who did this?" I asked BJ. He looked at the paper, "I don't know," BJ said, "Musta been my nephew, he was here while you were gone." I looked at the paper again, the writing didn't look masculine, more like a woman, big circles or hearts for the I in Tina. I threw the paper away.

BJ became suspicious of everything I did, he started accusing me of cheating on him, sometimes he worked himself into a jealous rage, shouting and throwing things, threatening to beat me. We started arguing on a regular basis.

BJ and I were laying in the bed, I was reading a book when BJ asked, "Do you think a person can love two people at the same time?" I put down my book and looked at him, he was laying on his back, staring at the ceiling, a dreamy expression on his face.

"Why do you ask? You think you're in love with two people?" I replied, with suspicion in my voice.

"Oh, not me, I was just thinking," he laughed nervously, "I got this friend who thinks he's in love with two women. Forget it, go back to your book." He realized he'd made a mistake asking me this question, and wanted to change the subject.

"No" I said, "I think there is room for only one in a person's heart." I picked up my book, but I wasn't reading the page, I wonder why he asked me that!

The obscene phone calls had stopped, but business at the club got worse and worse. There was a lot of tension between BJ and I when Kelly called, wanting me to cover for her on an out of town appointment.

"I don't know," I hesitated.

"Please Rita, Toni's up to something, and I can't go. I GOTTA stay here."

"Where is it?" I asked.

"In Arizona, down by the Mexican border, little town called Yuma. The appointment is for a month..."

"A MONTH!" I gasped.

"Yeah, but it's worth it! You're the only girl, down in the desert, you'll clean up!"

"Ever been there?" I asked Kelly.

"Sure have, and it's great!"

"Okay," I said, "Give me the number and I'll call."

I'd been back from my California vacation for 6 months, things weren't going well at the club, if I could make a lot of money and bring it home in a lump sum, maybe he'd get on his feet. And I wanted a rest from all the arguing, I didn't like fighting, but BJ was so jealous, picking at me about everything I did. I thought he could read my mind, knew the guilt I felt about my affair in California, knew that I enjoyed myself with tricks more than with him, knew that I thought about Joe occasionally. I denied all his accusations, but I still felt guilty.

Yuma isn't that far from L.A., I thought, I'll call Sandra and tell her I'm going to Arizona. BJ didn't like the idea of me leaving town, after he'd lost me for two weeks in California, but Yuma was supposed to be one of the best spots in the United States for a girl to work. BJ needed that big hunk of cash, so he relented.

Working downtown had changed over the years; businesses were closing, downtown was dying, old buildings were being demolished and parking lots to take their place, stores were closing and moving to the newly built malls. All the activity was leaving downtown, except for the whores, they'd made downtown a regular ho's stroll, there was one on every corner.

Without the Vagrant Prostitution Ordinance, the vice didn't have any control, so they were given a new law to work with; any prostitute with three prior convictions, would do a mandatory 30 days at the Correctional Farm. Karen and I already had three convictions, all we needed was another bust, and we would be locked up for 30 days.

I didn't like the idea of doing time. Before, as long as I had money for a bondsman, attorney and fines, I was free to ply my trade.

A MANDATORY 30 DAYS! Karen laughed, "They sure make it hard for a ho to make it!" Karen looked at me and the laughter was gone, replaced with a seriousness Karen didn't display often, "I'm not doin' 30 days! If I get busted again, I'm leavin' town, jumpin' bond!"

"Karen, if you do that, I might not ever see you again."

"You're not gonna stay here are you? Do 30 days locked up?"

"I don't know, there's gotta be a way around it." But we both knew that wasn't true, we watched the whores disappear from the streets, doing time at the farm.

"What about the club?" I said, "I can't just walk away, I've worked awfully hard. BJ wouldn't leave KC. I don't know what I'd do. I guess the best thing to do is be very careful, and not get busted."

When Kelly asked me to go to Arizona for her, it seemed like a perfect time to get out of town a while and make a pile of money without worrying about the police. It was also a perfect time to get away from BJ for a while, and all the arguing.

I was going to have my 26th birthday in Yuma, I'd been living in my illusions with BJ for over three years.

*****

Pearl had run her house in Yuma for over 20 years. She was in her 50's (at least), a short fat woman, of mixed Hispanic/black blood. Her whorehouse was located in an industrial area, away from the town, and it was a popular place. Service men, lettuce pickers and drug smugglers were in and out all night long, and all day, I have never fucked so much in my life.

Pearl took 50% of the money and charged $5 a day room and board. Once a girl arrived at Pearl's, she didn't go out the door until her month was up. There was no reason to go out, I ate all my meals at Pearl's and could watch TV or read when I wasn't busy, which wasn't very often. Pearl's was the only whorehouse within a 100 miles if not more.

Whores came from all over the United States to work at Pearl's. She never used local girls, she didn't want problems with the community, and local girls could only mean trouble. Like all successful madams, Pearl ran a low-key place, and the police turned their heads the other way. She hadn't been busted in 15 years.

Pearl was from Los Angeles, but had lived in Yuma for almost 30 years. She was married to a Mexican man, and owned a home in town. She gave to all the charities and community projects, belong to all the women's clubs, she was an outstanding member of the community. Her husband ran a popular Mexican restaurant in town, and most of the female portion of the town had no idea she was running a whorehouse in their backyards, but the men knew.

Early each morning, Pearl would arrive at the whorehouse, and be "open for business." She kept regular hours, she wasn't open 24 hours a day, if a guy got a hard-on at 3 in the morning, he was going to have to wait until Pearl opened at 9 a.m., or resort to other measures. She usually went home around midnight, but stayed until 1 a.m. on weekends.

"I'm going home now," Pearl would say, "Watch TV, read a book, do whatever you want. But DON'T answer the phone or the door. We're closed until tomorrow morning." A girl never turned any tricks unless

Pearl was there to greet and screen them.

From the time Pearl opened in the morning until she closed at night, I was busy turning tricks. All the tricks were "quickies"; straights, half and half and French's. Pearl didn't want the girl tied for an hour with a trick, and she didn't like kinky stuff. Pearl wanted her customers to get their "jollies" and leave cause there was usually another one waiting, and she only kept one girl at a time.

Pearl and I got along well together. Pearl talked of the "glory days" of her house when she worked 5 or 6 girls at a time. She had lots of pictures and showed them to me. In one of the pictures I recognized a famous soul singer. I held the picture out to Pearl, "Is this who I think it is?"

Pearl chuckled, "You bet! He used to bring his girls down here to work, but he hasn't brought anyone in 10 years. Once he made it big, he dropped all his girls, and married that square woman, turned his back on em. After they'd stuck by him while he was trying to make it in Hollywood! Truth is, he wasn't a very nice person, violent. You know what I mean?"

There were several military bases in the desert, and soldiers were a large part of Pearl's business. But there were drug smuggler's too, because Yuma was a border town. I dated one drug smuggler a number of times, he was bringing cocaine into the United States via Mexico. For a tip, he gave me a baggy of the white powder. I didn't like cocaine, but Karen did, so I took the baggy and placed it in my make-up case, next to my money. I would give it to Karen as a gift when I got home.

I'd been at Pearl's for two weeks when Sandra, Lou and the psychic Paul, drove to Yuma to see me. Lou engineered the whole trip, when he discovered I was only a few hours drive from Los Angeles, he wanted to see me, surprise me, he talked Sandra and Paul into coming along.

If Lou had told me he was coming, I could have saved him a lot of trouble and myself a lot of money. I wasn't in Yuma vacationing, I was working, and Pearl wasn't having any reunions in her house, she was strictly business. Pearl wouldn't let the three of them come to the whorehouse. Lou's car had broken down when they arrived in Yuma, his transmission was shot. Sandra and Paul had to get back to LA, so I bought them airline tickets. Lou was broke until his next paycheck, so I paid to have his transmission replaced. I spent freely, I was showing off for my sister and her friends, playing the "big time" whore. I was making over $1,000 a week at Pearl's. I put the money in my suitcase and watched it pile up, counting the days until I went home.

Once Sandra and Paul were gone, Lou called Pearl and was very charming, so she let him come to the house after she'd closed for the night, but only for a short while, when Pearl went home, Lou had to go, too. Once his car was fixed he headed back to LA with promises of paying me back the money.

One more week, I thought, and I'll be able to go outside again, with my pockets full!

A man rang the doorbell, and Pearl put him in the trick room. When I got to the room, the man gave me $25, a twenty and a five. I took the money and left the room, as I did with every trick. This was Pearl's rule, bring the money out of the room before you turn the trick. When I got back to the room, the man spoke.

"You're under arrest for prostitution." He shoved a badge in my face and pulled out handcuffs. I was speechless, this was the last thing I expected. He led me out of the room and placed Pearl under arrest, then he called his back up to come on in! He asked Pearl for the money.

"What money?" Pearl said, "I don't have any money." Pearl wasn't about to give back any money.

"She took the money out of the room and she gave it to you, where is it?"

"She didn't give me any money." Pearl stated matter-of-factly.

The cop pulled a gadget from his pocket, a small flashlight, he shined the light on Pearl's hands. "Northing" the cop said, "She hasn't touched the money." Then he shined the light on my hands, my finger tips glowed fluorescent green where I'd touched the "marked" bills.

"What did you do with the money?"

"I don't know," I replied, "Did you give me some money?"

I didn't know what to do, I didn't know anything about Arizona law, the cops back home didn't give the girls money, all they needed was a verbal solicitation in order to make an arrest. I followed Pearl's lead and denied any knowledge of the marked bills, even though my fingertips were shining under his light.

"I'm gonna call and get a search warrant."

The cops searched Pearl's house from top to bottom. They threw things out of the closets and ripped mattresses, they had no trouble finding the "marked" money, and they also found my $3,000, tucked neatly next to the baggy of cocaine I was saving for Karen.

"Hey!" the officer called, "Come look at this!" The money was stacked in neat little bundles, fives, ten and twenty dollar bills...$3,000, and he held the bag of cocaine in the air for everyone to see."

"We'll have to confiscate this money. Must be drug money." He grinned, everyone knew it wasn't drug money, but money I'd earned at Pearl's house.

The cops took the money and the cocaine, "It's evidence" they said. I was booked for prostitution, I spent the night in jail, and was taken to court the next morning to be arraigned on drug charges. Pearl had posted bond the night before. One of the arresting officers escorted me from the jail to the courtroom, which was in the same building. I sat, waiting on my name to be called. I was scared, I was a long way from home, I didn't know anyone but Pearl, and I didn't know her very well, and I was in a lot of trouble. What are they going to do to me? There were only a few cases, cause Yuma is a small town. The Judge called everyone on the docket and adjourned the court for the day. I looked at the officer sitting beside me.

"He didn't call me!" I said to the officer, I wondered if I would have to spend another night in jail.

"Must be a mistake," the officer said and he took me back to the jail.

Thirty minutes later a detective took me to his office, "There was a little mix-up in court today. Judge overlooked your name." He was smiling, friendly, "Where you from?"

"Kansas City" I said.

"Never been there."

"When are they going to set my bond?" I wanted to know.

"Well, probably won't be until tomorrow. Where'd you get the cocaine?"

"One of the tricks at Pearl's gave it to me, I don't know who he was."

"That was a lot of coke, pure, hadn't been cut yet."

"I don't know anything about coke, he gave it to me as a tip. I'll get my money back, won't I?"

206

The cop frowned, "We'll have to hold the money and the drugs as evidence. If you can prove it's not drug money, it'll be returned to you."

"It's whore money, you know that."

"The money was found with drugs, it's up to a Judge to decide where the money came from." The cop paused, looking at me, "Your bond has already been set for the prostitution charge. If I let you make bond today, you won't leave, will you? I can send an officer to Pearl's in the morning, bring you for the arraignment on drug charges."

"I won't leave," I said, already planning my escape, "I don't have any money to leave."

"Okay," the cop said, "There's a bondsman waiting for you. You're free to go. I'll send somebody over at 8:30 in the morning."

When I got to Pearl's, she was gone, but her husband was there, "Pearl said to wait until she gets here, she's taking care of some business. Don't answer the phone or door." and he left.

I've gotta get out of here! I was panicky. I couldn't believe that cop had let me make bond, but I wasn't going to wait around for him to change his mind, if they think I'm gonna sit here and wait for them to come back and put me in jail, well, they didn't know me!

When the phone rang, I answered it, I turned two tricks, enough for plane fare to L.A. I turned the tricks, packed my stuff and was at the airport before Pearl ever returned. I took the next flight to Los Angeles.

I did exactly what the police in Yuma wanted me to do. They hadn't "forgotten" to arraign me, there was no "mix-up", they wanted the $3,000, and they wanted me out of town so they could keep it. That's why they let me make bond.

After I was safely out of Arizona, I called BJ and told him what happened. He bought me a ticket to come home, he was angry and disappointed, he'd been counting on the money from Yuma. I was furious, I'd fucked day and night for 3 weeks and I was determined to get my money back. Legally, they couldn't keep it.

I hired an attorney in Kansas City to help me get my money. I wasn't going to let them have it without a fight!

Karen and I went to JJ's to have a drink and catch tricks, Karen had been going there quite a bit while I was in Arizona, she had a flirtation going with Jimmy, Joe's partner in the bar. We sat down and ordered a drink, Joe joined us at the table.

"Heard about Arizona." He said, "What happened?" I told him the story, then I looked at Karen.

"If I hadn't been savin' that coke for my partner, they'd have never taken my money! But I'm goin' to get my money back from those fuckin' bastards! I talked to a lawyer to day, and he said I got a good case."

"You better leave those people alone!" Joe advised me, "You're lucky they let you go. They coulda kept you and the money. Don't go fuckin' with them, you'll regret it! This is one hand you better fold, cause you can't win, they hold all the cards. It'll cost you more than $3,000 if they wanna get rough. Leave them alone, Rita. You'll get more money, but you ain't never gettin' that money back!"

I didn't take Joe's advice, I hired an attorney, he wrote a letter to Yuma, demanding the return of my money. Up to this point, Arizona had filed no charges against me, once I'd left Yuma, they forgot all about Shirley Sandy, until they received the letter, then they filed drug charges against me, issuing a warrant for my arrest as a fugitive from justice. I didn't know Arizona had issued a warrant, and I was surprised when the police in KC picked me up.

"We've got a warrant for you." They had stopped me while I was downtown working with Karen.

"For me? You must be kidding." I wasn't thinking about Arizona, that was 1500 miles away.

"Yeah, fugitive from Arizona."

My heart sank, oh no! I was taken to jail and bond was set at $10,000. BJ didn't have enough money for my bond, and I sat in jail while he tried to raise the money. I guess Joe was right, I thought as I sat in the jail. I should have left those people alone. Well, it's too late now!

Karen gave BJ half the money and he got me out of jail. My court date was two months away. It was to be an extradition hearing, if Arizona wanted me, they had to be in Kansas City, ready to take custody of me on that date.

"Karen" I asked after I got back to work, "There's no way you put up $400 without Tony knowing. Where'd you get it?"

Karen laughed, "I promised I wouldn't tell nobody, but you know I'm gonna tell you, Rita. Hell, I was wondering' what took you so long to ask! I've been bustin' to tell ya! Joe give it to me. I told him that jerk

BJ didn't have enough money for your bond. He gave me the money, told me not to tell anyone, especially BJ. Hell I wouldn't even talk to that creep, much less tell him anything. Don't tell Joe I told you."

*****

I was sleeping when the phone rang. Who can this be? I glanced at the clock, 9 a.m., I tried to ignore the phone. I picked up the receiver, and hung it up without saying anything, but it started to ring again, it rang 20 times, I finally rolled over and answered.

"BJ wants to suck my pussy. He wants to get a motel, I'll call you back and give you the room number. I want you to catch him, okay?"

It was a woman on the phone, and her voice was familiar, I'd heard it on the phone many times before, only this time she didn't try to disguise her voice. "Okay" I said.

"As soon as we get the room, I'll find a way to call and give you the room number. You be ready," and the woman hung up.

I sat on the edge of the bed in a daze, I wasn't awake yet. Is this a dream, I thought, some kind of joke? The woman probably won't call back. But she did call back, 15 minutes later, I had gone back to sleep.

"We're at the Admiral" she whispered into the phone, Room 205" the woman hung up.

What is this? Some kind of trap? I got dressed, called a cab and went to the Admiral Motel. I found room 205, I stood at the door, I could hear voices inside, I knocked.

"Who is it?" It was BJ, he sounded irritated, impatient.

"It's me, you ass-hole! Open the door!"

Silence, BJ didn't say another word. I beat on the door, yelling for him to come out, "I know you're there, BJ! Open up!" No one answered from inside and I continued to pound on the door until a man grabbed my arm.

"You'll have to leave, miss." It was the desk clerk.

"But my husband's in there!" The clerk looked me up and down.

"You've made a mistake, there's a black couple in that room. They called the front desk and said someone was banging on their door, asked me to get rid of you. You'll have to leave the premises or I'll have to call the police."

It was raining, not lightly, but pouring down in sheets, thunder and lightening, a regular spring thunderstorm in the Midwest. I stood on the sidewalk, off the motel property, keeping an eye on BJ's car, which was parked in back.

I knew he was in that room, but I had to make sure, I wanted to see him come out. I stood in the rain quietly crying, overcome by grief and pain. There's nothing sadder to watch than a young woman with a broken heart.

I waited all day for BJ to come out of that motel, and just as it was getting dark, BJ emerged, headed for his car. I'd been standing in that same spot for 6 hours, it had rained the whole time I'd been there. The rain was cold and my teeth were chattering away, I was completely drenched.

"B-b-bout time!" I shivered as I spoke, he turned and saw me.

"What're you doing here? You're soakin' wet! Poor thing! Let's get you home!"

I let BJ take me home, I didn't say anything, I didn't feel like talking. What was there to talk about? I'd caught him red-handed. I was cold and wet, and emotionally rung out, I felt numb.

"How'd you know I was there?" BJ asked.

"She called me, told me you wanted to suck her pussy." I said this matter-of-factly, no emotion in my voice. Was I in shock? Maybe?

"She made me go! Held me at gun point!" BJ was trying to explain.

"BJ, I don't feel like talking about it right now. But I don't believe you were forced to go to the motel. Why would she do that?"

"I don't know! She's crazy!"

As soon as we got home, I went to bed. BJ couldn't understand my reaction, I wasn't angry, and I wasn't crying, I'd stopped crying when BJ came out of the motel, I was sort of lifeless. I really didn't have any more tears left to shed. I'd cried enough in those 6 hours outside the Admiral Motel to last a lifetime.

PART III: THE AWAKENING

The only constant is change; it can be subtle, occurring over a long period of time, or it can be sudden and dramatic.

In the eight years I'd been a prostitute, I saw many changes take place in my profession. Most of the whorehouse hotels were closed, torn down for urban renewal, but massage parlors and houses ran by madams were taking their place. Bars with topless dancers were opening around the city, and most of the dancers turned tricks after work.

Working downtown had changed. No longer did the best girls work downtown. Many of the businesses were closed, there was nowhere a girl could hide in the crowd, she was visible to the public, the pressure was on the vice squad to "clean up" downtown.

No longer did the police round up girls once a month, laughing and joking with them while they took them to jail. Now they were bitter enemies, it became a game of cat and mouse, but the girls knew eventually the police would bust them. If a girl got busted and had three prior convictions for prostitution, she was off the streets for 30 days. Many whores left downtown, rather than take the risk of going to jail, they became dancers, worked in houses and massage parlors.

I was 26 years old and I had salt-n-pepper hair. I thought it looked distinguished, so I let my hair grow out. Everyone commented on how unusual it was, and I was proud of it.

When things first got rough downtown, I'd went to Yuma which turned into disaster, but before I went to Arizona, I thought I'd try to work in a house in town. I had the number of a house in Independence, Missouri. The woman was named May. I called and May invited me to come by the next day for an interview.

When I found the address, it was a row of shops, and May's place was upstairs over the stores. May was probably in her 60's with flaming red, dyed hair. She was short and fat, and wore lots of make-up and flashy jewelry, her hair was stiff, in a beauty parlor bouffant hair-do. "My girls get here at 10 every morning and we close at 5 in the evening. My girls wear negligees, no street clothes." May looked me up and down, evaluating my appeal.

"I hear you've got a Negro man. It always ends up in trouble. But I do make exceptions, that depends on the girl. I NEVER want him anywhere near my place. He can't drop you off, and he can't pick you up. Not even around the corner. I prefer my girls to take a cab. And he can't call you here."

"That's no problem," I said to her, "I can handle my own affairs in business."

"I've got a spot open next week, let me think about it and I'll call you."

I knew I was getting the brush-off. May wasn't going to call, I got up to leave, "Okay," I said as I headed for the stairs, "If you need a girl, give me a call."

May stood up and followed me to the stairs, "If you were to work here, you'd have to do something about that gray hair. My customers like young girls, and 26 is gettin' kinda old."

It was the first time anyone had told me I was "gettin' old." It's true, I thought, most of the whores working are younger than me. I'm considered an old whore now, I've been around 8 years.

As long as I was the young girl making all the money, I never gave it much thought. I'd been told for years that it was all down hill after a girl reached 25, but like most of the things in my life, I didn't think about it, prepare for it. Now I had to face the fact that money was getting harder to come by. I still did well, I made a living, but it wasn't as easy as it used to be. All the regular tricks knew me, and they wanted someone different, someone younger.

"That fat bitch told me I was old!" I told Karen that evening.

"Fuck her, Rita. Who wants to give her 50% of their money. I sure don't. We're doin' okay, we make good money."

"Yeah, but what if we get busted?"

"We ain't gettin' busted. You know you got that 6th sense working all the time. After everybody goes to the farm, we'll have the street to ourselves." Karen and I laughed. I dyed my hair the next day.

When I got back from Yuma, Karen had bad news for me.

"I got busted while you were gone."

"Damn, Karen! How'd you do that?"

"I don't know, I had a couple drinks, and this guy wanted me to come to the Holiday Inn, so I went. I thought he was okay, but he was a cop. He was drunk, too. It's your fault, Rita. If you hadn't been in Arizona, if you'd been here, you'da spotted him."

"I'm not infallible, I know they're gonna get me, it's just a matter of when."

"You may not be infallible," Karen replied, "but you're pretty damn good at pickin' em out. Best I've ever seen, you know who to leave alone. And I'll be damned if I know how you do it!"

"What are you gonna do now?' I asked her.

"I'm leavin'," Karen stated, "GOOD-BYE KANSAS CITY! I'm allowed three continuances, that could give me a few months to get together a little cash, and I'm OUGHTA HERE!"

"Have you talked to a lawyer?"

"Nothing to talk about, he can't help me, he can't change the law, he'll just take my money. You've seen the girls going to the farm. No, Tony and I are leavin', when my court date comes, I won't be here."

*****

For about a week after I found BJ at the Admiral Motel, I was in a state of shock, going through the motions of life, not feeling, and of course, not thinking.

I'd been asleep, when something important woke me up, a thought in my mind, not fully awake yet, the thought came back...BJ has another woman, he's always had another woman, he's lied to me and strung me along all these years, I even know her name. I thought of the paper I'd found after returning from California. Her name is Tina and he's had her in my apartment. They've been together longer than he's been with me, she's the one who made all those obscene phone calls, she was at the theater with him, not his cousin's wife, she bit my eyebrow off and she called me to come to the Admiral Motel. Whenever these things happened, BJ always left with Tina, making it obvious where his affections lay. He doesn't care anything about me, and he never did.

I opened my eyes, with these thoughts in my mind. But it wasn't really a chain of thought, but rather a picture that flashed in my mind, instant knowledge of the facts. Everything looked different, maybe it's the light, I thought. I didn't realize that I'd taken off the rose-colored glasses and from now on everything would look different. I looked around the apartment, 3 1/2 years, and still the place was empty, a bedroom set, and a dinette table, that's all. He never spent any money to make a home for us. Why didn't I see that before?

Everything was crystal clear to me now, I hadn't thought about it, but when I woke up that morning, I KNEW how blind I'd been. It was as if I'd been asleep all my life, in a dream world. A world that had existed only in my head, and for the first time I'd awakened from the dream.

I've made a fool of myself! Everyone knew about BJ and Tina, they tried to tell me, but I wouldn't listen. Where there's smoke there's fire is an old saying, I guess it's true. The mind is a powerful thing, a person can want love so badly, they invent love in their mind, create a situation that in reality doesn't exist at all. BJ never loved me, and he never tried to hide his other woman. I refused to see the truth, because it didn't fit in with my ideal relationship.

I knew this all along, I just wouldn't face it, pushed it to the back of my mind. The evidence was always there for me to see, all the facts were stored in my brain, but I wanted someone to love me, so I ignored them.

I wasn't angry, I wasn't even sad, I was relieved, I felt a new sense of freedom. Last night, when I went to sleep, I was in love with BJ, but this morning, the love was gone, and I was glad. It was the closest I ever came to a "religious experience", a light being turned on in my head. One minute the light was off, and a second later, it was on, showing me the truth that I'd avoided for so long. It was a sudden and dramatic change in my whole outlook on life.

"Nobody cares about a whore." the words Liz spoke when Bea died echoed through my mind. Except a pimp, I thought, he really cares because his livelihood depends on it. But does anyone really care about a whore? Her thoughts? Her emotions? Her ambitions? What ambition have I had? To be the best whore in KC. I did that, and what did it get me? AM I HAPPY?

A whore can never have true love. As long as she's fucking other men, no one will love her. Why should they? Do I know what love is? Probably not, but I know it's not what I've got with BJ. I wanted love, but I wasn't willing to stop whoring, I wanted both, but you can't have your cake and eat it, too, as the saying goes.

I was so proud, I acted so cocky. I wouldn't be with a pimp, I thought I was better off than the other girls, when actually, they were smarter than me. At least you know where you stand with a pimp, it's an honest relationship, not full of lies and deception. But BJ didn't invent this fairy tale in his head, I did, and I can't blame anyone but myself. BJ shouldn't have taken advantage of a young, emotionally naive girl, but I let him do it.

When I woke up that morning, I realized my relationship with BJ had been a dream, a nightmare. I was awake for the first time, and I wasn't going back to sleep.

*****

"BJ, could you come home? I'd like to talk to you." I called him at the club, it was early in the day and I knew he wouldn't be busy.

"Now? Can't it wait? I gotta watch this bartender." He shouted irritated and he was. He'd planned to have lunch with Tina.

"This is more important than the few dollars your bartender might steal. I think you better come."

BJ detected the difference in me, something's up he thought, "Okay, give me 20 minutes."

I couldn't wait to tell BJ about my revelation, I thought he should be the first to know. When BJ arrived home, I was waiting, I told him I knew about his affair. "I even know her name," I was laughing, I felt light, bubblely, "It's Tina!"

BJ was shocked, his mouth fell open, but he quickly recovered, "Somebody told you that! Who was it? Who told you those lies about me?"

I laughed some more, "Nobody told me."

"You're lyin'!" BJ shouted, "Did somebody call you this morning?"

"It's the funniest thing," I said in a dreamy voice, with a smile on my face, "I woke up this morning and I knew. I guess I've always known, I just never put it together before. I guess I didn't want to."

When he heard this, he breathed a sign of relief, maybe I can still talk her out of it. "You lettin' your imagination work over time! Rita, you think I've been havin' an affair? That's crazy! You know that ain't true!"

"BJ, I don't want to debate whether it's true or not, I know it's true, and I'm lettin' you know that I know."

BJ was worried, he didn't know how to handle this, I'd always been so easy to deal with, so quick to accept his excuses, he'd taken it for granted that I would always believe him. "What're you gonna do?" he asked.

I looked at BJ, and for the first time I saw him in a new light; an old, foolish man, he disgusted me. This image of BJ gave me a jolt.

When BJ saw the look on my face, he too, experienced a moment of truth. I've lost her, he thought, I made a big mistake, Tina is another man's wife, she doesn't really want me, and she doesn't want anyone else to have me. Tina has tried to run Rita off and now she's done it. I let her do it. I should have left her alone years ago. If I can get Rita to give me one more chance, just one, it'll be different this time. All these thoughts flashed through BJ's mind.

"Rita, I know I haven't done right by you." He reached out to put his arms around me, but I slipped out of his embrace, "But it's not too late."

"Please," I said moving across the room, away from him, "I don't want you to touch me. I don't feel like holding someone who's lied to me for over 3 years. You said you loved me, you used me for money. When you wanted love, you went to Tina. How do you think that makes me feel? After she bit a hole in my head, did you have enough respect for me to leave her alone? No, you've done nothing to show you love me. That club you got? You better make it work, because you're never gettin' another penny from me. I'm through being used by you or any other man. Believe it or not, I saw the light this morning. As long as I'm a whore, I'll be alone. Because I don't want just any relationship, I want true love, I won't settle for less, and I can't have it as long as I'm hookin'. I know now that I don't want a man that lets me turn tricks. When a man really loves, he won't allow it, and that, BJ, is what I'm lookin' for."

"You wanna quit working? That's fine, you don't have to work. We'll fix up the apartment, Peter can live with us." BJ was pleading.

"It's too late, BJ. I don't think I can forgive you."

*****

I didn't move out of the apartment, but continued to live with BJ. I wouldn't sleep with him, I made a pallet on the floor in the empty 2nd bedroom. At first he wouldn't let me sleep, trying to coax me to bed, after about a week of this, he left me alone. She just needs a little time alone, he thought.

I continued to work, or rather, I went to work and partied most of the night with Karen. I didn't care if I made any money, and I didn't give BJ any of the money I did make. He accepted this, but he didn't like it. He felt guilty, and as long as I was still living at the apartment, he felt he had a chance to patch things up.

BJ used to be gone all the time, but now he was always there, bothering me. If I wasn't going to give him the money, then he didn't want me working. BJ sincerely felt guilty about the way he'd treated me, he wanted to make it up to me. He really meant it, it wasn't an act. BJ always like women he couldn't have, women who treated him bad, this turned him on. Now that I didn't want him, he found me more exciting.

I tried to stay out of BJ's way, I couldn't stand the sight of him. He was a reminder of what a fool I'd been. And yet I didn't leave. I took pleasure in treating him like shit, turning away from him, seeing the hurt in his eyes. I knew I should leave, I knew I was never going to patch things up with him, but I didn't have anywhere else to go, I wasn't sure I wanted to leave just yet.

*****

Karen wanted to go to JJ's every night, she was "in love" with Joe's partner, Jimmy. She'd even talked about leaving Tony! Karen and I were having a drink when Joe walked into JJ's, ordered a drink, and stood in the back by the restrooms, watching the bar. I got up and headed for the women's restroom, moving sensuously, I passed Joe and whispered:

"BJ and I broke up." and I went into the restroom.

He didn't say anything, he lit a cigarette, his eyes watching me, our eyes locked for a second, and I joined Karen at the table. Joe watched me all night, he didn't approach the table, I would smile at him, and he'd look intensely at me.

Karen wanted to wait around until the bar closed so she could be with Jimmy, and I waited with her. At closing time the customers were put out, Karen and I waited at a table while Jimmy and Joe counted the money and paid the help. After the bartender and dancers left, Joe locked the door. Then he walked up and spoke to me for the first time that night. He was angry.

"What in the fuck you tryin' to do? Me and BJ's broke up!" he mimicked me. My mouth fell open, "Whata you think I am? HUH? A toy you can play with? Pick me up when you want, put me away when you feel like it!"

"Hey Joe, calm down. I didn't meant it like that. Forget it! Okay?" I turned away from him and he sat down beside me.

"Why'd you tell me you and BJ's broke up? It's not true, you're still there." He was talking to my back, he put his hand on my shoulder and turned me to face him, "What're you tryin' to do?"

"I'm not tryin' to do anything. I was just lettin' you know it was over between me and BJ. I thought you might be interested, but I was wrong. I haven't moved yet, but it's over. BJ had another woman, a square woman all these year."

"I was wonderin' when you were gonna wake up," he said.

I laughed, "That's just what happened. One morning I woke up, and it was over. Did you know about her?"

Joe looked at me and shook his head, "Rita, Rita! Everybody knew. You was running around bragging about not being with a pimp, bragging about your man and your club, when everybody knew that was BJ and Tina's club, not yours. It wasn't exactly a secret."

Joe had always wanted me, he wanted me to be his woman, and he desired me sexually. Joe was hurt when I'd decided to be with BJ, and when he saw how BJ treated me, he got angry. He'd warned me not be with BJ, and he was now taking satisfaction from telling me so. But when he saw the hurt on my face, he softened, "Hey, you still care about him, don't you?"

"NO" I said, "That's the funny part, I don't care about him at all. I'm not even mad, but I feel humiliated to know that everyone was laughing at me behind my back. I feel like such a fool!"

"Everybody plays the fool some time," Joe sang off key, "No exceptions to the rule!"

I started laughing cause Joe wasn't a very good singer, "Oh stop."

"It's true," Joe replied, "We all do foolish things, you ain't the only one. Don't worry about what other people think, or what they say. We've all been fools at one time or another. Just pick up the pieces and go on. What're you fixin' to do now?"

"About what? BJ? Leave, I guess."

"No," he grinned, "I mean right now, this minute. You and Karen going somewhere?"

"She's waitin' on Jimmy, I hadn't made any plans, I'm just here with her."

"Why don't you go with me? I know a place out on the highway where no one will bother us. No money," he said, "If you go, it's because you wanna be with me."

I didn't have to answer, my eyes said it all, I'd been waiting for him to ask.

He took me to a motel on the highway towards Bonner Springs. When we got to the room, a weird feeling came over me, I felt awkward and shy. Jesus! I thought, I've been with him before! What's the matter with me?

"Joe, you're not gonna believe this, but I feel shy with you, embarrassed. Be patient with me, I'll be okay in a minute. I guess I've been a whore too long." I laughed nervously. "I'm like a fuckin' machine, put the money on the table and I operate smoothly, but without the money, I become insecure, I have no confidence, I'm not sure what I'm supposed to do. I want to be with you, and I'm nervous about it. I know it sounds silly, I'm a whore, not a virgin, why should I be nervous? But I am."

Joe was sitting in a chair, smoking a joint, laughter in his eyes, "Are you shy, little girl?" he was teasing me, "Come over here and let the Big Bad Wolf show you what to do!"

*****

"You should be with me, Rita" Joe said, watching as I dressed, "I'd make you my bottom woman."

I didn't know what I wanted to do with my life, but I didn't want to be with Joe. I'd made up my mind that as long as I was turning tricks, I didn't want any man. Joe might love me, but it's not the kind of love my heart was aching for. I knew I had to say something, give Joe an answer, and try not to make him angry.

"Joe, I haven't even moved yet, I need time to get my head together."

A dark look came over Joe's face, "I always felt like you were MY woman. You belong to me, you just didn't realize it yet. I'd get mad because BJ was treatin' MY woman so bad, and I'd get even madder cause MY woman let him do it. You made more money than any girl out there, and you gave it to that fool. Every time I'd see BJ and Tina, I'd get sick to my stomach. Tina's married and she's playin' BJ for a fool." He saw the surprised look on my face, "You didn't know? Yeah, she's married, got a bunch of kids by her husband. She ain't gonna leave her husband, she's out to get as much as she can from BJ."

"It's bad enough to be a fool, but to be a fool for a fool. How could I have been so blind? I look at BJ now, and he's different, I can't figure out why I ever liked him. Whatever it was I saw, I don't see it anymore. I don't know who I was or what I was thinking about, I don't feel like the same person. It's almost as if I'm two different people, the one I used to be, and the one I am now."

"Rita, I'd never treat you that way. I'd always be truthful, honest, no slipping around behind your back, you'd know everything I was doing, and you'd know I was doing it for us. I'd make you a star, that's what you deserve." I made a face and Joe saw it, "I doubt if you'll ever be with another man," Joe said, "BJ ruined you. You'll never work for another man like you did for BJ."

"Joe, I'd like to stop hustlin', but I don't know what I'd do, I have no skills or education."

"You'd have a hard time, you're well known in this town, and you know we're in the middle of the Bible Belt. If you wanna square up, you'll probably have to leave town."

*****

Karen wanted to drive to Louisville for the Kentucky Derby, and she wanted me to ride along with her. Karen needed to get some money so she could move from KC, and she wanted to look Louisville over while she was there, she'd lived there before and thought she might return. We were going to spend Derby Week in Louisville and drive back Saturday night after the Kentucky Derby Race.

On the long drive to Louisville I asked Karen, "Have you ever wondered what you're gonna do with your life?"

"I know what I'm gonna do," Karen replied, "I'm gonna be a whore."

"I don't mean now, but later, after the whorin's over?"

"I'm gonna be a whore until I die," Karen laughed, "I don't wanna be anything else. Why, Rita? You wanna go to school or some other shit like that? Get some training? You're already trained! You can sit in a classroom for years and not make the money a whore makes."

"But you won't make that money when you get old, Karen."

Karen was belly laughing, "If I can't walk, if I'm in a wheelchair, I can still give a blow job! Don't worry so much!"

"You might be able to GIVE a blow job but will anyone BUY it? I'm not gonna whore all my life," I told Karen, "I'm gonna do something else, I don't know what, but something. And the next time I fall in love it will be different."

Karen stopped laughing, "No man is gonna want you if they know you was a whore, Rita. And if you try to start over here, somebody will come along and recognize you and that would blow it. Too many people know you in KC, you'd have to leave town."

*****

Louisville was overflowing with people. We couldn't find a vacant room anywhere in the city. We slept in the car, but we weren't alone, lots of people were camping out in the parks around town. Everywhere you went; the restaurants, bars and stores were full, with long lines of customers waiting to be helped.

Karen drove around Louisville, pointing out hi-lights of the city, "I used to live there," Karen pointed to an old apartment building. Everyday we went to Churchill Downs for the races. Karen showed me how to work the race track, meeting men at the betting windows or in the stands, finding out where all the parties were being held, and setting up dates for later. And drinking Mint Juleps as we worked.

We had no problem finding somewhere to stay. We had numerous offers from men willing to share their room, but we declined the offers. We stayed long enough to shower and put on clean clothes, but we slept in the car. We had more fun when it was just the two of us. If we spent the night with a trick, he'd wanna fuck all night.

"This is probably the last thing we'll ever do together, Rita. When I get back to KC, we're movin'. I might never see you again."

"We'll be in touch, Karen. We've been friends for years, we'll always be friends."

"Why don't you come, too. You said you wanted to start over."

"Right!" I said. "Move with you and Tony? Tony doesn't know I exist. Remember?"

"I didn't mean WITH us, but you could come to the same town, we could still work together."

"I don't know, Karen. I don't wanna go somewhere and be a whore. You wanna be a whore forever, but I don't. I really wanna start over, do the square thing, I'm just not sure how I get started. I've been a whore since I was 18, and before that I was in a reform school for four years. I have no idea what a square life is like, I haven't lived a normal life since I was 11 years old. Might be fun to work a little job, have Peter at home with me, learn to cook. I'd just like to try it."

"You'll be bored to death in two weeks." Karen said.

It was Saturday, Derby Day. Karen and I were at the track when we met two guys from New York. Black men from the Bronx, con artists. One was very tall, very big and very ugly, but the other man was handsome and charming. They said they were brothers but I couldn't see any resemblance.

The handsome one started talking to me and the ugly one tried to talk to Karen. They invited us to their motel to watch the race on television.

Karen pulled me aside, "Can I talk to you privately, Rita?"

"Sure" I said, turning to the handsome man, "I'll be right back."

"Rita, I ain't goin' nowhere with that ugly bastard! These are creeps from New York! Let's ditch em, okay?" Karen hissed between her teeth.

"Well, I think the one guy is really cute. You just sayin' that cause the other guy's so ugly. If he was cute, you'd be the first one at the motel."

"That's right!" Karen said, "But he's not even remotely cute, he looks like a monster. I'm not goin'!"

"Suit yourself" I said. "Cause I am."

We made plans to meet later at the car, and I left with the man from New York City. His name was Dewey, he wore fine clothes, flashy jewelry and drove a Lincoln Town Car. I told him I was a whore in KC, and I'd come to work the Derby with my friend Karen.

"You wastin' your time in KC," he said to me, "You need to go somewhere big like New York, KC's small time. Ain't no small potatoes in New York. Big money up there! You oughta come to New York, I'll show you how to make money without turning tricks."

I was interested, I wanted to start over, I wanted to make money without hooking, and I really wanted to get away from KC, away from everyone who knew about my foolish affair with BJ. I was ashamed of how I acted, how people had laughed behind my back. I wanted a fresh start.

"I don't know," I told him, "I'm on a fugitive bond from Arizona, I'm not supposed to leave the state of Missouri. I have to appear every 30 days for 90 days. Give Arizona a chance to extradite me if they want to. If they don't show up within the 90 days, I'm free, but I can't go to Arizona."

"Well, you're not in Missouri now," he said, "You're in Kentucky, you don't seem to be worried about it. After the race we're drivin' down to Birmingham to visit our mama. Why don't you ride with us?"

"I gotta get back to KC," I replied, "I gotta be in court this week."

"Hey, we'll drive down, and you can fly back to KC from Birmingham. Whata ya say? We'll get to know each other a little better, and I'll tell you more about New York."

"Foolish Pleasure" won the Derby that year. It was appropriate, because foolish pleasure is what I was about to embark upon. When I told Karen I was going to Birmingham and she'd have to return to KC alone, she was not happy. "Rita, I can't believe you're gonna go off with those guys! You don't know anything about them!"

"We go off with guys we don't know all the time." I replied.

"We came down here together," Karen shouted angrily, "I think you're bein' shitty for lettin' me go back alone! You don't know what they'll do. You better not go if you know what's good for you!"

"I'll be home about the same time as you. I'm flyin' home from Birmingham."

Karen got in her car and slammed the door, "This is your last chance, Rita, I'm leavin'. You comin' or not?"

"I'll see you back in KC." I said and walked off.

*****

The ugly guy drove the car while Dewey and I sat in the back seat and talked all the way to Birmingham, or rather, Dewey talked and I listened. Dewey was a smooth talker, he liked to hear himself talk, and didn't feel what other people said was of much importance. Talking was his business, he was a con artist and could talk his way out of or into anything. He told me how exciting life was in New York. He'd grown up in Birmingham, leaving when he was a teenager, and he was never going back to another small town.

The ugly guy in the front told me how Dewey and some other men wore NYC Policemen uniforms, went into a dope dealers house, pretending to bust the dealer, they handcuffed him and stole all his money and drugs. The dealer thought the police had actually ripped him off.

"Dewey's good," the ugly guy laughed, "He's got a scam for everybody."

"I'd like to leave KC." I told them, "Maybe I'll come to New York, but I've gotta take care of this Arizona thing first."

Dewey's mother was dirt poor. No wonder he left. Dewey gave his mother money and bought her groceries, but his mother wasn't happy about me being there. "Colored and white don't mix down here." she said. "You know that, Dewey. You be careful."

"Oh, Mama," Dewey told her, "Them crackers won't bother me."

"Yes they will, ain't nothin' changed down here, it ain't like New York." she warned him.

Although Dewy acted like he wasn't worried, his mother's anxiety brought back memories of his childhood in the South, and early the next morning he took me to the airport. He wrote his phone number in New York, "I'll be home in a couple days," he said as he pushed the paper in my hand, "Give me a call."

It was Tuesday, three days after the Derby and Karen was already back in KC. When I got home, BJ was waiting for me and he was fuming. "Where you been?" he yelled.

"I went to Louisville," I replied calmly, "You know that."

"Yeah, I know, but how'd you get home?"

"I came back with Karen." I lied.

"You didn't come back with Karen. She come by here lookin' for you. Wanted to know if you was back yet. She said you left with a niggah from New York, and she was worried. She left your luggage here."

I didn't deny anything, I sat looking at him, letting him know by my silence, it was true.

"Rita," he said, losing the anger in his voice, "I can't live like this anymore, if you stay here, you can't be goin' out with other men. I won't have it!"

"You don't mind if I go turn a trick," I replied with acid in my voice, "What's the difference?"

"Why don't you stop workin' and we'll try again."

"It's over between us." I said.

"Then why do you stay here, to torture me? Are you tryin' to get some kind of revenge?"

I got up and started to pack my clothes. I called a cab, BJ refused to give me a ride, BJ pleaded for me to stay, "How can you leave everything we've worked for?"

I looked around the empty apartment, "How can I leave everything I've worked for?" I let my gaze rest on his face, "It's easy, there's nothing here I want."

I rented a studio apartment in an old hotel downtown. There were only two apartments in the hotel, both on the first floor, the remainder of the building were rooms. I had a small kitchen and enjoyed being alone, away from BJ. It was my own place, all by myself. I painted the room, fixed it up with new curtains and even tried my hand at cooking without much success.

I called Dewey in New York and we started burning up the phone lines, talking long distance. We weren't in love, we just really liked talking to each other. A week after I'd flown back from Birmingham, Dewey flew to KC for a visit.

I'd been to court and no one from Arizona was there to take me into custody. I had to appear again in 30 days, and I wasn't supposed to leave the State of Missouri, because I still had a fugitive warrant in the other 49 states.

When Dewey came to KC, I showed him around, "What a hell hole!" he said, "How can you stand it here? There ain't nothin' to do, even if you had some money, there's no place to spend it! Come to New York!"

"What about my fugitive case?"

"When the time comes to go to court, you can fly here, it's only a few hours away."

Dewy flew back to New York and I followed him a week later.

*****

There was no passion between Dewey and I and neither one of us pretended there was. I wanted a new life away from KC, Dewey was opening a door for me, and I was going to cross the threshold and see what was on the other side. There was no talk of love between us, this was foolish pleasure, and grand adventure!

When I stepped off the plane, the first thing I noticed was the energy of New York City, it was a pulsing Metropolis, I could feel the pounding of millions of hearts.

Dewey met my flight at LaGuardia, and he drove around New York, showing me the "Big Apple." It wasn't a very pretty sight, the garbage men were on strike and uncollected trash was piled two stories high in some places, trash every where, and it stunk, it was almost summer, and the smell that hung over the city was odiferous.

I knew I wouldn't be staying with Dewey, he lived in the Bronx with his woman, Dino. Dewey assumed the role of teacher, and I was the girl from the sticks; that was our relationship.

He drove across the George Washington Bridge into Jersey and I got a motel room on Tonnelle by the Lincoln Tunnel. Dewey had another woman staying at the motel and her name was Penny. "Penny, you talk to her about the game. I'll be back tomorrow and see how it's goin'."

Penny was short, slightly overweight and plain, absolutely no sense of style. Penny and I disliked each other immediately, I felt superior to her and she could sense this.

I feel like I'm in a pimps stable, I thought to myself. I wonder how many women Dewey has? I knew Dewey was a hustler, and that was fine, I just wanted to escape KC.

Penny sat on the side of the bed and started talking. "Before we get started, let me warn you. You are NEVER to reveal the game to anybody. Do you understand?" I nodded, and Penny went on, "Tellin' the game is like snitchin' to the cops. Players don't like it and you could get hurt. Dewey must trust you or you wouldn't be here. Con game is serious business and it's about serious money, If you get caught, it's serious time. Remember that."

I thought Penny was getting a little over dramatic, but I sat there silently, waiting for her to go on.

"Ready?" Penny asked and I nodded, "First you get your play money together."

"Play money?" I said.

"Yeah" Penny picked up a brown paper bag and pulled out imitation money, the kind found in a toy department. It was the same size as real money. She opened the packages and began wadding up the fake bills.

"You crumble up the money so it looks like it's been used." She was throwing the bills in a pile on the bed and I began to crumble the bills with her. After the last bill was thrown in the pile, Penny picked them up and smoothed them out, putting the bills in stacks. When all the money was smoothed and sorted, Penny reached into her pocket and pulled out authentic U.S. currency.

"You put real money on the top and bottom of each stack." Penny instructed as she placed two bills on each side of the stack, and twisted a rubber band around it to hold it together, then placed it in the brown paper bag.

"Okay" Penny said as she put the last bundle in the sack, "This is your play money. This is what you work with."

Penny took out a piece of paper and started to write, "Next, you wanna put a note in the bag with the money. You want the note to go something like this AT, (use initials, that always looks good) DEPOSIT $100,000 TO OUR SWISS ACCOUNT. WAITING FOR SHIPMENT FROM SA. SIGNED L'. You want it to look like it's illegal money; drug money, gamblin' money, tax evaders. Always keep the note as simple and short as possible."

Penny folded the note and placed it in the bag. "Once you got your play money together, you're ready to go to work. We'll be working together, you're not strong enough in the game to work by yourself, that takes experience. You wanna pick an old person for your "mark" (victim), the older, the better."

"Why?" I asked.

"Old people are easier to sting, and if anything goes wrong they can't beat you up." Penny laughs at her joke, "I guess they're lookin' for that one last chance at life, hoping for that pot of gold at the end of the rainbow."

"I wouldn't feel right takin' some old person's money. Be like robbin' your grandparents." Then I thought about Buck and Jean.

"Look" Penny broke into my thoughts, "Don't feel sorry for a mark! You can't con an honest person. Just wait until I tell ya the game, you'll see what I'm talking about. You pick a mark, I like old ladies best. You'll be at a bus stop, park bench or somewhere like that and I'll be down the block, I'll be watchin' to see if you get someone. Pick up the bag and say Excuse me, you left your bag." Usually the person will say it's not theirs, you open the bag and "oh my God! Look at this!' you'll say. Have your mouth hangin' open and show the mark what's in the bag, don't give them the bag, don't let them take the money out, you keep possession of the bag at all times. At about this time, I'll come down the street, you're very excited and I join you to see what's up, we don't know each other, as far as the mark knows, we're complete strangers, in your excitement you tell me about the money you just found. The mark might not like this cause most of em wanna split up the money and leave, but you won't do that, and you got possession of the money. You play the honest role, you wanna do the right thing, and you don't want to take any chances on getting in trouble, you'll only take the money as long as you don't feel you are jeopardizing yourself. Maybe we should return it,' you say. Open the bag and look inside, pull out the note, no way to identify the owner with only initials. I'll say it's probably drug money. You'll worry about getting in trouble for keeping the money. Then I'll say I work for an attorney. I'll offer to call the attorney and ask if we can keep the money legally. You agree with me. It's your job to pull the mark. You met the mark first, you discovered the money together, you'll have a stronger influence on the mark. But you really have to play it by ear. Sometimes the mark will lean towards the other person. But one things for sure, the mark will lean towards one of us, not both, and it's that person's job to pull the mark in."

Penny stopped to take a breath, "Another way we can start is you talk to someone, oh, ten, fifteen minutes, establish a chitty-chatty friendship, then I approach and ask if either of you lost the bag, and we all look inside together, but I keep the bag. Everything has to happen quickly, you don't wanna give the mark a chance to think about what's goin' on. I go to a pay phone and pretend to call my boss. I come back and say Yes, there is a way we can keep the money legally. In order to claim the money legally, we have to give the lawyer $15,000 for filing fees, etc.' I'll handle that part. At this point we'll find out if the mark has any money. The $15,000 is supposed to be put up before we can claim the $100,000. I'll say I don't have $5,000 to put up, you say you do have it, we'll see what the mark says. If they got the money and are willing to put it up, of course, you're willing, we take em to the bank. Don't ever let the mark out of your sight, talk all the time, keep em from thinkin' about what's goin' on.

Once I've got the money, I take it and go into an office building, once I'm out of sight, you get away from the mark. Tell em you gotta go to the bathroom, tell em you're gonna look for me, but for them to wait in case I come back. Tell em what ever you want, and we'll meet back at the motel."

"And that's it?' I asked, "People actually go for that? That's wild! What if the mark only has $3,000 to put up? What do you do then?"

"I'm not gonna turn down $3,000. I tell em they can still claim a percentage of the $100,000. Don't worry about that part, I'll handle all that, and you watch me. Each sting is different, and has to be handled differently. Your job for now is to agree to everything I suggest and pull the mark. Got it?"

"I think so." I replied.

"Remember, everything has to happen quickly, no laggin'. You're countin' on that person's greed to get the best of em. Okay?" Penny stated, "Let's go over it again."

*****

Penny tutored me daily on what to do and say while playing the "game." I flew to KC for my second court appearance, and no one from Arizona was there, I had one more appearance and I'd be free. As soon as court was over I caught the next flight to New York.

Penny didn't think I was ready to play con, but Dewey thought I was almost ready.

"Dewey," I asked him, "When are we going out? I think I can handle it, I'm out of money."

"About a week" he said, "I gotta get everything ready. Rent a car, I'm sendin' you two out of town. Too hard in New York, too many people already know the game here."

"A week! How am I supposed to pay the motel?"

"You told me you was a ho, there's lots of places you can work in New York. Go to Times Square."

I was hoping Dewey would pay the motel bill, after all, he invited me to come here. I didn't want to hook in New York; too big, too many people, New York overwhelmed me, it was frightening. I knew I had to do something, I didn't have any money and it's obvious Dewey wasn't going to help.

I should have left New York right then, but I was determined to stick it out a little longer. I picked up a publication that advertised for girls, I answered one of the ads, making an appointment for an interview.

The place was in Manhattan, and I could tell right away it was a Sadism/Masochism house. The interviewer wanted me to strip, he said he had to inspect the merchandise first. I got a bad feeling from the man and I wanted out of there.

"I've changed my mind." I said, and fled through the door. I was shook up, New York was nothing like KC, I knew I was a country girl and out of my league. I was in Greenwich Village, I stopped in a bookstore and browsed, I was killing time, I didn't know what to do, but I knew I had to have some cash.

I walked until I ended up on the Avenue of the Americans, I walked up and down the street for an hour or more. Everyone was rushing by in a hurry, no one wanted to stop, the people were unfriendly, suspicious.

After a few hours the police picked me up and took me to jail. The officers didn't book me, they didn't even ask my name, they put me in a holding tank with other prostitutes.

"What's the deal?" I asked one of the girls, "They put you in jail and they don't even ask your name?'

"That's right!" the one girl spoke up, "If someone calls lookin' for you, they ain't got no record that you're here!"

"Seems to me, they're violating our rights." I said.

All the girls started laughin, "Where you from? The Moon? This is New York City, the cops do what they want here. Just be glad that all they did was put you in jail."

"Yeah," another girl said, "Bout 6 or 7 in the morning, they let us go. They do it all the time, especially if your around the tourist spots. Sit tight, you'll be out first thing in the morning."

I was relieved to hear this news, if I'd been booked and fingerprinted, they might have discovered I was a fugitive from Arizona. When the Sun rose in the morning, the jailers unlocked the doors and freed the whores.

I called Dewey and told him I'd spent the night in jail. He reluctantly paid my motel bill.

"I can't afford to take care of you," he said, "I'm sendin' you and

Penny out this week."

*****

Dewey arrived with the rental car. Penny and I drove to Boston, and Penny registered at a motel. "We meet back here," Penny said. "Make sure you remember where the motel is at."

We went to an area called Boston Commons, trying to pull our scam, but no one was biting.

"Better move to another area," Penny said, "It's not good to stay in one place too long."

Penny went to an older, poorer section of Boston, and we found an old woman sitting on a park bench. I sat down and struck up a conversation with her, we talked awhile then Penny showed up with the bag. The woman went for it hook, line and sinker! Once Penny showed up with the bag, the woman had nothing to say to me, she leaned towards Penny (Penny had the bag), the mark followed that bag like a bloodhound!

We took the woman home to get her savings account book, she had $5,000 she could put up for the lawyer. The mark didn't want me in her apartment, she didn't trust me! The old woman kept hanging onto Penny, whispering in Penny's ear.

I waited in the car and watched as the old woman, leaning on Penny's arm, entered the old, shabby apartment building. This woman has nothing, I thought, and we're gonna take what little she's saved over the years! I feel like shit! I'm glad the woman didn't lean towards me. This isn't like whoring, getting paid for a service, and everyone walks away satisfied, this is stealing. It leaves a bad taste in my mouth!

I felt sorry for the old women, I wanted to tell her to run, run as fast as she could away from Penny. But I didn't say a word, I was silent, I played my role, doing everything Penny suggested.

Penny went into the bank with the old woman, and when Penny disappeared into the office building, I had no trouble ditching the mark. "I've gotta call my babysitter," I said, "I'll be right back." I headed for the motel.

Penny was waiting, pleased with herself, "Five grand!" Penny hollered, "She was easy!"

"Where's the money?" I asked. I didn't feel good about what I'd done, I was going to get my part of the money and leave.

"That's Dewey's money." Penny replied, "He'll be here any minute. When I pretended to call the lawyer, I called Dewey, told him we was on our way to the bank. He'll give us what we need, don't worry."

When Dewey arrived, Penny presented him with the $5,000, proud she could do this for him, it made me sick. He took us to dinner at the motel restaurant. Is this our reward for stealing an old ladies life savings? Dinner? I didn't like anything that was happening, but I was afraid to speak up. What have I got myself into?

"Order anything you want!" Dewey announced. That's big of him, I thought as I looked at the menu. I wasn't feeling very hungry.

"This is a celebration!" Dewey continued, "This is Rita's first sting!"

"The mark hated her," Penny said to Dewey, ignoring me, "I had to do everything, set up the deal with the lawyer, pull the mark, EVERYTHING! The old woman didn't want Rita in her apartment." Penny bragged to Dewey, trying to impress him with her skills at the game.

"I just wonder," I said to Dewey, ignoring Penny, "How that old woman felt when she realized we weren't coming back with her money. What little dab she'd managed to save was gone!"

Dewey frowned at me, "That old woman got what she deserved. She was greedy, wanting something that didn't belong to her. When you start to feel sorry for a mark, just remember, you can't con an honest person, if that old lady knew the game, she'd play it on you!"

I looked at Dewey and Penny, I ate my dinner and remained silent for the rest of the meal, Penny was talking enough, and of course Dewey was talking, he was the maestro of this operation, he was like Fagin in "Oliver Twist", and Penny was hanging onto every word. Wake, up Penny! I thought, as I finished my dinner, you're the biggest mark of all, and so am I, he's conned us both!

Can't con an honest person? That old woman wasn't hurting anybody, sure, she'd like to have a bigger nest egg, a sudden windfall. What's wrong with that? Does that mean the old woman is on the same level as Dewey and Penny? NO! I don't think so! Dewey says you can't con an honest person to ease our conscience about what we're doing. Well, he can save his breath, I've spent years listening to bullshit, but those days are over.

"We're going to another town tomorrow," Penny announced.

One more time, I thought, and I'm not letting Penny give all the money to Dewey, I'll get my hands on some of it, some way, and I'll go back to KC, away from this madness.

I didn't like New York, I didn't like what we were doing, I didn't like Penny, and I didn't like Dewey anymore. If I tell them I'm leaving, what will they do? Will they react like the pimps in KC? Kick my ass? Hold me against my will? I better not say anything yet, I'll feel things out first, and slip away if I can.

*****

The next day Penny and I drove to Bridgeport, Connecticut. This will be my second and last sting, I thought on the ride down, cause Penny and I didn't talk to each other and I had plenty of time to think. If I get some money, I'm out of here!

We tried a couple of old women who quickly got away from us. "Maybe we should go somewhere else." Penny said, then she saw an old woman, walking up the street, struggling with her groceries. "Let's try her. I'll let you out here, and I'll be up the street with the bag."

So, I thought, Penny's going to handle all the money! I've got to figure a way to get my hands on some of the money. I approached the old woman and offered to carry her groceries, she eagerly handed the bags to me, "Such a nice girl! Your parents raised you properly. Most young people aren't so polite." When we turned the corner, Penny was in plain sight and she was arguing with two police officers.

One of the officers ran up to me, "You're under arrest!" The old woman was wide-eyed, "Not you," the officer said, "You," he nodded his head towards me.

"Why? I'm not doing anything. I'm just helping this lady with her groceries. Is that against the law?"

"You're under arrest for Flim-Flam." the policeman pulled out his handcuffs. "Give the groceries back to this woman."

"Don't try to play dumb with me. We got your bag of money, we know what's going on. Somebody called the station and reported you. Just put down the groceries and let's go." The officer turned his attention to the old woman while he put the handcuffs on me, "You should be more careful. Do you know what this woman was going to do? She was gonna try and steal your money. Be careful who you talk to."

"She seemed like such a nice girl." the old woman replied, looking at me with a puzzled expression.

Penny was arguing with the police, making smart remarks, she wouldn't let them handcuff her, so they had to overpower her, which only took a few seconds. That wasn't too smart, I thought. I was scared, if they found out I was a fugitive from Arizona, my goose was cooked! When we got to the police station, the officer removed my handcuffs.

"Mind if I smoke?" I asked him.

"Go right ahead," the officer said, offering me a light.

Penny and I were told to sit down on a bench and wait. Penny was escorted to an office and I was taken to a different room, we were being interrogated separately.

"What were you doing?" the detective asked me.

"I don't know what you mean," I said, "I don't even know why I'm here. I was only trying to help an old lady with her groceries."

"We know what you were doing. You scumbags come up here from New York and pull your shit. Well, we're not putting up with it here in Connecticut. What's your name?"

"Ann Jones" I lied. The officer was filling out a report, every time he would bend his head to write, I took my cigarettes and burned my fingertips, rolling the glowing end across my fingers in hopes of distorting my fingerprints. Please God! I prayed, (something I'd recently started doing, praying) don't let them find out who I am! I promise I'll never con another soul! If they find out I'm wanted, I'll never get out of jail.

"Where are you from, Ann? You're not from around here."

"I'm from Texas," I lied, "Dallas area."

The officer finished his report, pushed his chair back from the desk and looked at me. "Look, Ann, if that's your real name, which I doubt, I don't know how long you been doing this, or how you got hooked up with that other woman, but you're in a lot of trouble. That woman you were with, we've already got three people who can positively identify her as the person that flim-flammed them. She's going to prison for a while. If anyone identifies you, you're going with her."

"You con artist are hard to catch, but if we get you one time, we've got a line of people waiting to pick you out. That woman you were with, she conned my aunt out of her savings, believe me, I'll make sure she does time. You people disgust me!"

The detectives led me out of his office, my fingertips were swollen from the cigarette burns. I was fingerprinted, photographed and booked on charges of Flim-Flam.

We spent the night in a small jail in Bridgeport. The next morning we were arraigned on the charges and our bond was set at $20,000 each. I expect Dewey to be there to post the bond, but Dewey was nowhere around.

The towns and villages in Connecticut had no facilities to hold someone for long periods of time. Anyone not being able to make bond right away was held at the women's penitentiary in Nianik. Prisoners awaiting trial were kept separate from the regular prison inmates who were serving a sentence. But those awaiting trial and those already sentenced, shared the prison library, and it was there I met a woman serving time for flim-flam.

"I only got picked up once," the prisoner said, "Kinda like you, they didn't catch me doing anything. I got picked up in Pennsylvania, they had nothing to hold me on, but I think every sting I made was waitin' to finger me. I got two cases in Connecticut that I'm doin' time for now, when I get out of here, Jersey is waitin' on me. I wish I could go back and change it, now I won't see my kids grow up. If somebody identifies you, that's it! One of the cases they hung on me, I didn't do, but the mark identified me, so it's my case."

Penny was being held at the prison also, but she didn't talk to me, she blamed the bust on me. "I'll never work with another greenhorn," Penny told anyone who would listen.

I have news for you, I thought, you won't be working with anyone for a LONG TIME! I couldn't understand why Dewey hadn't bonded us out.

The prison was similar to the reform school I'd spent so many years at. If he doesn't get us out, I can survive here, I've lived this kind of life before, but this isn't what I want. If I get out of here, I'm never doing anything to get myself in this kind of trouble again.

I didn't know if burning my fingertips had helped, but no one discovered I was Shirley Sandy.

*****

After sitting in prison a week, Dewey bonded me out, but left Penny in jail. On the ride back to New York, I asked him "Why'd you leave me in jail so long?"

"That was a big bond. Had to put my car up as collateral." That was a lie, but what could I expect, he was a con man, his whole life was a lie.

"Why didn't you get Penny out?" I wanted to know.

"That dumb-ass bitch can sit for awhile. Teach her a lesson. Maybe next time she'll listen to what I say. She always wants to do everything her own way. Hard-headed! I told that dummy a hundred times, if you try a couple people and no one bits, move on, get out of town."

"She's in a lot of trouble, Dewey, they're gonna send Penny to prison."

"Aw, I'll get her out of it," Dewey said.

"I met a woman in prison for con, this isn't anything like I thought it would be. This whole New York thing, it isn't me. Maybe it's too fast paced. Maybe I'm just a hick, but I don't think I'm tough enough to handle it. Look what happened when I tried to hook in New York, and now, the second day I play con, I end up in jail."

Dewey looked at me, I didn't know how he would take it, I held my breath waiting for his reaction. "New York is fast paced," he said, "It's not for everybody, I know that, I understand."

That was easy!

"Where do you wanna go? I'll buy you a plane ticket anywhere you want. You're a nice kid, I like you, and you're right, you don't belong in New York."

"I've gotta go back to KC. I've still got that Arizona case."

"You've got a case in Connecticut, too. If I send you home, you gotta promise me you'll come back for court. I put my car up as collateral, and if I lose my car, I'll be pissed."

"I'll be here for court."

"You know, I believe you. I'll send you home first thing in the morning. You can spend the night at my place in the Bronx."

Dewey lived on the 5th floor of a high-rise. His woman Dino was there, and they had a small baby only a few weeks old.

"A few more weeks," Dewey said proudly, "And Dino's going back to work!"

Dino was a "big time New York con artist". But I wasn't impressed,

236

I'd seen enough of the con game. I thought they were all crazy and I just wanted out of there.

Two men came to the apartment and Dewey led them to the bedroom, "Hey girls!" Dewey called, "Come look at this!"

Dino and I went to the bedroom, in the middle of the bed was a pile of money, more money than I'd ever seen before.

"Quarter of a mil'!" Dewey says, "We're gonna turn it into millions!"

More men came to the apartment and everyone was packing a gun, they didn't conceal their weapons but displayed them openly, laying their pistols on the table, pushing back their jackets to show a shoulder holster. I tried to stay out of their way. If I live through this night, I thought, it'll be a miracle.

Dewey was buying cocaine from the men, the biggest bag of cocaine I'd ever seen. But this coke looked different, it had a pinkish tint to it.

"That's cause it's pure." Dewey told me.

The deal was made, the men put away their guns and left with the money, and Dewey left with the coke, "I'll be back in a little while." he said as he walked out the door.

All the time Dewey was there, Dino had gone out of her way to be nice to me, but once he left, she took off her mask. "So, you're the country girl Dewey met at the Derby. He told me you had class, you'd be a great con artist! Get the big money! HA! You got busted the second day out. I ain't never been busted!"

"Well, when you get busted," I said, "You're probably going to prison like Penny."

"I ain't nothin' like Penny," Dino said, "She doesn't listen to Dewey. It's her own fault she's in jail. Dewey knows this business, Dewey says your stupid, he's worried about you, that's why he's sendin' you home."

I didn't like being called stupid, I guess no one does, and especially by Dino, I wanted to knock her down a peg or two. "If Dewey was worried about me, he wouldn't have pulled that big drug deal in front of me. He's sending me home because he likes me, because I asked him to."

Dino didn't want to hear this kind of talk, "Dewey don't like nobody but me and little Dewey (the baby), the rest of you girls are here for us."

"If that's the case," I said, "Why are you going back to work? Taking the risk? Why not let the other girls take the chances?"

"Because I'm the best." Dino boasted, "These other girls can't touch me when it comes to makin' money. That's why I've got Dewey!"

I didn't want to argue with Dino, I didn't care who Dewey was with. I'm going home tomorrow, I thought, Dino shouldn't care about me, but I guess she feels threatened by any girl Dewey brings around. If a new girl makes more money, Dino could lose her spot! I know how you feel Dino, and I'm glad it's you and not me. I jumped up and went to the door, unlocked the numerous chains and deadbolts on the door, "I'm taking a walk, I need some fresh air."

"You can't go out!" Dino shouted, "Dewey'll be pissed. It's dark out."

"I'll be back," I said.

I went downstairs in the elevator and stood in front of the building. I couldn't stand being in the apartment with Dino, I'd wait until Dewey got home, then Dino could put her mask back on. I was outside for only a minute when Dino showed up. "Please come back upstairs." She pleaded, "If Dewey comes back and finds out I let you leave, he'll kick my ass! You ain't in the country, you're in New York, the Bronx, and women don't go outside after dark. Hell, it ain't safe in the daytime."

"I'm fine," I told Dino, "I can take care of myself." Dino's talk was scaring me, but I didn't want Dino to know. If she asked me one more time, I thought, I'll go back to the apartment.

Dino placed her hand on my arm, "Come on, you're going home tomorrow, it'd be terrible if something happened."

"Well, if your gonna carry on like this, I'll go, on one condition."

"What's that?" Dino asked.

"Don't talk to me!"

"Okay" Dino agreed, "I won't say anything to you, and let's not mention any of this to Dewey."

"My lips are sealed." I told her.

I didn't want to cause Dino any problems, I felt sorry for Dino. Maybe Dino wasn't a whore, but her situation wasn't any different. She worked, taking risks with her freedom, and she gave all her money to Dewey. Dewey did whatever he wanted, and he had as many women as he wanted. Dino wasn't in a very good position, if another woman came along and gave Dewey more money, Dino would be out in the cold.

I'll never, I vowed to myself, have a man involved in the hustling life. From now on, it's only square men for me, but in order to have a square man, I gotta be a square woman!

The next morning Dewey took me to the airport. "I know you gotta go back to KC for court, but don't rot away in that town. Go somewhere else. Didn't you say you had a sister in California?" I nodded, "Well, go there. Lots to do in California, but it's not' as fast as New York, more laid back."

"Maybe I will." I said.

"And don't forget, I'll see you for your court date in Connecticut."

*****

I had been on the East Coast for over a month.

"I was worried you wouldn't get back before I left." Karen told me. "I knew you'd be back, though. I'm leavin next week, we're goin' to Louisville. Now that you're back, we'll party before I leave!"

I was glad to be out of New York, the lifestyle wasn't what I was looking for. Dewey was mixed up in all kinds of stuff! But now I was back in KC where I didn't want to be.

Although I wasn't happy and wanted a new life, I didn't know how to go about it. I was unsure of myself. Could I get a job? Would I make enough money to support Peter and myself? I was afraid, so I kept on hooking.

Karen I went to JJ's the night before Karen was to leave. Karen had been my only friend for many years and I was going to miss her. "It won't be the same when you're gone." I told Karen.

"You don't have to stay here," she replied, "We can have fun in Louisville, too."

We hugged and cried while saying good-bye. We swore we'd keep in touch. I talked to Karen on the phone a few times, but I never saw her again.

*****

I went to court on the Arizona fugitive warrant, and for the 3rd and last time, no one from Yuma was in court to take me into custody...it was over...and I was free.

I flew back to Connecticut for the Flim-Flam charges, the Judge gave me a "floater" (leave the state and don't return) out of Connecticut, and that was fine with me. I'd had it with the East Coast. Too fast for me. I'm a mid-western girl and I always will be.

Penny was in court. Dewey had finally made her bond. Penny was confident she'd beat her cases. Dewey's really done a snow job on her, I thought, he'll have her out there, giving him money, until she walks through the prison door!

I flew to KC, leaving New York and the con artist behind forever.

*****

"Hey, Rita!" a black prostitute greeted me. "There's a trick at the Midwest Hotel, wants a white girl. He's in 202 if you wanna go."

"Okay, I'll try it." I went to the Midwest and knocked on the door of room 202.

"Doors open!" a man called out.

I entered the room and a trick was laying on the bed in his underwear, smoking a marijuana cigarette. We talked for a few minutes, when suddenly there was a loud BOOM, and the door flew open. Three men rushed into the room with their badges drawn.

"You're under arrest for prostitution. Both of you. Stand up, hands against the wall."

The trick jumped out of bed, "What is this?" he yelled.

"What have we got here?" one of the detectives had spotted the joint in the ash tray.

"That's mine." the trick said. The cop turned his back on the trick and looked at me. I knew the cop, I knew all the cops.

"I was listening at the door," he said to me, "I heard you offer this joint to the guy. I'm charging you with possession of marijuana, too." the cop was grinning, he knew it wasn't my pot, but he didn't care. I just shook my head and muttered.

"I don't believe it!" But I did believe it, I knew the cops could do just about anything they wanted.

"It's my pot!" the trick said, "Not hers."

"You're in enough trouble," the cop said, "Don't worry about her, worry about yourself."

I was taken downtown and booked for prostitution and possession of cannabis. The trick wasn't charged with anything, he promised to return to KC to testify against me in court. The charges were a misdemeanor, but if convicted on the prostitution charge, I'd go to jail for 30 days.

The trick was a truck driver from Indiana, and everyone knew he wasn't coming back for court. But there was always the possibility that the trick would show up. I consulted my attorney.

"I don't think you have anything to worry about." the lawyer told me, "Without the trick, they have no prostitution case, and possession of half a marijuana cigarette will probably be a $25 fine."

*****

A week had passed since I'd gotten busted at the Midwest. It was morning and the phone was ringing.

"Yes" I answered, not yet awake.

"You better get to the school, FAST!" It was Alice, Grandma's daughter, and Dorothy's mother, "Dorothy's on her way to the school and she's got a gun, says she's gonna kill Peter!"

"WHY?" I screamed.

"Dorothy thinks mama cares more for Peter than her own flesh and blood! She's crazy! She threatened mama, too. You call the school and I'll call the police."

I called Peter's school, I told them Peter was in danger, that his life had been threatened. "Take Peter out of class, to the office, and keep him there until I can pick him up. I'll be right there."

As the taxi pulled up at the school, I could see the police cars and Dorothy was pulled over. The officer's were searching Dorothy's car. I gave the cab driver some money and asked him to wait until I could get Peter. As the driver pulled away from the curb, Dorothy stared with hate in her eyes. What did I ever do to her? Why doe she hate me so much? She hates me so much, she'd kill my son!

I had the driver take us downtown. Peter couldn't stay at my motel, they didn't allow children, and he can't go back to Grandma's, it's too dangerous!

BJ still lived in the empty apartment we had shared together, and he lived alone. I called him up, "BJ, I need a favor, I have Peter with me and I need somewhere to stay until I can get a place of my own."

BJ was more than happy to let me stay, he thought he was getting another chance.

*****

Once I arrived at BJ's with Peter, I called Grandma. "What happened?" I asked her. Grandma and I had grown close over the years. Grandma loved Peter and Peter loved her. She took care of Peter and I loved her for giving Peter the home he needed. This is what Dorothy didn't like.

"I don't know, girl!" Grandma said, "I don't know what's the matter with Dorothy. Her mama says she's on drugs. She came over here wavin' that gun around, tellin' me she didn't want Peter here no more. She said I cared more about Peter than her daughter, but she don't understand, I raised Peter, he's like my own little boy. You never interfered, you let me raise him like I wanted. I couldn't do that with Dorothy's daughter, she wouldn't let me."

"I didn't interfere because I knew you loved Peter and would only do what was right for him. I never worried about him. I knew he was safe with you. But now I don't know."

"Don't pay Dorothy no mind." Grandma said. "Peter'll be safe with me. If she comes back, I got somethin' waitin' on her."

"Grandma, Dorothy is your granddaughter, this whole thing is crazy. I can't take a chance with Peter's safety. Dorothy is nuts and for some reason she hates me. Maybe it's for the best this happened. Peter's 8 years old, it's time he lived with his mother, it's time we had a real home together. I should have done this a long time ago."

"I won't know what to do without Peter here!" Grandma said. "He's my baby, I'll miss him, but I suppose you're right, he needs to be with his mama, and Dorothy IS crazy. You take care of my baby."

"I will." I told her.

The next day I put a deposit on an apartment, but I couldn't move in for two weeks, until the other tenants had moved out.

*****

I was an old whore, my prime money making years were over. I didn't want to end up some old whore scrounging around for every dollar, lowering my prices to compete with the young girls, and that's what was ahead of me if I didn't change my life. I'm tired of whoring, I'm tired of going to jail, and I'm tired of not being loved because I'm a whore.

I don't regret being a whore, I learned a lot about human nature, whoring made me financially independent, but I do regret the money I gave away. If I'd been smart, Peter and I could be secure, but I wasn't smart, I ended up like all the other whores...broke, but at least I'm alive. I didn't care about money, it was so easy when I was young to get money, I thought I could buy love. Love is priceless, I can no more buy someone's love than they can buy mine.

I'm going to California, flashed through my mind, I'll start over, maybe I'll go to school, or get a job. I'll go where no one recognizes me, where my past won't influence their opinion of me. I'll start fresh with Peter. I'll call Sandra right now. Once my mind was made up, I was ready to go.

I hadn't spoken to Sandra in a year, I didn't know what Sandra's situation was. Sandra had gotten married and she asked me to come to California, just like I hoped she would.

"Well, Sandra, would two days be too soon?"

"Two days!" Sandra laughed, "I guess you were ready to come!"

"Yeah, I'm ready, I'm ready to start over. I don't wanna be 12th Street Rita anymore, I wanna be Shirley Sandy again. I wanna be myself."

*****

The next day I purchased two large trunks, one for Peter's things and one for myself. I was excited and at the same time I was scared. I was afraid of the "square" world, I didn't know what it was like, I'd been a whore all my adult life. But no matter how afraid I was of the future, I knew the time had come for change.

When I told BJ I was leaving, taking Peter with me, leaving for good, never coming back, he started to argue with me.

"My mind's made up," I told him, "I've gotta do this. I'm gonna square up, and I can't do it here, you know that."

"I suppose you're right." he said, "I'd rather you be with me, but maybe you need to do something different. At least if you're in California, I won't have to see you with other men."

BJ took us to the airport. We boarded the plane to Los Angeles. As the plane took off I held Peter's hand, he smiled up at me and I smiled back. I looked out the window and watched as the skyline of downtown KC faded from view. Good-bye Kansas City, I thought to myself, good-bye 12th Street Rita.

About The Author

Shirley Sandy lives in Kansas City with her husband, four dogs, ten cats and calls her home Paradise. An oasis of love in the middle of the city.